Defying
LIMITS

Defying LIMITS

How Extraordinary People Redefine Strength And Success

Vítek Formánek
Eva Csölleová

Sastrugi Press
Jackson, WY

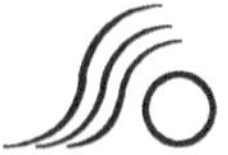

Sastrugi Press / Published by arrangement with the authors

Sastrugi Press: PO Box 1297, Jackson, WY 83001
www.sastrugipress.com

Defying Limits: How Extraordinary People Redefine Strength And Success

The authors have made every effort to accurately recreate conversations, events, and locales from records and memories of them. To maintain anonymity, some names and details such as places of residence, physical characteristics, and occupations have been changed. The activities described in this book are inherently dangerous. The publisher does not have any control over and does not assume any responsibility for author or third-party websites or their content.

Any person participating in the activities described in this work is personally responsible for learning the proper techniques and using good judgment. You are responsible for your own actions and decisions. The information contained in this work is subjective and based solely on opinions. No book can advise you to the hazards or anticipate the limitations of any reader. Participation in the described activities can result in severe injury or death. Neither the publisher nor the author assumes any liability for anyone participating in the activities described in this work.

Library of Congress Cataloging-in-Publication Data

Names: Formánek, Vítek, 1963- author
http://id.loc.gov/authorities/names/nb98092693
http://id.loc.gov/rwo/agents/nb98092693 | Csölleová, Eva author
http://id.loc.gov/rwo/agents/n2013050556
Title: Defying limits : how extraordinary people redefine strength and success / Vítek Formánek and Eva Csölleová.
Description: Jackson, WY : Sastrugi Press, [2025]
Identifiers: LCCN 2025006134 | ISBN 9781649222435 paperback
Subjects: LCSH: People with disabilities--Biography
http://id.loc.gov/authorities/subjects/sh2008109034 | Success--Case studies http://id.loc.gov/authorities/subjects/sh2010112509 | LCGFT: Biographies http://id.loc.gov/authorities/genreForms/gf2014026049 | Case studies. https://id.loc.gov/authorities/genreForms/gf2017026140
Classification: LCC HV1552.3 .F67 2025 | DDC 362.4092--dc23/eng/20250522
LC record available at https://lccn.loc.gov/2025006134

ISBN-13: 978-1-64922-243-5 (paperback)

910.4

15 14 13 12 11 10 9 8 7 6 5 4 3 2

Table of Contents

Table of Contents

INTRODUCTION

Through difficulties towards dreams

Life is meant to be lived to the fullest. Dreams are meant to become reality. The only true limits are the ones we create in our minds. While these words might sound like clichés, this book demonstrates their undeniable truth.

The first part of the book shares the extraordinary stories of individuals with disabilities, told in their own words. Despite immense challenges, they accomplished incredible feats through determination and effort. Missing limbs didn't stop them from winning Paralympic gold medals, climbing mountains, running marathons, playing tennis, swimming, dancing, or even driving race cars.

Even total paralysis from the neck down didn't deter them from composing music, making films, or creating breathtaking works of art. These remarkable stories from across the globe highlight people who, despite drawing a "short straw" in life, refused to give up. They became inspirations for us all.

Jamie Andrew, Jennifer Bricker, Louise Hunt, Simon Fitzmaurice, Alex Zanardi, Sam Schmidt, Jason Becker, Rob Jones, and others featured here know exactly what it means to truly live life to the fullest.

The second part of the book is a collection of interviews with people who pursued their dreams against all odds. Their stories were so compelling that some became the basis for films. Eddie "The Eagle" Edwards, Homer Hickam (*October Sky*), Benjamin Mee (*We Bought a Zoo*), Dr. Patch Adams (*Patch Adams*), and Margaret Keane (*Big Eyes*) are just a few of the inspirational figures you'll meet in these pages.

We live only once, and it's our life to shape. There are no do-overs, no second chances. How we choose to spend it is entirely up to us.

AARON FOTHERINGHAM

A Wheelchair is Not an Obstacle. It's My Toy.

When we were looking for interesting people, we came across Aaron Fotheringham by accident. Born with Spina Bifida, a condition that prevents him from using his legs, Aaron went to a skatepark at the age of nine and attempted to do in his wheelchair what others do on BMX bikes or skateboards. The incredible pictures we saw made him an obvious choice for an interview, and he kindly obliged.

What sort of childhood did you have, and how did you react when you realized that others could walk while you couldn't?

I spent much of my childhood in hospitals, having surgeries linked to my Spina Bifida. I realized at an early age that I was a bit different. Even though I was different, I felt like I had an advantage. I viewed my crutches and wheelchair as tools to help me get what I wanted!

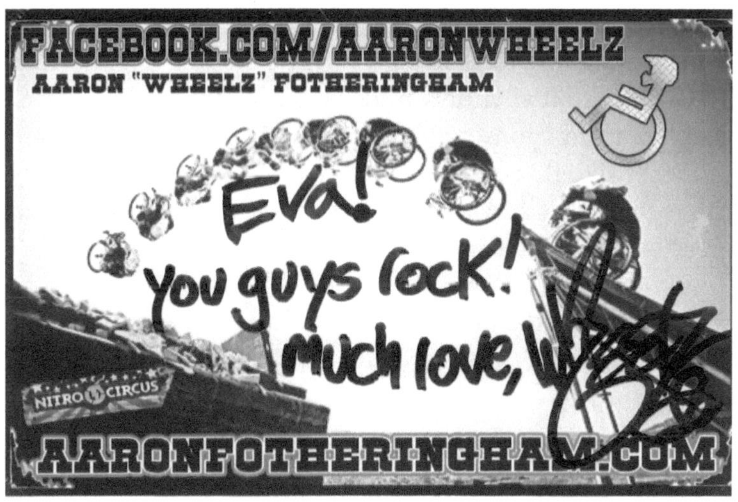

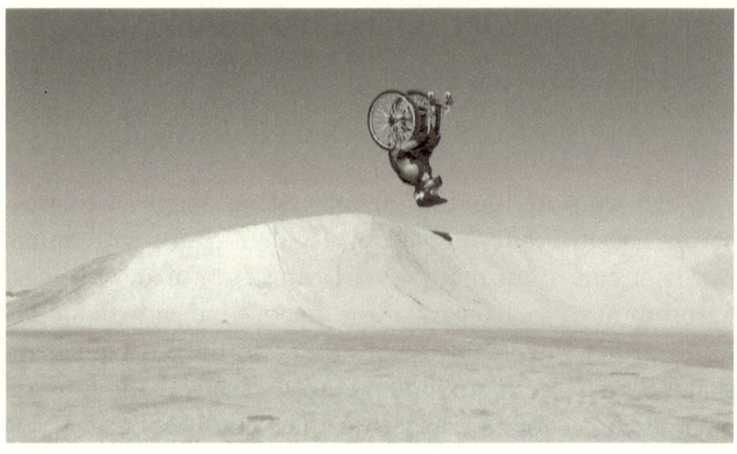

Did you feel like an outsider? Did your schoolmates show disrespect or malice towards you?

At school, a few kids bullied me, but I felt like there were twice as many kids who stood up for me!

Did you start doing your tricks in an ordinary wheelchair? When did you realize it was too heavy and fragile for sports? When did you start making your own improvements, like adding a new suspension?

I started going to skateparks with a standard wheelchair and destroyed it after only nine months! Thankfully, a wheelchair company sponsored me in the early years, which led me to meet Mike Box of Box Wheelchairs. Mike still builds my chairs today. We added shocks, skateboard wheels, and extra cross-bracing to make the chair hold up to the abuse!

You had many knocks and heavy falls before succeeding in your stunts. Aren't you scared that you could break your neck and become fully paralyzed?

I am always concerned about serious injuries, of course. Even though it may not seem like it, I am very cautious about certain tricks and won't attempt anything unless I feel ready or confident. I also wear a neck brace on the big ramps just to be safe.

How do you work on your stunt jumps, backflips, etc.? Do you talk first with BMX and skateboard jumpers about techniques to avoid unnecessary danger, or do you simply go onto the ramp, do it 20–30 times, and slowly improve?

I do a little bit of both. I usually talk to BMX riders or skaters and get their advice, and then it's time to try it over and over. I learn something from each crash. I just make adjustments after every attempt, and eventually, I enjoy success!

Do you use the same technique as BMX jumpers and just apply it to the wheelchair, or do you have to find new ways and test them to see if they work?

Some tricks and techniques are adapted from BMX, but some are unique to WCMX. There's only so much you can borrow from BMX because a wheelchair is a bit different.

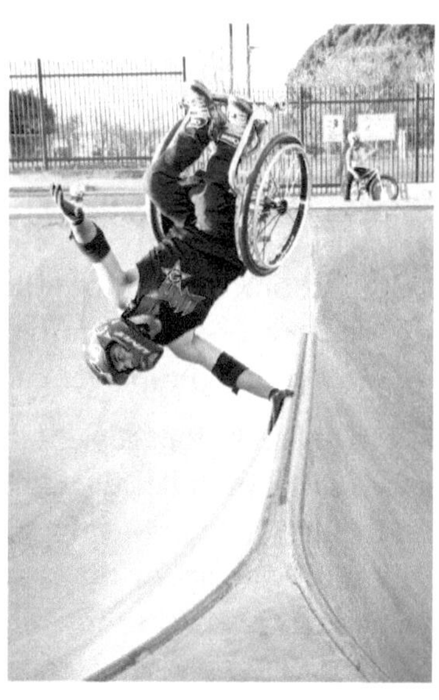

Did you approach any wheelchair builders to help you with special devices, suspension, seats, tires, lighter frames, etc.? Did any of them visit or call you to test their designs, and did they sponsor you?

Mike Box has been building my wheelchairs since I was nine! We've worked together to build very tough chairs. Each one gets stronger

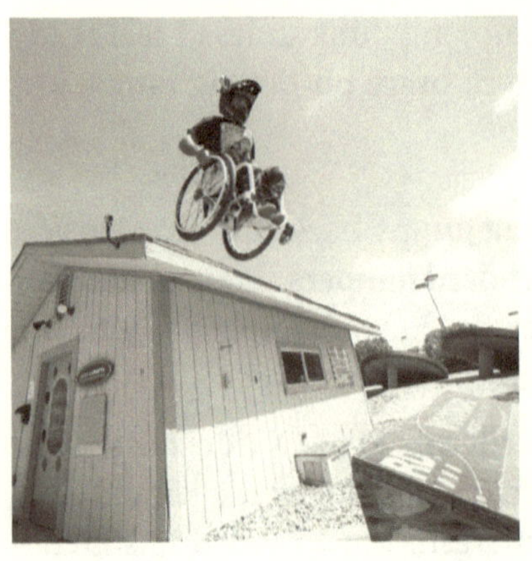

to handle new styles of riding and tricks!

Do you do all your jumps in an improved wheelchair only for your own use, or did you decide to be a kind of guinea pig and pave the way for others, maybe creating a new discipline for the Paralympics in the future?

One day, I hope to see WCMX in the Paralympics! The sport has grown a lot over the years, and one of my big goals is to elevate it to the Paralympic level so people worldwide can have fun with their chairs.

That Nitro Series you toured with—was it just an attempt to earn a few bucks, or were you asked to inspire people to follow their dreams and push the envelope?

I joined the Nitro Tour back in 2010. At first, they invited me just to test the ramp. After I succeeded, I was invited to tour the world with the crew. It's been a huge blessing to be part of the shows and have a platform to inspire people!

Tell us about that 50-foot jump in Brazil. How many times did you try it before landing successfully? Do you intend to go further and jump over cars or buses like Evel Knievel?

I tried the 50-foot gap about five times before Brazil with no success. But in Brazil, during the Mega Ramp event, I landed it on the first try without any practice—it was amazing! I'd love to jump over cars or buses someday—maybe even throw in some fire and sharks too!

Do you intend to invite more disabled people, teach them the tricks, and establish your own "Flying Circus" to tour and earn a regular living?

I think it'd be cool to get more people into WCMX and show that a wheelchair isn't just a medical device—it's an extreme sport!

You won $20,000 on a TV show. Did you start your own business with those funds?

I used the money to buy tools to start my metal shop so I could build and repair wheelchairs. I'm not quite at the level of doing it as a business yet!

Now you are kind of a celebrity, the first in the world in many ways. Do you regret not being able to walk? Would you rather be able-bodied and anonymous, or are you happy with the way you are now?

I don't consider myself a celebrity or anything like that. I've been able to experience some really cool stuff, but with or without the spotlight, I'd choose to remain in a wheelchair—it's too much fun!

Do you intend to break into the film industry as a stuntman?

I've done a few things in the film industry as a stuntman and some acting, and I really enjoy it. I'd definitely like to get into more film projects in the future.

2017

ADRIAN ANANTAWAN

No One is Perfect, and We All End Up Making Great Art

This Canadian musician was born without a right hand and picked up the violin at the age of nine. Doctors aren't sure why his right arm didn't develop normally, but they believe the umbilical cord wrapped around his arm, cutting off the blood supply and halting its growth. His forearm is only 12 cm (less than 5 inches) long.

As if the missing hand wasn't enough, young Adrian didn't learn to talk until he was three years old. His mother emigrated from Hong Kong to Canada in 1971, while his father arrived from Thailand in 1975. To play the violin at all is no small feat, but despite the obstacles his physical disability posed, Adrian was well supported by his mother, who hoped playing the instrument might one day become a hobby.

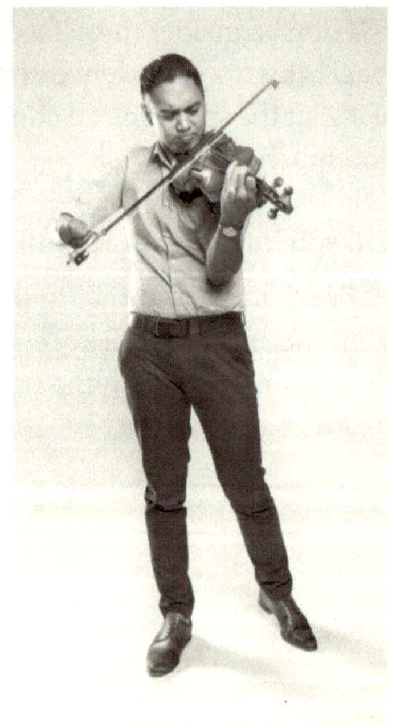

Adrian worked hard, training for six to ten hours a day, and went on to win numerous prestigious accolades and seats in Canadian youth orchestras. He was accepted to the Curtis Institute of Music, considered the world's most selective and prestigious music conservatory. Over the years, he performed for Pope John Paul II, the Dalai Lama, and at the White House.

We admired his style of playing and reached out for an interview. He kindly replied within three days.

What brought you into the world of classical music? Were your parents musicians, or were you somehow more inclined to Mozart and Vivaldi than to Boney M and Michael Jackson?

My parents weren't formally trained as musicians, but my father played as an amateur when he was younger. There was always classical music in the house, so I ended up listening to it on the radio, in TV shows, or in movies. It was something I always appreciated. My big inspiration was Itzhak Perlman, who was also a disabled musician and one of my idols growing up.

Were you just a naturally gifted musician, or did you discover a love for the violin and want to play it despite your disability?

I think I always had a good ear. Teachers always told me that the most important thing is to listen to yourself. It was a good philosophy for me because I was disabled and had just one hand.

Were you first told 'no' by your parents or teachers when you asked for violin lessons? Did they try to make you play with your left hand, which would probably be easier for you?

I was very lucky to be sent to a teacher who showed me how to play. We started with the left-hand technique first, and then we had to figure out the bow. Later, we went to a rehabilitation center for about a month, where they made a device for me.

Playing the violin is difficult for able-bodied people. Was it doubly difficult for you since you had to master the movement and touch of an artificial hand first? Was it a tough experience as a beginner, or were you in tune from the beginning?

The difficulties of the instrument are universal. I don't know what listeners thought when they first heard me play, but I hoped they would close their eyes and hear the music first.

Players have to train many hours every day to keep their fingers 'soft.' How does it work for you when you don't have fingers? Can you play longer since you don't get cramps? Does the bow ever disconnect from your stump after long hours of playing, or is it fixed solidly?

I have a bow holder for my right hand. I don't use my fingers, but primarily my shoulder. I have to continually monitor my shoulder movements to ensure they're correct. I used to go to therapy a lot for this in the past.

You are a master of your instrument now. Do you approach public performances thinking, "Well, if it's not perfect, people will excuse it because I don't have a hand," or did you ask your teachers to be hard on you until you were equal to or better than able-bodied top players?

It's about expressing the story of where I come from, regardless of disability. I share a story that I feel is unique to my listeners. No one is perfect, but we can all create great art. I think it's important for people to say I'm a good musician and player—not just a good musician and player for someone without a hand.

While playing with orchestras, did you feel people focused more on watching for mistakes than enjoying the music? Did musicians ever doubt your abilities when you were introduced?

I've never had an issue with an orchestra seeing my disability as a problem. I am very adaptive, and I'm lucky to be among great colleagues. I aim to show that I can achieve the same things as anyone else. I think I demonstrate the potential of humanity—people see me as someone with a challenge who can be a role model for others.

Could you tell us more about the 'Spatula'? What is it, and how does it work?

The spatula cast is something I wear around my small hand to hold the bow. It's attached to a tube fitted to the cast, enabling me to play. Holding it isn't as difficult as mastering the technique. It rotates at an angle, allowing me to manipulate the tone on my violin. I can also feel the vibrations of the notes as they travel through the device.

Ideally, an orchestra should represent inclusion—people with and without disabilities learning and working together to create music. The same should apply to educational organizations. We must find people aligned with the mission of enabling all learners to flourish, regardless of ability.

Are you working as a 'guinea pig violinist' for instrument makers to build devices for other disabled musicians?

Not at the moment. Maybe one day I'll try to work on experimental bows. I had some difficulties using the full bow at first, and it was very tricky to figure out how to play pizzicato or staccato. I don't use the entire bow—I switch from up-bow to down-bow more often than other violinists do.

You've played for Pope John Paul II, the Dalai Lama, and at the White House. Were these solo performances? Were you specifically invited, or were you part of an orchestra?

The concerts for the Pope and the White House were quite different. The White House was a solo performance for an invitation to the performing arts. The Pope's concert was for his birthday. Both were big honors and great experiences that showed me how music can take you to places you never dreamed of.

You've won many awards and scholarships. Do you have a specific goal, like emulating Paganini, or do you simply love playing and want to keep progressing?

Whatever you do in the arts, it's a never-ending journey. You're always developing techniques and striving for growth. Musically, everything has to come together. It's wonderful because you never plan to retire. Over time, you become more humble, gain more knowledge, and realize there's always more to learn.

2019

ALESSANDRO CAPOCCETTI

I Try to Capture the Beauty of Each Person Whose Picture I Take

When we were looking for a subject for an interview, we came across the Italian photographer Alessandro Capoccetti. He was born with the very rare Gollop-Wolfgang syndrome, a condition that affects only about 200 people worldwide. Growing up with such a condition in a small Italian village wasn't easy, but Alessandro didn't give up. Despite not having a right leg, he became a professional photographer. He now takes pictures of people with physical disabilities and supports the *Models of Diversity* campaign, which aims to encourage acceptance of models with disabilities in the fashion industry.

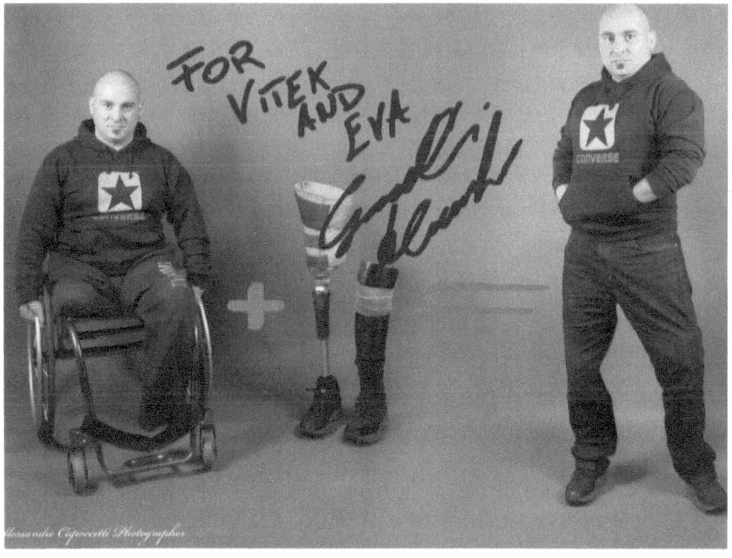

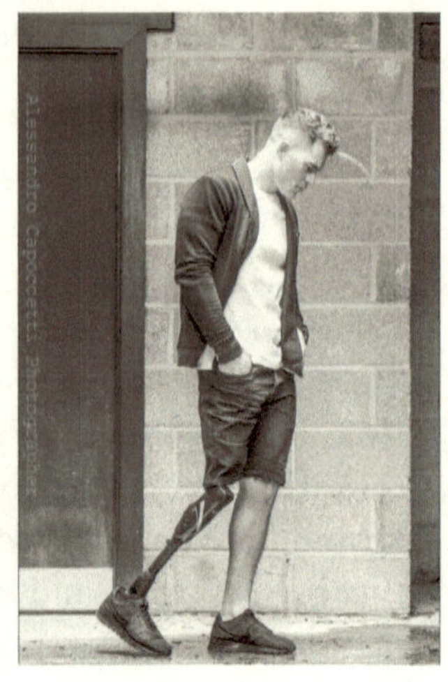

What sort of childhood did you have, and how were you treated by your schoolmates and neighbors? What have you taken from childhood into later life?

Despite being born with Gollop-Wolfgang syndrome, I had a nice childhood and the right upbringing to prepare me for life's challenges. I learned early that I would have to face many obstacles and troubles. I had good friends, and if someone harassed or bullied me, they would put them in their place. My father taught me to take life positively and with optimism. He encouraged me to enjoy life to the fullest. I had some rough times in my youth, but my father always supported me and stood behind me.

You have an artificial right leg. Did you get it from the insurance company, or did you have to pay for the care yourself?

The artificial leg was paid for by our health insurance. However, if I wanted a more modern or advanced model, I'd have to cover the extra cost myself, as the insurance only pays for basic medical care. If I could, I'd choose some models made with avant-garde technology.

Did you become a photographer because, through the lens, you could see a better world than the one you saw around you in reality?

I love pictures and imagination. In every shot, I see a unique story or moment that can be preserved forever. I met a photographer whose art I fell in love with, and that inspired me to start taking photos. I began with a classic film camera and loved the freedom of expression it gave me. I love my job because it's important—many things are hidden from the eyes, but you can't deceive your heart.

Some people take portrait pictures, others photograph nudes, and still others focus on landscapes. How did you decide?

I love capturing the ordinary beauty of people and trying to convey their emotions through photography. My goal is to highlight what makes each person unique. That focus naturally led me to the *Models of Diversity* campaign.

Within this campaign, do you seek out disabled models to photograph, or do you meet ordinary disabled people and convince those who interest you to pose?

Models of Diversity is a social campaign that supports diversity and fights discrimination in the fashion industry. It was established in London by model Angel Sinclair. I've worked with her since 2010. Everyone involved works for free. Often, the models themselves contact me, expressing their interest in contributing to the campaign. Occasionally, I'll spot someone

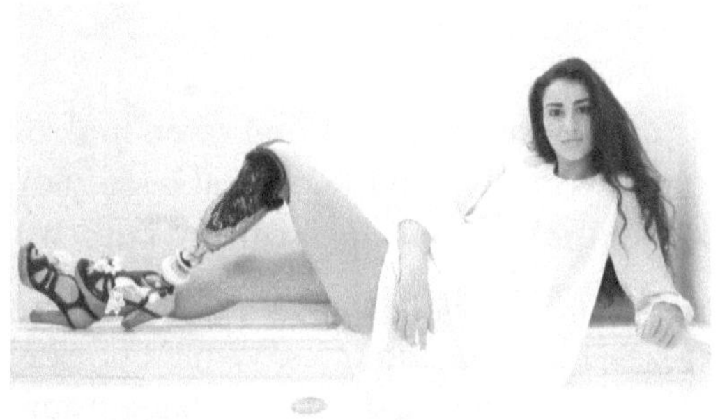

Alessandro Capoccetti Photographer

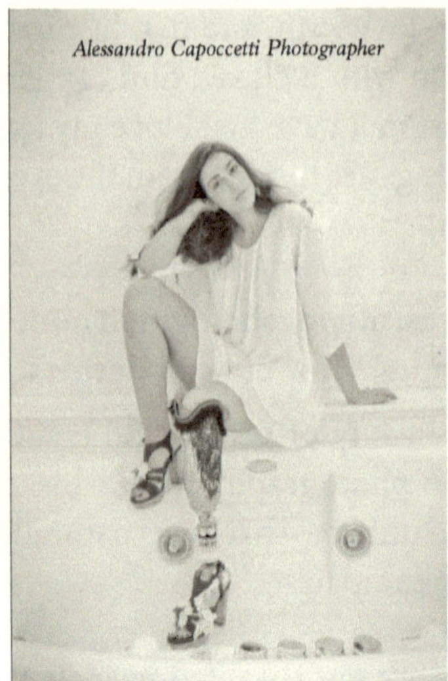

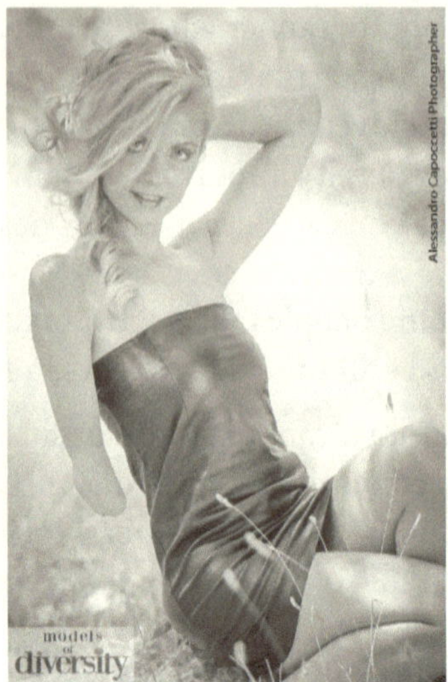

with great potential and reach out to offer them a chance to work with us.

Do you plan projects like creating an annual calendar featuring disabled models to either raise funds for them or increase awareness and promote tolerance?

I have many plans, but one key focus is getting our models onto the stages of major fashion events. It's essential to educate people to see the beauty in diversity.

Top models maintain strict diets and often look like Barbie dolls. Do you try to capture the natural beauty of ordinary people, without makeup, to show real and authentic beauty?

In the *Models of Diversity* campaign, we look for models of all ages, sizes, races, and abilities. While I don't like hiding disabilities through retouching, a good makeup application is often an important part of a photo session.

Is it true that you use your prosthesis as a tripod? Do you talk to models before a session to ease their nerves and build trust?

Yes, it's true—the prosthesis can be modified to serve as a tripod, so I always have a reliable one with me. I spend a lot of time talking with models before each session. It's vital to understand their unique beauty so I can bring it out in the photos.

When you started with the campaign, did you face misunderstanding or contempt for your work? Have you seen any change in people's attitudes since then?

Not really, to be honest. Many people appreciate our work, and there's a growing number who admire our models and learn to see beauty in diversity rather than stereotypes. Of course, I've faced some difficulties, but my passion for this job helps me overcome them. When you're as motivated as I am, even big obstacles seem manageable. I've learned to focus on the bright side, stay optimistic, and turn challenges into advantages. People like my work and the way I approach problems, which encourages me and keeps me moving forward.

Is taking pictures of disabled people your sole source of income, or are you on a mission?

I earn my living as a professional photographer, but I work for free on social campaigns and humanitarian causes. The mission of the *Models of Diversity* campaign is to change the face of the fashion industry. Professional models are often required to be flawless, self-confident, and sometimes even have acting ambitions. But not everyone possesses those qualities, even though they may have natural beauty. Our goal is to show the beauty of all races, shapes, sizes, and ages without limitations. In my opinion, a model shouldn't just be an empty figure but should express themselves through gestures, expressions, and movement. 2018

ALANA JANE NICHOLS

My Injury Led Me to Become a Top Athlete in Two Different Disciplines, and I Am Grateful for It

When Czech skier Ester Ledecká won gold medals in two different disciplines at the Winter Olympic Games in 2018, it was a sensation that landed her in the history books. Now imagine a sportswoman winning two Olympic gold medals in both the Summer and Winter Paralympics, in two completely different disciplines, despite being disabled. The story was so incredible that we immediately reached out for an interview.

American Alana Jane Nichols was born in March 1983. Growing up in Colorado, she loved snowboarding from an early age. At 17, she miscalculated a jump, landed on her back, and broke her spine. Despite being paralyzed, she went on to graduate from the University of Arizona, where she was introduced to wheelchair basketball. She began studying kinesiology and went on to win a gold medal with the basketball team at the Beijing Paralympics.

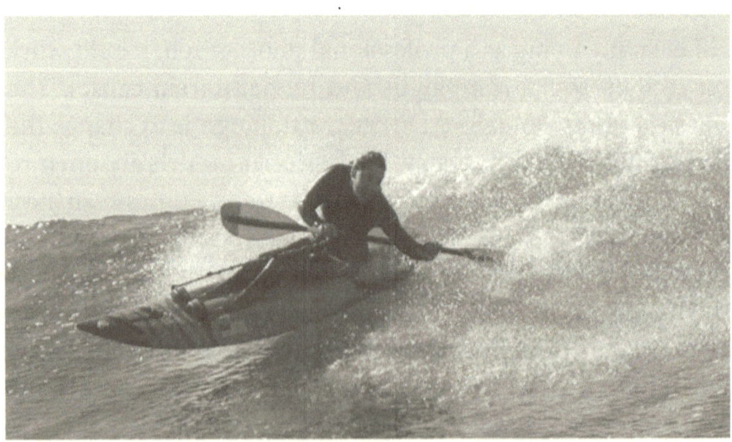

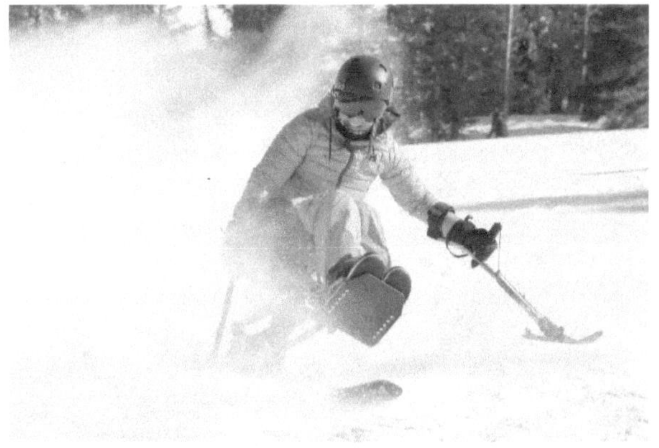

Afterward, Alana moved back to Colorado and started alpine skiing just a month after her basketball triumph. She began training with the National Sports Center for the Disabled (NSCD) and soon won multiple events, including the Super-G, downhill, and combination. At the Vancouver Winter Paralympics, she achieved an extraordinary feat: two golds, one silver, and one bronze. Later, at the Paralympics in Sochi, she won a silver medal, and two years after that, she finished seventh in sprint kayaking.

Could you say something about your accident? Was it just having fun snowboarding, or was it a planned, trained jump that went wrong?

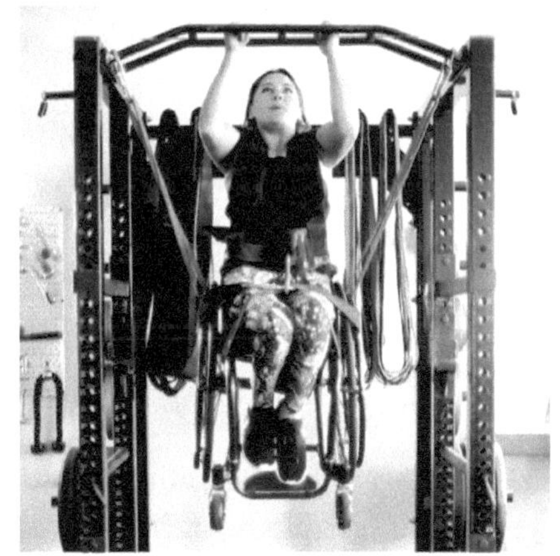

When I was 17, I attempted a backflip on my snowboard. As I approached the jump, I threw my feet hard over

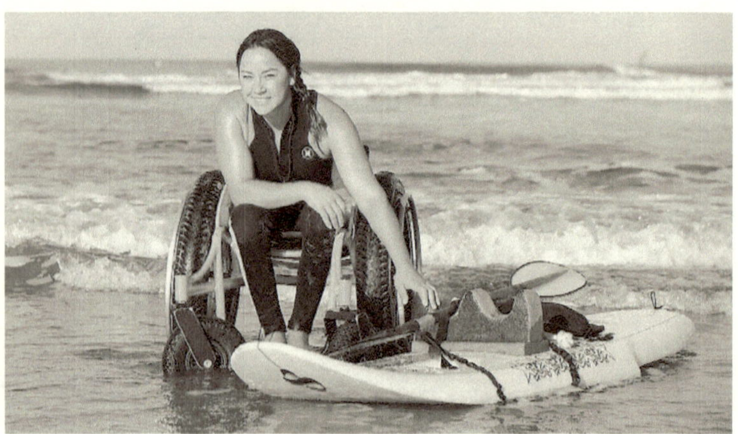

my head, but I over-rotated, completing one-and-a-half flips. I landed on my back in the snow, with my feet over my head. Unfortunately, I hit a rock under the snow, breaking my back in three places.

Did you realize you were paralyzed immediately after the fall, or was it confirmed later? How long did you spend in the hospital and rehab before returning home? Was your home adapted for a wheelchair in the meantime?

I knew immediately that I was paralyzed. I felt the sensation leave my body in a wave from my waist to my toes. I spent two weeks in the hospital and two months in inpatient rehab. By the time I was ready to return home, it had been adapted with a ramp, and the bathroom was remodeled for accessibility.

At 17, your life turned upside down. What were your plans for the future before the accident, and how much did you have to change them? Did you receive any insurance money to cover living expenses?

I had always been an athlete, and in high school, I focused on playing fast-pitch softball. I was hoping to earn a college scholarship when I broke my back during my senior year.

Luckily, I was already on social security because my father had passed away when I was young. All my hospital expenses were covered, and I began receiving disability insurance income, which helped me pay for college.

You loved winter sports. What brought you to basketball? Was it a desire for change, or did you want to avoid skiing because of the accident?

I had played basketball for nine years before my accident. I always loved team sports and taking on hard challenges. When I saw wheelchair basketball, it intrigued me because it required so much coordination. I was hesitant and nervous to return to skiing.

What inspired you to study kinesiology? Did it stem from wanting to understand your body and its capabilities, or was it a backup plan for your future? Do you see yourself working as a personal trainer or in a hospital?

I studied kinesiology to better understand how my body and disability interacted with high-performance sports. I also wanted to learn how people with disabilities could improve their performance. While I'm not sure if I'll work as a personal trainer, I currently coach basketball and alpine skiing, applying what I've learned to help my athletes perform better.

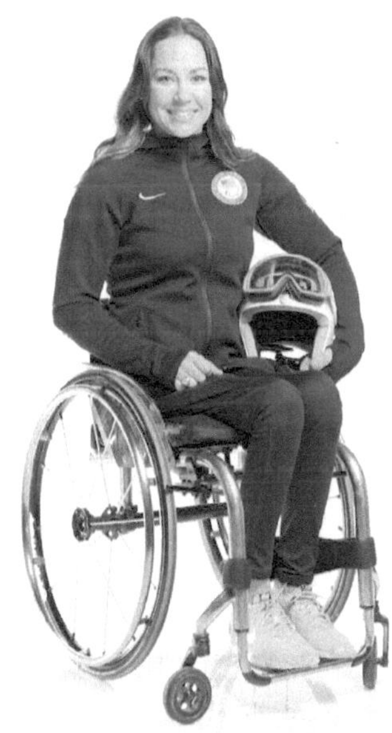

Some athletes dedicate years to a single discipline to reach

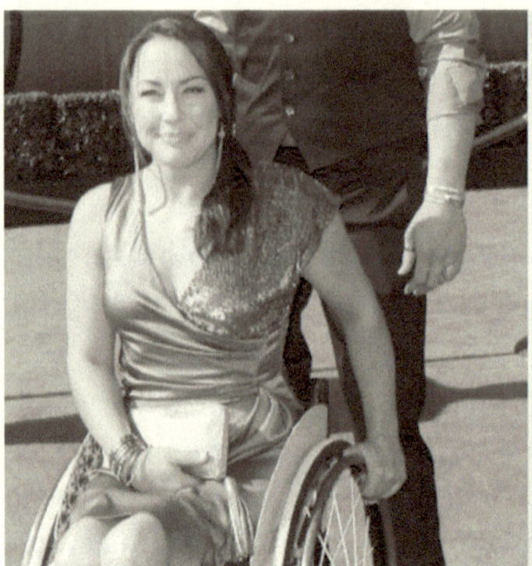
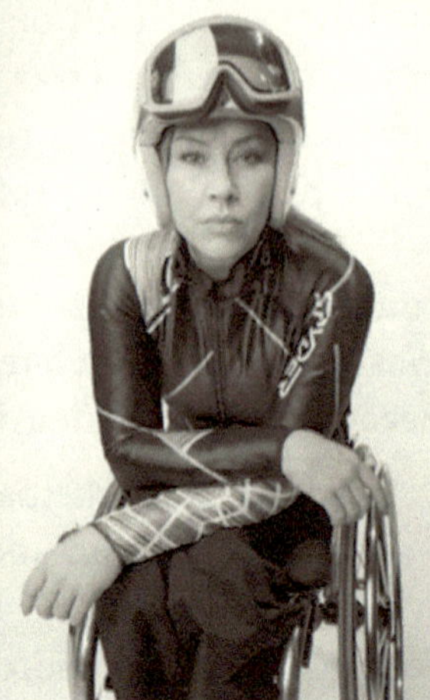

the Olympics. You've won gold medals in two different sports across both the Summer and Winter Paralympics. Was this a deliberate goal, or did your talent naturally lead you to success in both?

It was a combination of both. I was one of the first athletes to succeed in two sports at the Paralympics. Wheelchair basketball was a great cross-trainer for alpine skiing and vice versa. Training year-round for one sport prepared my body physically to compete in two. I just had to develop a stronger mindset to excel in both.

Can you compare the feeling of winning a team gold at the Summer Paralympics versus an individual gold at the Winter Paralympics? Do you prefer one over the other?

They're both special in their own ways. Winning a team sport gold required twelve women to work together toward the same goal. It takes incredible coordination, dedication, and focus from every athlete. If even one of us hadn't done her job, we wouldn't have succeeded. Sharing that victory made it very meaningful.

Winning an individual gold in alpine skiing was also incredible. I had no one else to rely on—or to blame—if something went wrong. The pressure was entirely on me. Crossing the finish line and achieving my goal was an unforgettable feeling.

You also took up sprint kayaking. What are the rules of the sport, and do you plan to compete in it again? How do you balance training for multiple sports?

Sprint kayaking is a 200-meter flat-water sprint, and the goal is simple: the first person across the finish line wins! I don't plan to compete in the sport again. I initially trained for sprint kayaking to become a world-class adaptive surfer. You should check out adaptive surfing online—it's amazing!

Do you work as a motivational speaker or focus on helping specific groups, like disabled women? Are you involved in any campaigns?

I do motivational speaking to encourage everyone, especially people with disabilities, to reach their fullest potential. I'm passionate about helping others see what they're capable of, and speaking allows me to do that.

2019

ALESSANDRO OSSOLA

There is More Life to Live

Life can be turned upside down in the blink of an eye, as young Italian Alessandro Ossola experienced when a motorcycle accident took both his leg and his new wife. He went from a high point in life to the lowest through no fault of his own. We reached out to him through Alessandro Capoccetti, a talented photographer, and received a response within hours.

How did the accident happen, and whose fault was it?

On August 29, 2015, I was on a motorbike with my wife, heading to an appointment to see a bigger house so we could start our family. During our trip, a car crossed the line and hit our motorbike. We fell, and in the accident, I lost my wife and severely damaged my leg. After a month in the hospital, I requested an amputation, and the doctors agreed. It took a lot of courage to make that decision, but I preferred to lose the leg. With the prosthesis, it may not be aesthetic, but it's functional.

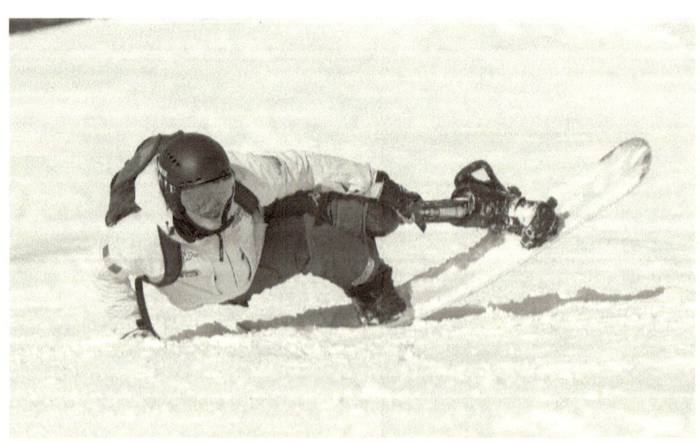

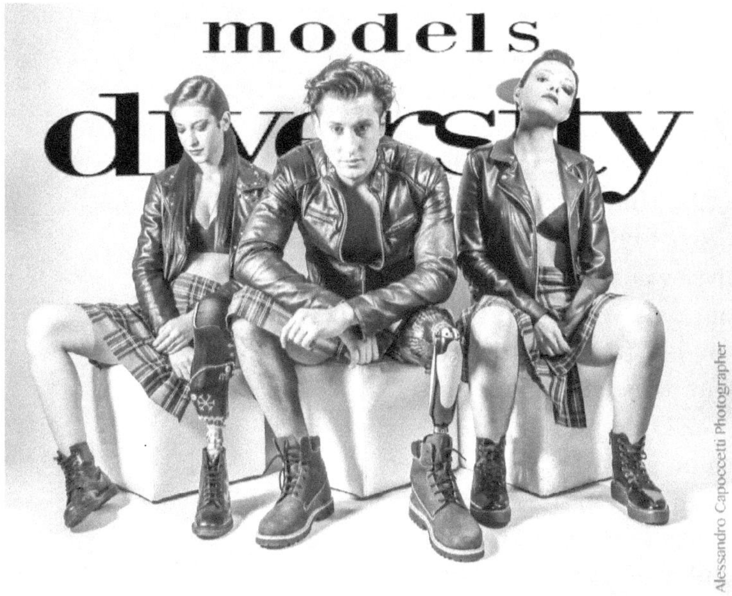

When you woke up and realized you had lost your leg and wife, which pain hurt more—the physical or the mental?

I immediately realized I had lost both my leg and my wife. I was on the ground when the doctors delivered the devastating news about my wife. It was incredibly hard. I had to stay calm—there was no time for panic, screaming, or crying. I was losing a lot of blood, and panicking could have cost me my life. I called my mother while waiting for the ambulance and told her: "Mama, come to me. I had a motorbike accident. I am gonna die." Without a doubt, the mental pain was far greater.

How long did it take you to pick yourself up and return to normal life? How long does it take to learn to walk with an artificial leg?

The path to returning to normal life wasn't easy. I spent two weeks at my parents' house after leaving the hospital, but then I returned to my own home and went back to work. Staying at home alone felt sad and unproductive. I'm an independent person, so I needed my own space again.

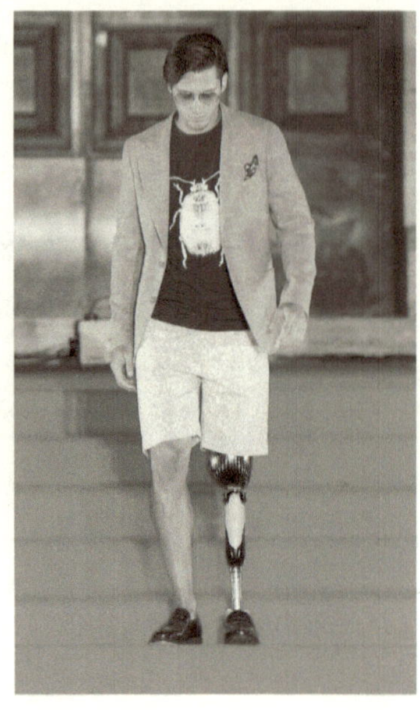

I also started going to the gym to build strength and improve my balance. I tried to live as normally as possible—not only for myself but also for my family and friends, who trusted and supported me. One pivotal moment came when I saw my father with tears in his eyes. I had never seen him cry before, and it shocked me. That was when I decided to move forward and start smiling again.

Between February and March 2016, I went to an orthopedic hospital in Bologna to set up my new prosthesis and start walking. It wasn't easy, but I worked hard. After a month of effort in the gym with my technician, Maria Grazia, I started walking again. The orthopedic staff was satisfied with the results, and I was proud of my progress.

Did you snowboard before the accident, or was it new for you afterward? If you snowboarded before, did you have to change your style with an artificial leg? If you started after, was it difficult to find balance with one leg that doesn't react as quickly?

I started snowboarding in 2008 as an amateur. With two legs, it's definitely easier to correct mistakes during slaloms. My style now is quite similar to before, thanks to my coaches, Igor Confortin and Paolo Di Pietro, who helped me improve quickly and become competitive.

I use an Ottobock knee prosthesis and a socket system from Officine Ortopediche Maria Adelaide in Turin. It includes a 'BOA' lever that increases pressure on the socket to address issues like leg volume changes caused by mountain temperatures.

After a year, you joined the national Paralympic team. How many disabled snowboard racers were competing against you? Are the next Paralympic Games your goal? How often do you train, and do you focus solely on snowboarding or include freestyle?

After a year of training with the Italian National Paralympic Snowboard Team, I competed in my first European Cup race in November. It was an amazing experience in an international environment, and I felt very positive about it. I competed against 18 other people.

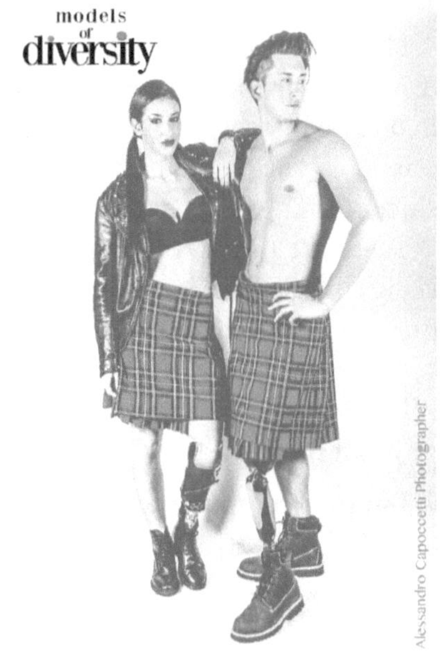

There are three categories: one for people with amputated arms, another for those with above-knee amputations, and the third for below-knee amputations. Participating in the next Paralympic Games is one of my goals, and I'm working hard to achieve it.

I go snowboarding two to three weekends per month and do intense gym training during the week. In

Para Snowboarding, there are two disciplines: Banked Slalom and Cross Snowboarding. While I continue to focus on these, I'd love to try freestyle tricks in the future.

Golf is quite technical. How much harder is it to master with an artificial leg, especially in terms of balance and the swing?

I chose golf as a summer sport because it doesn't require running or complex movements—just mastering the 'SWING.' People often think golf is easy, but it's the second most difficult sport in the world after pole vaulting.

Achieving a good swing requires synchronizing many movements. With a prosthesis, it's possible to play well, but it takes much more practice, especially to maintain balance. The type of prosthesis matters, too—electronic ones can be very helpful but are also more expensive.

You also box, right? Doesn't having a prosthetic leg give you an advantage, like never getting tired or hitting harder?

Ha ha, funny! Especially in kickboxing, you might think the iron leg could hit harder—ha ha, just joking! I don't compete in boxing matches; I prefer the 'peace and love' approach. But boxing is one of the best ways for me to get cardio training since running is challenging for me.

There are limitations during training. For example, delivering a hard punch requires good balance, and it's easy to fall. But we're 'Bionic People,' so we don't give up!

What is your job? Did your disability help you achieve more, or has it held you back?

I studied computer science and trained in AutoCAD 2D/3D, a CAD (computer-aided design) program used to draw mechanical parts. I've worked in this field since 2012 at a small factory in Borgaro Torinese called VIGEL. It's one of the world's leading companies for manufacturing technologies based on multi-spindle machining centers.

Tell us about the 'Bionic People' project. What is it, and what is its mission?

A few months ago, I spoke with Chiara Bordi, Miss Italia with prostheses, about creating a group of people with disabilities who could share their stories with schools, organizations, and others. We want to discuss disability in various fields—fashion, sports, and more—and how to overcome challenges after an accident.

In my opinion, the process involves three steps:

- Realize what has happened.
- React.
- Set achievable goals.

Our mission is to inspire people, disabled or not, to never give up and set new goals to find happiness and satisfaction. We believe, "THERE IS ALWAYS MORE LIFE TO LIVE."

How did you start working with Alessandro Capoccetti on photo modeling?

I met my friend Alessandro Capoccetti during a fashion-inclusive event in Avezzano, a city in the Abruzzo region of Italy.

2019

ALEX ZANARDI

The Extraordinary Will of an Extraordinary Man

Alex Zanardi is an extraordinary man, known for his resilience and incredible achievements both before and after a life-altering accident. His journey is marked by triumph over adversity, demonstrating courage and determination in the face of immense challenges.

He competed in F-3000 and Formula One from 1991 to 1994, scoring a solitary point and nearly losing his life in a severe crash during testing that left him hospitalized. Afterward, he moved to America and, despite some setbacks, secured a seat with the Target Ganassi team. He became a hugely popular champion in CART in 1997–1998. This success caught the attention of Sir Frank Williams, who offered him a contract in F1 for the following season. However, it was an ill-fated year, plagued by reliability issues and a lack of competitiveness in the car, leaving Alex disillusioned and without a single point.

He returned to the USA, but, as the saying goes, you're a hero one day and a zero the next. He struggled to secure a seat due to increased competition and a lack of strong results in recent years. Everything changed in 2001 during the Lausitzring race, where he suffered a horrific crash. T-boned by another driver, Alex lost 3/4 of his blood and both legs. The impact was so severe that it required immediate, life-saving intervention on the track.

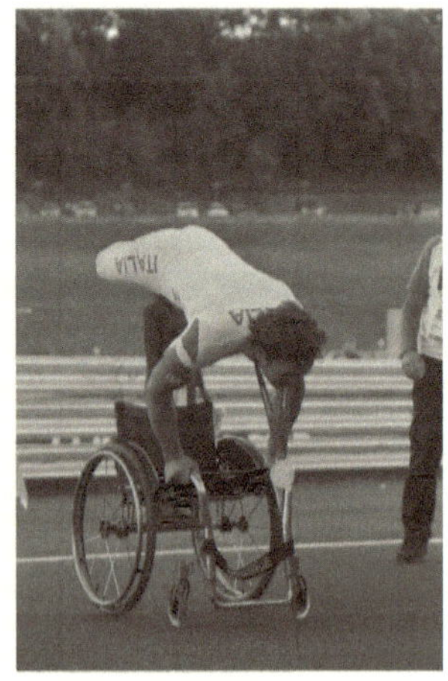

After receiving artificial legs that didn't meet his needs, he decided to design and create his own, tailored specifically for him. Over the next five seasons, he drove a BMW Italia car in the touring car championship. Later, he transitioned to hand-cycling, winning gold medals at the London Paralympics in 2012. He went on to win disabled marathons in Venice, Rome, and New York, and competed in the Ironman race in 2014.

In addition to his athletic pursuits, Alex builds kart chassis and runs his own foundation, *Bimbingamba*, which helps children who have lost their legs. Securing an interview with Alex was no easy feat—it took six months due to his busy schedule—but he graciously obliged, thanks to his supportive wife Daniela.

When you had your almost fatal crash in Germany, do you remember the feelings when you woke up and realized you had no legs? What were your immediate thoughts?

Understandable question. However, I have to tell you, if someone had asked me before the accident how I would react in such a situation, I could never have predicted it. I was just pleased to be alive. As bad—actually, terribly bad—as I felt at that moment, I knew I had already gone through the worst part. Therefore, I was happy for the opportunity to start all over again.

How long did the rehabilitation take? How long did it take you to learn to walk on prosthetic legs? Was it difficult to drive a car very fast with artificial legs? Did you face any limits, or was it just a matter of retraining your reflexes?

It took about a year to be up and standing properly. I began walking on prosthetic legs a few days after returning to Italy, 45 days after the accident. Rehabilitation is different for everyone—it takes time to transform a pair of artificial legs into tools that allow you to live better than you could in a wheelchair.

In that year, I not only learned to walk but also adapted my residual abilities to meet my personal needs. During this process, I began thinking about how I could drive a race car again. Having the right technology helps, but you need to know exactly what you want to achieve.

Was your only thought how quickly you could get back into a car, or were you considering other ventures? Did someone or something help you focus elsewhere?

Life is like shopping at a supermarket—you don't put everything into your trolley. You choose what suits you, what brings you joy, or what fulfills your needs, leaving the rest behind. One night, I was talking to an old friend who worked with BMW Italy, and he offered to prepare a car for me. The rest is what you saw.

I can also say that on January 1, 2014, I had no idea I'd be in Hawaii on October 11 to compete in the Ironman. Life happens incidentally, and you just go with it.

When did you decide to take cycling seriously and aim to become the best in the world? How long did it take you to become an Olympic champion?

At the end of 2009, BMW Italy didn't have an exciting project for the following season, and I was already passionate about hand-cycling. I saw it as the perfect opportunity. I decided to dedicate more time to training and set a goal to qualify for London 2012.

Was it natural for you as a sportsman to set another challenge? Could you use any of your reflexes or experience as a driver? Was the Olympics your ultimate goal, or did your progress even surprise you?

London was just a good excuse to pursue something I loved. Success doesn't come simply from ambition—it comes from loving what you do. The same was true in racing. My best talent might be knowing where to go in life.

Can you compare the feelings of winning at the London Paralympics versus winning the CART championship? Are they similar or different? Which was harder to achieve?

The feelings were very similar. Whatever I'm doing at any given moment feels like the most important thing in my life. Achieving success in that context brings immense joy, whether it's car racing or hand-cycling.

Technically, the two activities are very different, but maintaining focus while racing a car with 100,000 people watching helped me stay calm and concentrated in cycling competitions.

In Formula One, you raced for a team. Now you race for yourself. Does that give you more freedom?

Yes! It's easier to deal with myself than with a team owner.

With your *Bimbingamba* foundation, what are you trying to achieve? Do you use your popularity to attract sponsors or media attention?

Bimbingamba provides prosthetic limbs for kids who need them but can't afford them. Since starting in 2005, we've helped over one hundred children at RTM (the orthopedic center where the foundation operates). We're committed to continuing to assist all kids who need us.

What kind of help does the foundation provide? Is it mainly technical, or does it include social and legal support?

Our primary focus is providing prosthetic limbs customized to meet the unique needs of each child. Sometimes we also help families navigate healthcare systems to secure the benefits they're entitled to. When that's not an option, we cover all costs, including travel expenses to get the kids to us.

Do you think the accident opened a door to a new and fulfilling life? Are you happier and richer—mentally—than you would have been as a retired Formula One driver?

Without a doubt! Everything I'm doing today is directly related to my new condition. Losing my legs became one of the greatest opportunities of my life. Life is like a good Italian coffee: you can add all the sugar you want, but unless you stir it, it won't get as sweet as you'd like.

2015

BROM WIKSTROM

I Believe Life is What You Make of It, Whether Disabled or Not

We came across Brom Wikstrom's story purely by accident. What drew us in was his participation in anti-war demonstrations in the late 60s and his adventures traveling across the country on freight trains. We admired his attitude and free spirit, which didn't falter even after a freak swimming accident. Brom has traveled around the world, including a visit to Kutná Hora, a town in the Czech Republic near where we live. With so many points of connection, we reached out to him for an interview.

Could you tell us about life in the USA in the late 60s, with the Vietnam War, J.F.K., Martin Luther King, etc.? It must have been a remarkable and tumultuous era. How many anti-war demonstrations did you take part in, and were they brutally attacked by police or peaceful with no incidents?

Growing up in the 1960s was both exciting and bewildering. From my earliest memories, the lingering

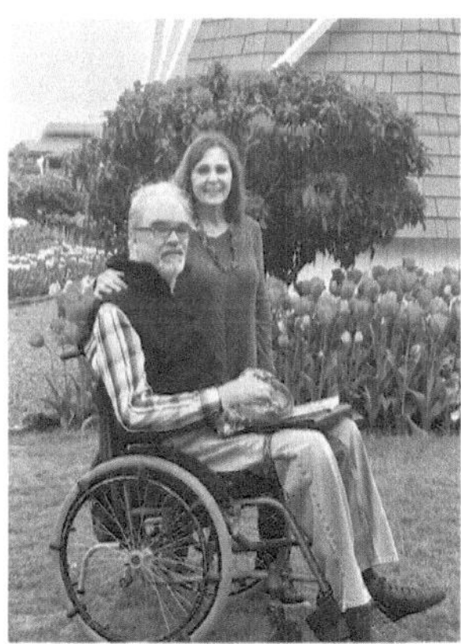

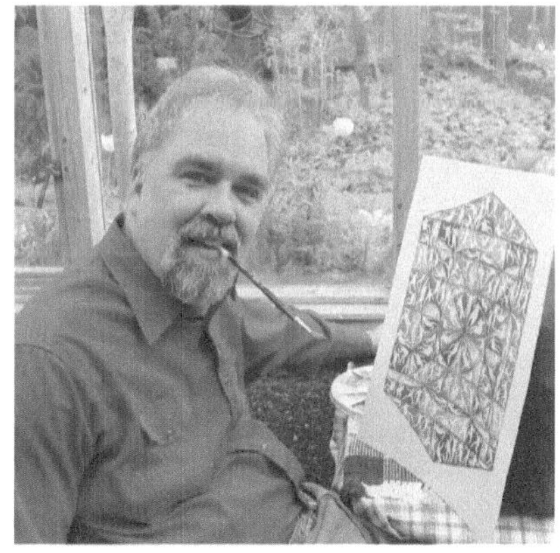

threat of nuclear annihilation was ever-present, with weekly drills at school. My father served in the Army Reserve, and his brother was lost in World War II, so the military presence was very real in our home.

The anti-war protests coincided with the Black Power movement, and I became involved in both while still in my early teens. Most of the demonstrations I participated in were peaceful, but I did witness violence on occasion. After the Kent State tragedy, where student demonstrators were killed by National Guardsmen, protests became more militant. I was part of a group that blocked car traffic on a state highway to disrupt commerce. Police overreactions were expected, but I avoided arrest by turning to more clandestine protests, like posting banners at night and writing anonymous articles in an underground school publication.

Fortunately, I avoided military service due to a high draft lottery number. Seattle, being the hometown of Jimi Hendrix and Bruce Lee, was a cultural hub. Though I never played an instrument, I was deeply involved in the music scene, attending concerts, festivals, and be-ins. My father, despite his conservative politics, was a big fan of modern jazz, exposing me to Miles Davis and other progressive artists early on.

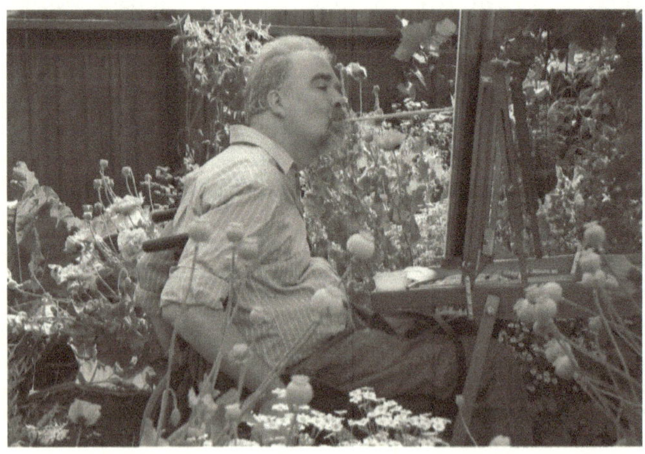

This later served me well when disco took over, and I happily shifted my focus to jazz and reggae.

You seemed to be an exploratory person—searching for Indian artifacts in Alaska, riding freight trains, and living in derelict buildings. Were you trying to see the real America, or just seeking freedom and independence? How did you ride freight trains, and was it dangerous or illegal? How did it feel to experience that kind of boundary-free freedom?

I grew up near the railroad tracks in Seattle, often seeing vagabonds warming themselves by campfires and sharing what they had. Hitchhiking was common, and I always traveled with a companion for safety.

Short trips around the state gave me the confidence to embark on longer journeys. The feeling of independence was exhilarating and addictive. Several friends traveled this way, including one whose father worked for the railroad and taught us the finer points. Traveling through freight yards was technically illegal, but by being discreet and avoiding trouble, we could figure out which trains were heading in the desired direction, find an empty boxcar, and wait for the train to pull away.

During the years I traveled like this, I never had any issues. However, by 1975, railroads had cracked down on unauthorized riders, and it became too difficult. Hitchhiking was another option, and as long as you were polite and willing to contribute—perhaps sharing gas money—you could meet wonderful people, stay in hippie communes, and pick up odd jobs like fruit-picking.

How did you sustain your spinal cord injury while swimming—was it an unexpected accident?

My injury occurred while I was living in New Orleans. I was swimming in a familiar part of the Mississippi River and thought I knew where the deep water was. Foolishly, instead of wading in to cool off on a hot day, I took a running dive from the beach. I hit shallow water—or possibly a submerged log—head-first and became instantly paralyzed. If my friend hadn't recognized my distress, I would have drowned. I must have held my breath for a couple of minutes before being rescued.

How long did rehabilitation take? Did you receive any insurance money, or were you left to fend for yourself? How did you acquire a wheelchair?

Thankfully, the federal Social Security system covered my hospitalization, and I received disability income, along with extra funds for a personal care attendant after rehabilitation.

I spent a year in rehabilitation due to complications like pressure sores and a throat tear from poor initial care. At one point, I fell from my hospital bed, tearing my breathing tube from my neck. I had a near-death experience during this ordeal, crossing into a light that was a glorious experience. It stayed with me and inspired my desire to help others, especially children with disabilities.

What was the situation for wheelchair users in the USA in the early 70s? Were public spaces accessible, or were people with disabilities ostracized?

Seattle was progressive for wheelchair users in the mid-70s. Most city buses had lifts, and curb cuts were being installed. Public reactions were a mix of pity and curiosity.

I became accustomed to stares and questions, particularly from children. I appreciated the kindness of strangers who helped me up hills or held doors open. I continued to visit museums, movies, and galleries, and eventually became a familiar figure in town.

A large cultural center near my home, the site of the 1962 Seattle World's Fair, hosted civic celebrations and non-profits.

I became involved in their programs and found a sense of community.

How did you adapt to your new circumstances? How did you resume painting, and how long did it take to learn to paint by mouth?

After rehabilitation, I moved back to my parents' house, where they set up ramps and a workspace for my art. Those were hard times, as most of my friends had moved on with their lives. I became very depressed.

Painting helped me cope, and after several months, I saw improvement in my work. I held a small exhibit at the hospital where I'd undergone rehab and gifted pieces to the nurses and therapists who had supported me.

You designed an art program for a children's hospital and became a teacher. What did that mean to you?

Volunteering at a local children's hospital gave me a sense of self-worth. Working with children who had severe disabilities or terminal illnesses gave me a new appreciation for my abilities.

I applied for a grant to expand the program, which introduced me to advocacy for the arts among people with disabilities. I began giving presentations at schools and festivals and pursued art therapy classes through state vocational services. This eventually led to my involvement with the Kennedy Center for the Performing Arts.

Tell us about your meeting with Andy Warhol. What was it like?

Through VSA Arts, a national organization supporting artists with disabilities, I participated in a festival in Washington, D.C. My art station was set up next to Andy Warhol's. He came over to examine my work and exchange pleasantries.

He was there to draw a Campbell's soup can, while I painted portraits of festival attendees. He later returned with Jamie Wyeth to watch me work. I like to think I taught Andy Warhol a bit about painting with the mouth. He was gracious and genuinely interested in my art.

You've traveled the world. Were your trips always for exhibitions, or did you travel as a tourist? Where were facilities for the disabled the best and the worst?

Most of my travels are for exhibitions and conferences, where organizers handle my needs. Tourist trips are always more challenging, but they're worth it for the people we meet and the experiences we gain. Italy is among the most memorable destinations, though access can be difficult. My wife, a seasoned traveler who speaks Italian, makes it easier.

You are active on the boards of many charities. Do you do this to fill your time fruitfully, or would you have done so even if you weren't disabled?

I began serving on non-profit boards as a way to give back for the assistance I received. Meeting compassionate, knowledgeable people in these roles inspired me to contribute more. My disability gives me a unique perspective, and I hope to be a better advocate because of it.

Do you think life gave you more than it took?

I believe life is what you make of it, whether disabled or not. Challenges may be great, but victories are sweeter. If I can inspire someone to try harder or help someone in need, then I've played my part in making the world a bit better.

2018

DENNIS FRANCESCONI

My Sense of Survival Was and Still Is Strong

We were looking for some interesting paralyzed artists and came across a few names of people who had made extraordinary and beautiful paintings—by mouth or foot. We asked them for interviews, and Dennis Francesconi replied within a day, which was very encouraging. So we worked out the questions and sent them to America. Interesting answers came back to us within 48 hours.

Could you tell us about the water-skiing accident, please? Was it a planned stunt, or was it simply an unexpected accident?

The accident was just that, an accident. The boat came closer to the shore than I anticipated, my speed was too great, and upon contact with the sand, I was thrown 30 feet, landing on the back of my head and neck, instantly becoming paralyzed.

Had you been interested in painting or art before the accident, or did you take up mouth painting while confined to bed as a way to pass the time?

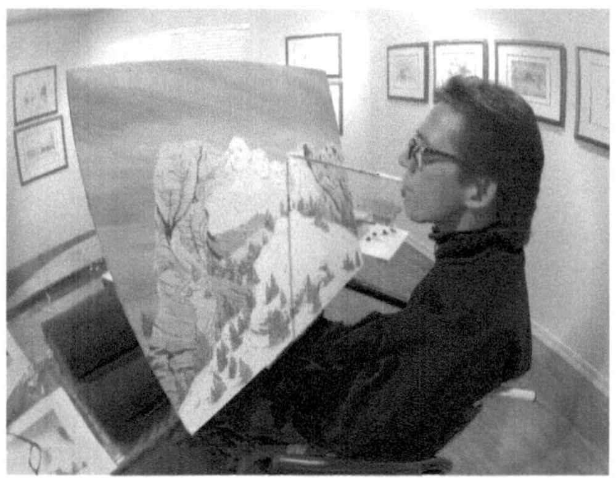

No, I had no interest in art or anything else at the time. I was mainly thinking about what would happen next. Going from having a 100% working physical body to maybe 10% was a drastic change, to say the least. Career choices weren't part of my thought patterns; survival and trying to determine how to fit into this thing called life were more important.

Do you think there is a difference between being an able-bodied painter and then, when paralyzed, transferring skills from hand to mouth, or starting from scratch with no talent and experience?

I know a couple of people who were artists before their injury and continued afterward by using their mouths. I believe that's an advantage. I had no artistic ability before my injury, although I did admire those who did.

Nine years passed between your accident and your first sketch. What did you do during that time? Did you ever struggle with thoughts of giving up, or were you able to overcome these

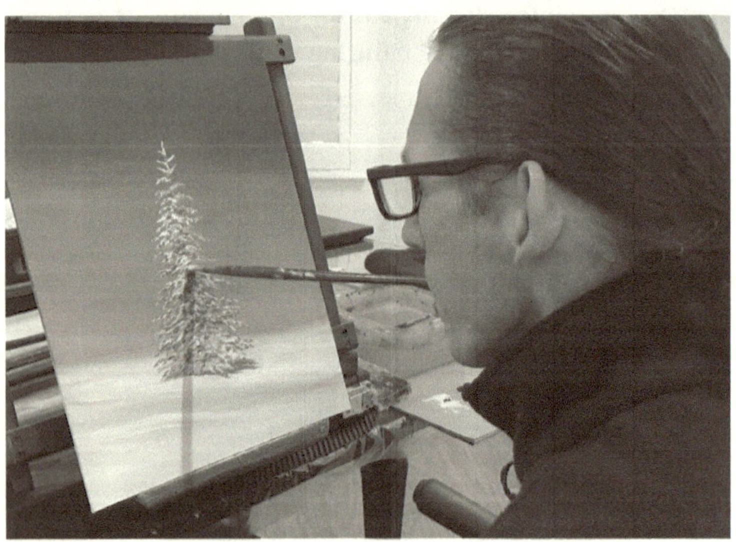

challenges more quickly before mouth painting entered your thoughts?

After my injury, I spent two and a half months in the hospital. For the first two years after that, I turned to Jack Daniels. Of course, thoughts like "Why am I here?" or "It would've been better if I'd died in the accident" crossed my mind, but I never thought about ending my life. My sense of survival was, and still is, too strong. Then, after I realized that this behavior wasn't making things any easier, I moved on.

With the encouragement of my mother and my girlfriend, I tried other things. I studied and earned a real estate license, but I didn't care for that line of work. I then tried a sales job, selling vitamins and food supplements. After a couple of years, I gave that up as well; I just couldn't maintain an interest in it. Around that time, my girlfriend became my fiancée, and I became interested in therapy and physical exercise.

Not long after that, I started writing about my experience in a notebook by mouth, and while thinking of what to write next, I created small sketches in the notebook. After about two years of doing that, the pen sketches became more elaborate, and I progressed to watercolor and started creating small paintings.

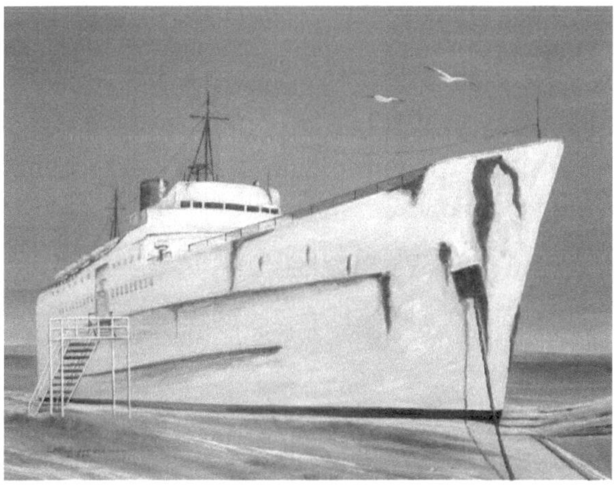

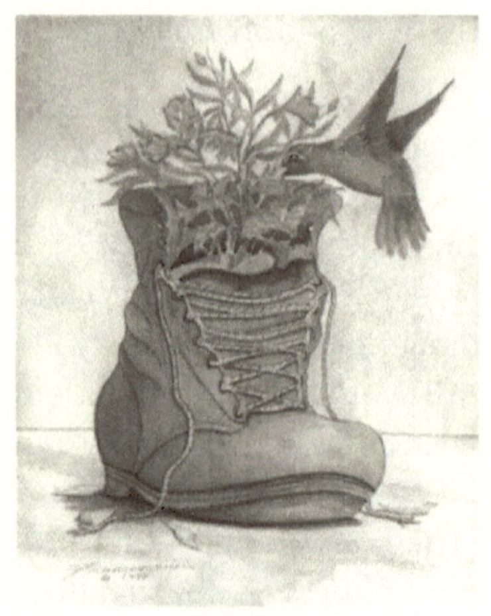

Our friends and family were amazed, and this encouraged me to do more. I then learned about the Association of Mouth and Foot Painting Artists of the World (AMFPA). I submitted samples of my work and was quickly offered a contract as a student member, which provided a scholarship that I used to purchase better-quality art supplies.

Did you join college to gain a safety net qualification, or was it a serious pursuit of art to develop your skills and knowledge?

No, my fiancée decided to get a college degree and invited me to go along and get one too. We both completed our college education with full honors, including membership in Phi Theta Kappa (an international honors society) and inclusion on the National Dean's List. I studied and passed all of the required classes first and then completed my degree by taking some art classes at the end.

Did you receive health benefits that covered your living expenses, wheelchair, and college, or did you face challenges in applying for financial support repeatedly?

After my injury, I was placed on public support, which covered my basic living and medical expenses. My college expenses were paid for by my scholarship from the AMFPA.

When you became a full member of the AMFPA, you declined public funds that supported your living. Does that mean that

as a full-time member, you get some kind of wages that keep you afloat?

Yes, after being promoted to a full member, I began receiving a very generous annual salary with great incentives and methods to increase my earnings. I removed myself from public support, although I didn't have to because the options presented and available to me at that time were not appealing. This change allowed me to fully embrace my new career as an artist and focus on my role within the AMFPA without the limitations or expectations that came with public assistance.

Your paintings are beautiful and clean. How long did it take you to find your style, and was it always like that, or did it become better, nicer, and cleaner after hundreds of hours of painting?

My style, at least for me, has evolved over the years to become what it is now. I believe that was the case for other artists too—constantly learning and improving.

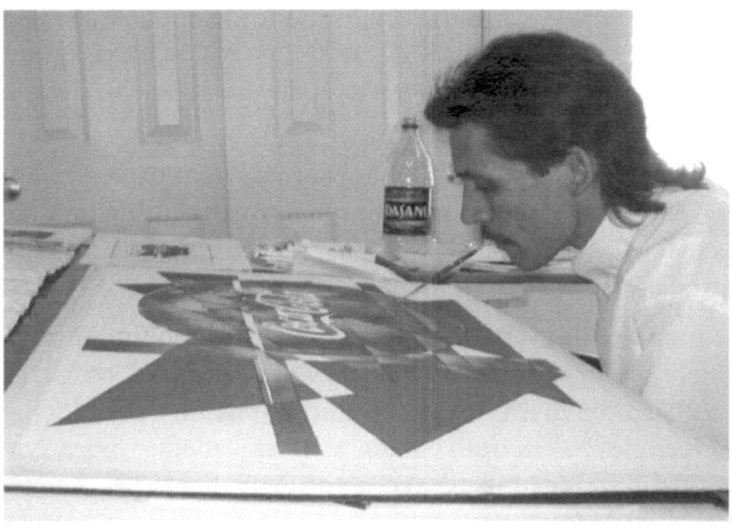

How did it happen that Governor Arnold Schwarzenegger chose your painting for his official Christmas card collection? Did you get any fee for sales?

Well, that opportunity just showed up in my email one morning. It turns out that Trish Fontana, the Director of Special Projects in the office of First Lady Maria Shriver, found me on the internet while searching for an artist for this project.

The Christmas card design that they selected went out to several thousand National Guard members and others close to Governor Schwarzenegger. And no, we didn't charge any fees. The press reports on television, in newspapers, and on the internet were enough, and very positive.

We saw some of your corporate paintings. Are you approached by companies, or do you market your paintings yourself? What is the normal fee that your pictures are sold for, and do you sell what you paint by your own will, or are you asked to paint something (customer order), so basically paint on demand?

Opportunities of this nature have come to me in the past; I've never chased them. I don't sell my original paintings. My income and assets are derived from my contract with the AMFPA and our investments. However, I'm always open to new opportunities.

Do you paint what you have in your imagination and mind or reproduce what you see? Your topics are very different, so you don't have favorite subjects to paint (e.g., forests, flowers, animals, faces, etc.).

I try to paint subjects that could be useful to the AMFPA publishers worldwide on cards, calendars, and other products, and also for them to use in international art exhibitions. Sometimes I work from photographs, and at other times, I'm inspired by something I've seen or simply thought of.

How long does it typically take to complete a painting? Do you receive exhibition opportunities through the AMFPA, or are you approached by exhibition halls directly?

It depends on the painting's subject, size, and complexity. The shortest time to complete a piece is about three or four days. The longest is three and a half months. My average now, I'd say, is one week.

The AMFPA is run by the artists for the artists, so yes, we all help each other as much as we can. I encourage everyone to learn more about the AMFPA at http://vdmfk.com.

Do you feel you are a better person and a more satisfied human being than you were when able-bodied? Do you enjoy life now, or do you sometimes reflect on the accident and ask, 'Why me?'

I'm satisfied with what "we"—my wife Kristi and I—have achieved together with the physical abilities I have. Without her, I'm not sure if any of this would have happened the way it has. No, I don't have any "why me" thoughts at this point. Since I've been paralyzed for 38 years now, I really can't compare my life experience as it is to a life of any length being able-bodied. That's just not possible, and it's something that we'll never know.

I ask that you include these important links with this story, in an effort to help others learn more.

For more information on Dennis A. Francesconi, http://sconi.com For more information on the Association of Mouth and Foot Painting Artists Worldwide (AMFPA), please visit their international website at http://vdmfk.com.

2018

DOUG LANDIS

Hidden Abilities Within Us

When I came across the beautiful paintings by pure chance, I couldn't believe they were made by a man who was paralyzed from the neck down, painting by holding the brush between his teeth. I checked the biography of that man – Doug Landis – and realized he embodies the Czech saying: "Through sport to better health and permanent disability." Doug became paralyzed in an instant during a wrestling match. He appreciated the interest from the Czech Republic, and the interview was conducted within a few days.

Could you describe the wrestling accident? Was it an official match? Did the other wrestler feel guilty?

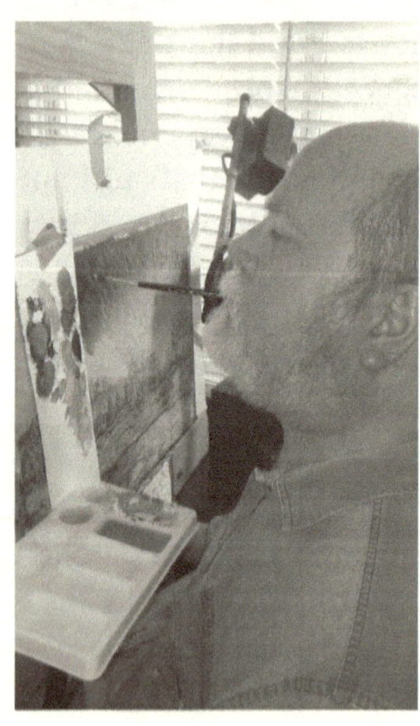

I was 15 years old when I was injured in a high school wrestling match in 1975. It was my sophomore year, and I was on the wrestling team. I had worked at a fast-food restaurant during the summer and missed football tryouts, so when school started, I joined the wrestling team because I had some training in judo when I was younger and thought wrestling would be easy. It wasn't—it was tough, but it put me in the best shape of my life, which ultimately saved my life when I was injured. I never considered myself a jock; I just liked playing sports for fun. I was just an okay wrestler, and our high school team was wrestling another high school to see who would qualify for the state championships. I was wrestling a freshman from the other school, and I thought it would be an easy win because I was older and slightly bigger.

I went for a takedown move where the correct way to execute it is to plant your face in your opponent's chest, wrap your arms around their body, and pull them down. That's how I was taught, but I did it wrong. Even the night before, during practice, I was wrestling with a teammate who was showing me how to do it correctly. I did it wrong, planting my head next to my opponent's hip and wrapping my arms around their body like a tackle. My teammate planted my face into the mat and scolded me, warning me that I could get hurt if I did it wrong because an opponent could grab my head and take me down.

Sure enough, during the match, I went in like a tackle, putting my head next to my opponent's hip instead of into his chest, allowing him to grab my head. I realized immediately

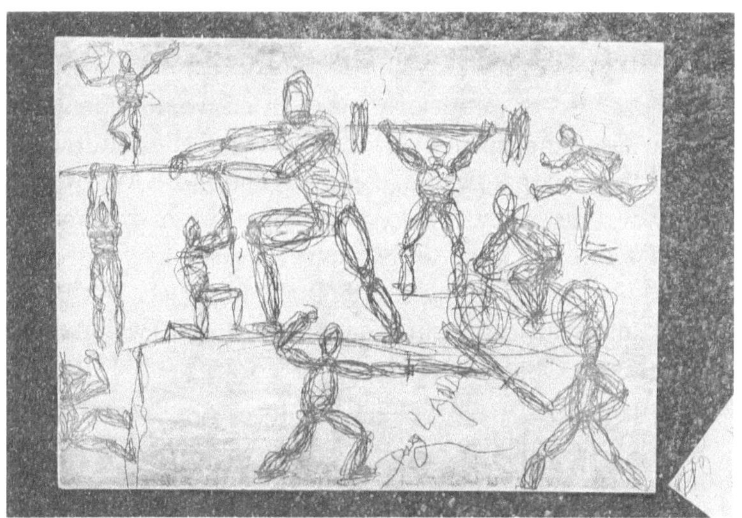

that I'd done it wrong and tried to pull away. My opponent naturally held onto my head, and due to the angle and pressure of my pulling away and my opponent holding on, my neck dislocated at C3-C4, paralyzing me instantly. I fell to the mat, briefly passing out. Somehow, I knew right away that I'd broken my neck and couldn't move anything—paralyzed from the neck down. My coaches tried to console me, saying they thought it was just a pinched nerve in my neck, as another football player from our school had been paralyzed briefly by a pinched nerve but fully recovered.

While waiting for an ambulance, my opponent and his coach came over to apologize. I told them not to worry; it wasn't his fault. It was my mistake, and he did exactly what anyone in his position would have done. We didn't keep in touch, but I heard he struggled with it afterward. I've been interviewed several times on local TV and in newspapers, and I've always said I've never blamed him—it was completely my fault, and I've accepted that. I truly hope he knows that.

How much has life changed since then? Was it difficult to adjust to having someone help you? Do you have a caretaker with you all the time? Is your house wheelchair-accessible?

Life changed dramatically. I was an active, independent person. Growing up in California, I loved the outdoors—riding bikes, hiking, fishing, camping, and more. We moved to Missouri just a year before I was injured. I had many life goals: I wanted to learn to fly, scuba dive, skydive, and rock climb. I also hoped to join the military to fly jets, but I had learned just before my injury that I needed 20/20 vision to fly in the military, and I wore glasses, so I wasn't sure if I'd join like many of my friends planned to.

Going from being so active to being completely paralyzed from the neck down, unable to move or feel anything, was devastating. It was hard learning to let people do everything for me. I had to learn patience and not take my anger and frustration out on my caregivers. I was fortunate that my mother was a registered nurse and took care of me for nine years. Later, I met an amazing woman in college, and we've been married for nearly 35 years. She's been caring for me by herself, and we live in a wheelchair-accessible house. I'm also fortunate to have a 14-year-old van with a lift.

Did you leave school or return in a wheelchair to finish your grade? Did you receive any social or health benefits?

I spent two months in the Intensive Care Unit. Shortly after moving to a rehab unit, tutors began visiting my hospital room to help me keep up with my studies. I spent six months in rehab, three of which were during summer break, so I was able to keep up with my classes. There was talk of me attending a Special School District for students with disabilities, but I wanted to return to my old school. I set a goal to graduate with my class. The school wasn't accessible, but they ensured all my classes were on the first floor in one building, which had only one step at the entrance that I needed help with. My parents advocated for me, and I was able to return to school at the beginning of my junior year.

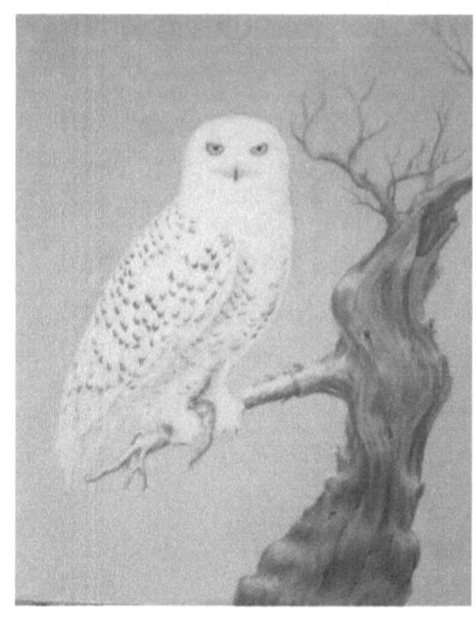

With morning tutors, a state college correspondence course, and classes in the afternoon, I graduated with my class—the first person in a wheelchair to do so at that high school. Once I turned eighteen, the state helped pay part of my tuition at the local community college and university I attended.

You studied at an institute for motion graphics founded by Walt Disney. Is that where you developed your passion for painting, or did you want to learn painting formally and adapt by painting with your mouth?

In rehab, they tried placing a paintbrush in my hand and putting my arm in a metal sling so that I could move slightly with my shoulder. The result was mostly rainbow paintings, as I could only swing my arm back and forth. It didn't spark my interest in art.

It wasn't until months later when my family thought I was watching too much TV, that they put a ballpoint pen on the end of the mouth-stick I used for typing and challenged me to a drawing contest. We drew a vase, and I won the bet. Shortly after, my mother found a book of biblically inspired poems with sketchy pen-and-ink drawings of the apostles by a Spanish artist. I thought I could replicate the style, and I started sketching faces and dancers. Then we received a Christmas card with a sketchy line drawing of a house, and I copied it, creating designs inspired by the Painted Lady houses in San Francisco and older homes in our area.

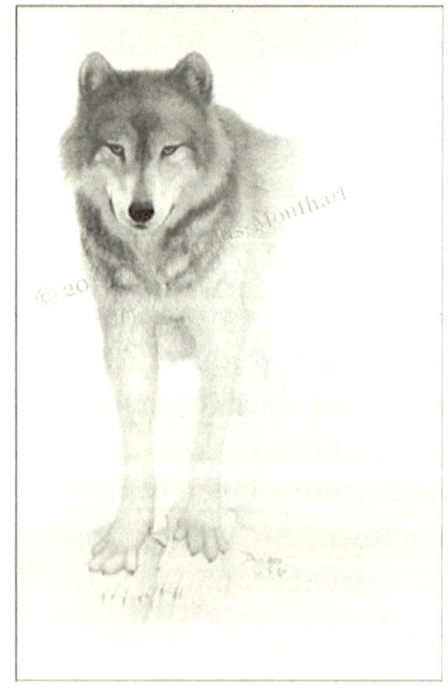

Besides using a ballpoint pen, I experimented with brush and ink, creating a few animal images. We had some of them made into prints and note cards to sell at local arts and crafts shows. At the time, I was attending high school, community college, and university, studying Communications, Film, and

Television Production. I only took one figure-drawing class, and even though I sold some artwork, I considered it just a hobby.

When I chose the California Institute of the Arts (CalArts) for my Master of Fine Arts, it was because they were one of the only schools in the U.S. teaching computer graphics in the mid-1980s. I went to study computer graphics, film, and video animation—what they called Motion Graphics. I thought it would be a good career path for someone with my disability, using a mouth-stick. Looking back, I really wish I had taken my art more seriously back then and taken art classes at CalArts—it's a fantastic art school, and many talented artists have come out of it.

I read that you learned to paint upside down and sideways. Why did you do that, and how long did it take you to learn?

I'm a self-taught artist. After graduating from CalArts, I worked as a computer graphic artist for a travel promotions company and started having neck problems. I also started struggling to control my art when using a pen in my mouth-stick. My wife suggested switching to art pencils, which came in very light grays to charcoal black, giving me more control and being gentler on my neck. I also designed an adjustable easel in school that a friend built for me, bringing the art closer to my face.

I would come up with an idea and then search for photos to guide my drawing—sometimes using up to ten reference images to get details like fur texture or muscle positioning right. I started drawing sideways and upside down when working on larger paper and creating larger images. I would also turn my sample images sideways or upside down to keep the perspective true. I've learned with every drawing, figuring it out as I went. I don't enjoy practicing, so each artwork is a new challenge and learning experience.

Why did you decide to paint animals instead of stationary subjects like flowers or stones? Did you try other subjects first?

When I switched to drawing in black-and-white art pencils, animals seemed like a natural transition. For years, I had used pens, trying to become more precise in my drawings, losing the spontaneous scratchiness of my early work, which hurt my neck. I was also trying to find my style. In the early 1990s, I was working in pencil, and one day, while drawing an eagle's face looking straight at the viewer, my wife said, "That's it—stop right there. That's your style." I created my Vanishing Breed series and realized this was something I needed to explore. With her encouragement, I started competing in fine art shows and won First Place and Best of Show in a few.

Your paintings are so lifelike. Do you paint from photos or observe animals on TV? Did you choose endangered species to contribute to conservation?

I get inspiration from everywhere—my imagination, TV, magazines, the internet, and more. I've always loved big cats and birds of prey, so they were the first animals I wanted to draw. Sadly, many of them are on the endangered species list. The style I developed, with parts of the animals fading away, represents how they're vanishing from the wild. I named my series "Vanishing Breeds" as a way to recognize and support conservation efforts.

I read that you don't sell your paintings. Why not? They could fetch good money, which would make life easier.

I do sell prints of my Vanishing Breeds series on my website (mouthart.com). I've sold some original pieces in the past, and I'm in the process of updating my website to sell more of my color paintings.

Mouth painting must be exhausting. Do you get neck aches or cramps? How long can you paint at a time, and how long does one painting take?

Yes, drawing by mouth is very exhausting—mostly on the neck. I hold the pencil or brush between my side teeth, and my neck does all the moving. Since I also type a lot with a mouth stick, it's taken a toll on my neck. I used to draw for six to eight hours a day until I started experiencing severe neck pain. At one point, a doctor told me I'd have to give up drawing—I found a different doctor.

I worked with one therapist for six months, which helped but then found another therapist who, after just two weeks, got me back to drawing, though not for as long. Now, with age and medical issues, I can only draw for one to four hours a day. My work can take anywhere from 40 to 200+ hours to complete. Some of my brush handles are made of plastic rather than wood, and when I've been painting aggressively, holding the brush between my front teeth, I've cracked them, needing my dentist to fix my teeth more than once.

Do you have any life goals besides painting? Have publishers asked you to illustrate a book?

My life goals are to keep painting and drawing for the Mouth and Foot Painting Artists Association (MFPA) and myself. My head is full of images I want to create. I love working with MFPA because it lets me challenge myself with all kinds of subjects and experiment with different techniques and styles.

I also like writing science fiction stories, though I haven't tried to publish anything yet. Maybe someday I'll finish a project enough to try. I also recently bought a GoPro and plan on making some videos. I was once approached to illustrate a book and help turn it into an animated movie, but the project fell through, which was okay. I'm not a very prolific artist, and there are many techniques I'm still not great at.

You've had exhibitions worldwide. Did they approach you, or did the MFPA help you get noticed?

When I first started drawing in the 1970s, my dad set up an interview with the MFPA. At the time, I didn't have confidence in my art and didn't see it as a career path. Also, MFPA primarily accepted color works, and I wasn't working in color then. Lacking confidence, I asked my dad to withdraw my application—something I regret. In the early 1990s, Very Special Arts asked me to show my work at a local event and later invited me to their international show in Brussels. There, I met Brom Wikstrom, a fellow mouth-painting artist, and his wife. They encouraged me to join MFPA, but I still lacked confidence and didn't contact them until the early 2000s.

After creating a series of color works, I interviewed with MFPA again and was accepted. MFPA has given me great opportunities to have my work seen across the country and worldwide. They also give me the freedom to continue learning and improving my skills. I believe we all have hidden talents, and I encourage everyone to explore and find theirs.

2018

ENOCK GLIDDEN

Living Without Limits

Enock Glidden was born with a condition called Spina Bifida, which meant he could not walk. Raised in Maine, he underwent 55 operations by the age of 12. Then he met his teacher, Bob Dyer, who became both a coach and a friend, introducing him to sports. Enock took the challenge seriously and tried almost everything—from cross-country skiing to paragliding, skydiving, downhill skiing, flying a plane, and mountain climbing. Since he even climbed the highest peak in Yosemite National Park, we thought it would be fascinating to interview him. His answers came within six hours. Bless you, Enock.

When does a child with Spina Bifida realize they are different and won't be able to walk?

Growing up with Spina Bifida, I knew I was different, but it never really bothered me because it was all I knew. So, I adapted and was able to do most of the things other kids were doing, just in a different way.

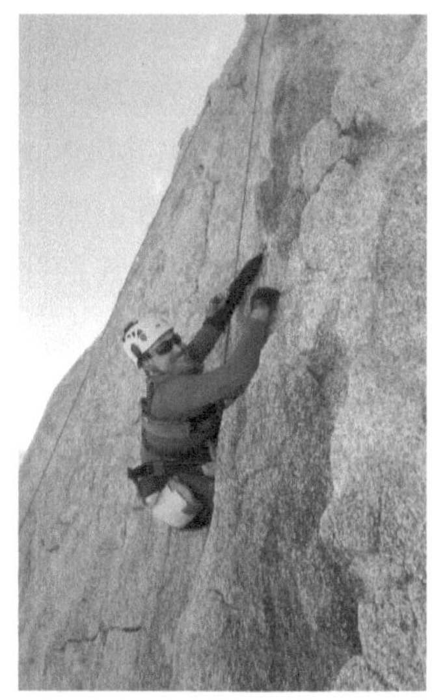

How did having 55 operations before age 12 affect your school life? Were you treated as an outsider or accepted by your classmates? Did insurance cover the operations, and did you ever hope to walk again?

Having 55 operations meant I spent a lot of time in the hospital. I was able to complete my studies because my teachers sent homework for me to do while I was there. Being disabled actually made me more popular with the other kids, as they enjoyed helping me and doing things with me. I was also the only disabled kid in my school, so everyone knew me. My father worked on the railroad and had good insurance, which definitely helped. The operations I had weren't meant to help me walk on my own, but I did use braces that allowed me to walk.

How did your teacher Bob Dyer get you into sports? Which was the first sport, and why did you choose it? When did you realize you could be equal to others and take on harder challenges?

Bob Dyer wanted to include me in everything he taught in class by finding ways to get me involved. That led to opportunities to try wheelchair racing and skiing. The first sport he introduced me to was skiing. I wanted to try it, and he found a way to make it happen. I think I always knew I could do everything others did—I just had to find a way to do it.

With all your activities, how do you meet the cost of living? Do you have a disability pension or a part-time job?

I'm on Social Security and am able to write grants to fund the activities I choose to do.

How does getting funding work? Do you approach organizations directly, and do you get the full amount?

I usually apply for climbing grants through the American Alpine Club and an adaptive grant through the Challenged Athletes Foundation (CAF). When I apply, they ask for a description of the climbing mission or equipment I need and the overall cost. They typically give a portion of the cost, but not the full amount. For example, if a climbing adventure costs $5,000, they might give me $1,500. I don't always get the grants, but I've been fortunate to receive the CAF grant every time I've applied.

How do you climb without using your legs? Do you need a partner, and do you train in the gym to build arm strength?

To rock climb, I need a friend to set ropes for me. I use a special ascender with handles that allows me to do pull-ups on the rope. I hope to do more of it on my own as part of a team in the future. I also train at the gym, doing pull-ups and weight exercises to build arm strength. In 2016, I climbed El Capitan by the Zodiac route, the highest rock face in Yosemite National Park.

What is your next big climbing goal? Do you rest during climbs, or go in one go? Have you ever felt like your arms couldn't continue?

I hope to climb a route in one of our national parks soon. For big walls, the climbs usually take several days with rest in between, but I hope to complete a route in a single day someday. So far, I've never felt like I couldn't continue during a climb.

When you climb for multiple days, do you always need a partner, and where do you sleep?

When I climbed El Capitan, we slept on a fabric platform called a portaledge, which was anchored to the rock face. I always climb with at least two able-bodied partners who carry the gear and assist me. They stay with me throughout the climb.

How do you do cross-country skiing, and is it just for leisure, or are there races?

I do cross-country skiing in the winter on a sit-down cross-country ski. For me, it's just for leisure.

Do you have a pilot's license, and was the plane specially adapted? How close are you to finishing, and how expensive is it?

I haven't completed my pilot's license yet, but I'm very close. It's the same license anyone gets—there's no adaptive version. The only adaptation I use in the Cessna 172 is a hand control for the rudders. It's a metal bar attached to the pedals with a ring at the top, allowing me to move it while keeping my hands free for other controls, like the fuel.

Was your paragliding flight solo or tandem? How did it feel, and how many times have you done it?

I went paragliding with an adaptive organization called Project Airtime. It was a tandem flight with an instructor behind me on a specially designed wheelchair. I've only done it once so far, but I'd love to do more. In the air, I was mostly riding while the instructor handled the controls.

Was your skydive a tandem jump? How was the experience, and do you plan to try scuba diving?

When I went skydiving, it was a tandem jump, though there are paralyzed people who jump solo. I enjoyed the freefall and also got to steer the parachute during the peaceful flight afterward. I'd love to try scuba diving in the future and have already discussed it with a few people.

Do you do all these activities because you're a sports enthusiast or because you want to pave the way for others and push boundaries?

I enjoy sports for the challenge, but I also hope to inspire others to try new things by showing what's possible. I write about my adventures on my blog at gobeyondthefence.com.

2018

ERIK GUNDERSEN

From Champion to the Hard Ground

In the 1980s, Danish Speedway rider Erik Gundersen was one of the best in the world. He won world titles in Speedway, the World Pairs Championship, the World Team Championship, and Long Track. Known for his friendly attitude and constant smile, he earned the nickname "Mr. Nice Guy." Then, on September 17, 1989—known as Black Sunday—his life changed forever at the World Team Championship final in Bradford, England.

The circumstances leading up to the event were unusual. At the nearby Donington Museum, a wreath fell off Erik's picture on the wall. The normally carefree and joyous atmosphere in the van that morning was tense and silent. During the first heat, a massive four-rider pile-up occurred. Erik lay motionless on the track, having swallowed his tongue. He was rushed to the hospital, where he could only breathe through a ventilator.

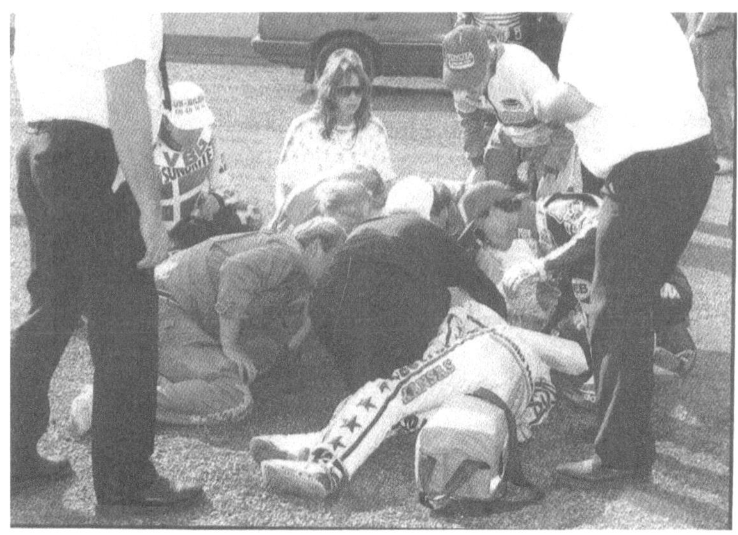

One of his neck vertebrae was broken, and it appeared he would be paralyzed. Later, doctors placed his head in a metal frame and stabilized his spine, preventing paralysis. Though he made a remarkable recovery, Erik never rode a bike again. Instead, he stayed involved in the sport as a coach.

Coincidentally, we sent him the following questions on September 17, exactly 24 years after the accident that nearly claimed his life.

I know you were always Mr. Nice Guy, but did you change your view and attitude toward life, as some people do after a brush with death? If so, in what way?

I don't think you can remain exactly the same person you were before. You do change, and for me, the change is in having an appreciation. I have a greater appreciation for things I never particularly valued before. I don't mean "trees of green and red roses too," like the Sam Cooke song. I was always very "happy-go-lucky," and I loved my lifestyle and the freedom it gave me. The difference now is that I appreciate life and everything in it. You've heard the saying, "Don't sweat the small stuff." I don't sweat the small stuff, and I appreciate the people and things around me.

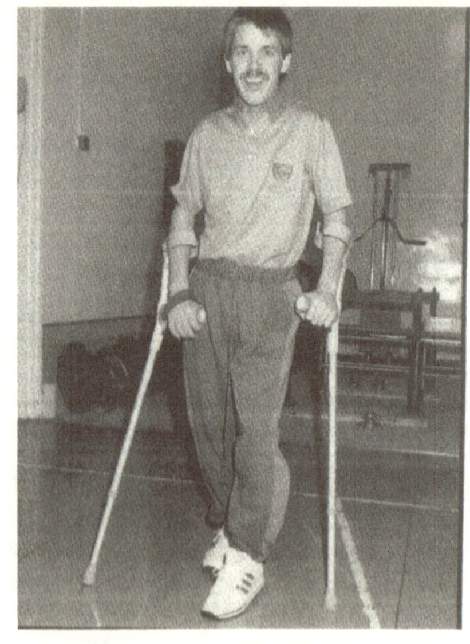

When you were lying in the ward, relieved of pain and with time to think, did you reflect on life, what lay ahead, and why this had to happen to you?

It's hard not to think, "Why me? Why now?" But I couldn't dwell on it. I was a realist before my accident, and I remain one. Of course, you get scared about what the future holds. In a spinal ward, you have a lot of time to think. I had dark days and moments of genuine fear about what lay ahead. I think it's natural to have those thoughts, especially when your injury affects not just you but also the people you love.

You were popular among fans, and thousands supported you with cards, letters, and donations. Do you think your recovery would have been longer and harder if you hadn't been a famous star but an ordinary working man?

I received tremendous support from the entire Speedway family, as well as good wishes from other sportspeople and strangers. I am forever grateful for that. However, like most people who experience a life-changing accident, the unconditional love and support of family are key to accepting your

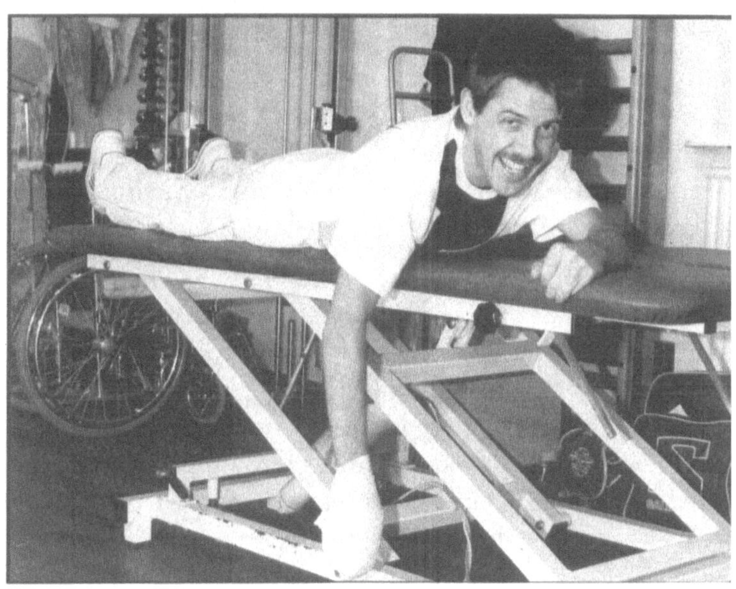

situation and recovering. I've often said that while I was dealing with my own demons and challenges during rehabilitation, my brother Preben and my wife Helle had to find their own inner strength.

In terms of societal attitudes, there have been improvements, and there's greater awareness of the need for inclusive communities. After the 2012 Paralympics, there was hope in England that it would leave a legacy of promoting positive attitudes toward disabled people and recognizing their abilities.

What helped you the most on your way back? Was it family, friends, determination, or the quality of healthcare and therapy?

Acceptance. What helped me the most was accepting my situation. You first need to accept that you have a spinal injury and are disabled. You need to accept yourself and your new reality. From there, you must accept that you can't do everything on your own; you need help from others. Once you've walked that road of acceptance, you can truly appreciate the care, therapy, and support from medical professionals, friends, and family.

When you returned to life, did you focus on your future in sports and life, or did you also want to give something back—like lectures for disabled people on how to fight back?

I've been involved with a few organizations that support disabled people, and I'm glad to have helped raise their profile. I also give speeches to various groups, which helps raise awareness of the challenges facing people with disabilities. However, I haven't directly addressed disabled groups on how to handle their challenges—I think there are people far more experienced and qualified than me who can do a better job. Still, I'm always willing to help if I can.

You were on top of the world, surrounded by fans and winning world finals. When you were lying in the hospital, did you think about how precious health is compared to the wealth and fame of a Speedway rider?

I think you go through a full spectrum of thoughts and emotions. I don't think I ever directly compared health to the fame and success I had in Speedway. Honestly, I don't think I fully appreciated the value of being completely fit and healthy before my accident.

Do you believe in destiny? Could the fallen wreath at Donington and the different atmosphere in the van that morning have been omens you misread? Do you think it was written in your destiny to conquer the world but also hit rock bottom?

I'm not sure. Everything happens for a reason, though sometimes it's impossible to understand what that reason is. Yes, strange things happened that day, but I don't think noticing them earlier would have changed anything. My destiny led to the life I have now, and my acceptance of it allows me to live it fully.

2014

EVŽEN ERBAN

My accident gave me a much needed kick

It was May 17, 1979, during a speedway league match at Prague's Markéta Stadium. The visiting team, ZP Pardubice, sent their rider, Evžen Erban, into his fifth and final heat. In the pits, he removed his back protector—he was the first rider in Czechoslovakia to use one. A decision that, within minutes, would cost him dearly.

On the penultimate lap, coming out of the last bend, his bike lifted, and he crashed heavily into the fence, hitting his back first. He lay motionless on the ground as medics rushed to him and unfastened his helmet. "Don't move me!" he shouted. "Something is wrong with my spine."

They took me to Motol Hospital in Prague and sent me to the ICU, but they made a mistake—they didn't free my spine. I had crushed two vertebrae, but my spinal cord was only compressed, not ruptured. A blood clot had formed, and because they left me in that state until the next afternoon, the nerves in my spine died before they could operate.

I spent six weeks there before being transferred to Pardubice, where I stayed until August. After that, I was discharged into home care and later sent to the Kladruby rehabilitation center,

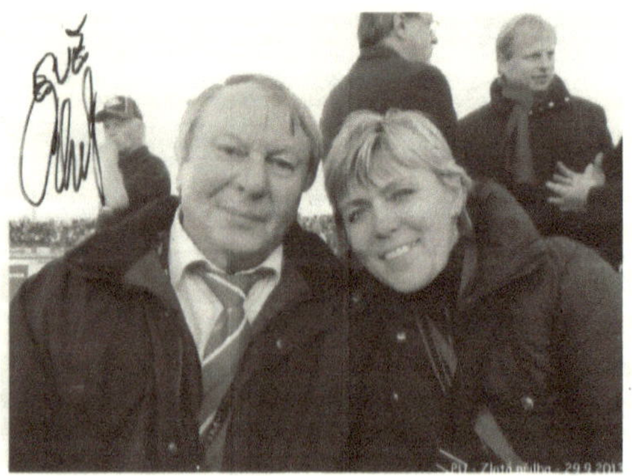

where I spent over six months. With intensive rehabilitation, I got onto crutches and was able to leave the wheelchair behind.

The most famous speedway rider and my friend, Ivan Mauger, organized my visit to Dr. Carlo Biagi, a Scottish specialist in cases like mine. He had helped dozens of injured riders return to racing. I had my visas arranged, but Red Star Prague—our archrival and a police club—blocked my trip. My accident had happened at their stadium, after all.

Instead, I went to Pinderfields Hospital near London, where they confirmed that my spine should have been operated on immediately. From there, I continued treatment at a clinic in Garmisch-Partenkirchen, Germany.

Do you remember what was going through your mind while lying motionless on the track?

I had seen enough serious crashes to know what they looked like, but I hoped something had just shifted in my spine. I remained optimistic. My mechanics were crying over me, and I told them, "Don't be stupid. Go home and say hello to my wife. Tomorrow, the specialists will come, and we'll know more—there's no point in talking about it now."

Under communism, wheelchair users were pushed to the margins of society. How were you treated? There were no

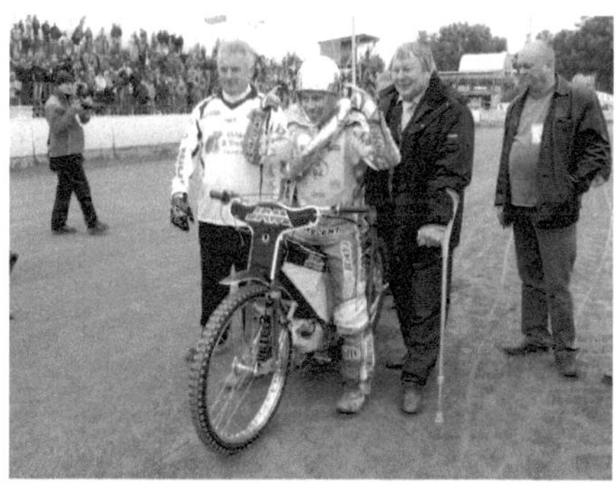

specialized fitness centers like today.

In Kladruby, there was a rehabilitation center where we were up by 7 a.m. and started therapy—exercise, swimming, or individual treatments. If someone was willing to work on themselves, the staff supported them. I don't know how it works today, but I must say the nurses were very attentive.

I trained intensively. At first, I could only walk 14 meters on crutches in 12 minutes. After continued exercise, I managed 750 meters. Improvement kept coming, but one day, it stops. The doctors told me that if progress doesn't come within a year and a half, it won't come at all—unless a miracle happens.

I also helped start a driving school for handicapped people. There was no such thing at the time, so I trained the instructor myself. Later, they received certification, and the school still operates today. After leaving Kladruby, I continued rehabilitation in Pardubice. Unlike today, where therapy lasts a week or two, my doctor allowed me to continue for as long as I wanted.

When you returned to normal life, did anyone help you? Did you have an idea of what you wanted to do?

There was a rule that after a serious injury, you were automatically placed on disability pension after a year. I had to take care of myself. Fortunately, there was a law that treated sports

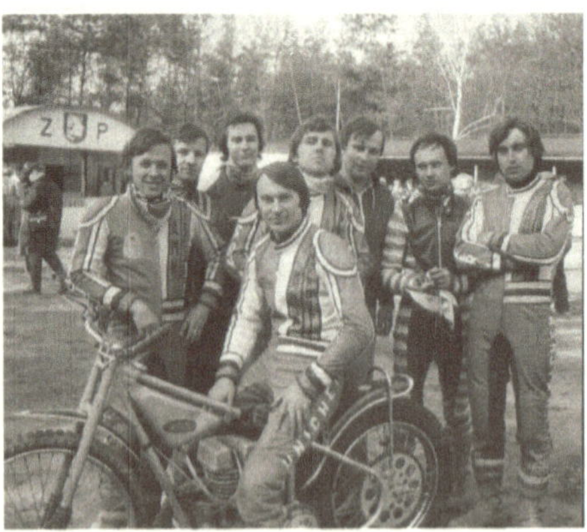

injuries as work-related, so I received a proper salary.

Still, I wanted to stay involved in speedway. My first opportunity came when the Finnish speedway federation sent ten riders to Czechoslovakia, and since I was the only rider who spoke some English, I became their trainer. That led to an invitation to Finland for six months.

I then earned my first-grade coaching qualification and later received an offer from the Italian Speedway Federation to train new riders. My contract lasted two years, alternating three weeks in Italy and one at home. After renewing it, I left due to rising violence—Red Brigades were bombing cars and trains. It was too dangerous, so I returned home to coach the junior team in Pardubice.

You were traveling around the world. Were you interested to know how do they care for handicapped people in foreign countries?

I think it was the same everywhere—those with money could afford better care. In that sense, things might have been even worse in the West than here.

After your accident, once you regained mobility, did your attitude toward life and people change?

Absolutely. Here's an example: Before, I'd see a car with a handicapped placard and think, 'Oh, someone disabled.' But once I had the placard myself, I became aware of just how many people shared my situation.

There's also a shift in mindset. Some handicapped people become selfish, envying others in slightly better condition. I saw this in Kladruby. I expected us to help each other, but most focused only on themselves. Everyone handles recovery differently.

How did you adjust to everyday life?

I had so many interests and activities. I set a goal: exactly one year later, I would sit on a bike again. At 6 p.m. on the anniversary, I went to the Pardubice racetrack, changed into my gear, got on a speedway bike, and rode two laps. I shed a few tears, realizing it was over. I sold all my bikes and equipment, but I knew how to make a living. Living on a disability pension meant limitations, but I refused to accept that. I worked as a coach, then started EE Tuning, an engine tuning business for England and Germany.

I thought to myself—I didn't give myself life, so if I screwed it up, it was on me to take care of myself. Since childhood, I had been a bad loser. On the track, I had accidents because I refused to finish second—I wanted to win. Maybe that was the wrong attitude but that's who I am. One thing is certain—sports helped me become both physically and mentally stronger.

I enjoyed watching hockey and football like anyone else. I never drank or fell into depression, though I saw many who did. In Kladruby, I knew four guys who hanged themselves. I always told myself—if I could survive this, then I had a responsibility to make something of it.

Have you thought about how your life might have been different without the accident? In what ways do you think your life might have been richer or poorer?

Well, I don't know if my life would have been richer in every way. The accident forces me to stay active and not dwell on what happened. But financially, yes, I'm sure I would have been better off. Even under the communist regime, I knew how to make money and live an above-standard life.

I would work myself to exhaustion every evening, but by the next morning, I was ready for a new day and another chance to earn. In some ways, the accident was a wake-up call—it pushed me forward. I was always thinking about what came next.

I don't regret what happened to me. It happened while doing what I loved, and I accepted it that way. 2014

FRÉDERIC SAUSSET

It was this or die

The involvement of disabled people in motor racing represents a significant step forward. We now have a quadriplegic driver controlling his car with a special helmet equipped with sensors. There are drivers with no arms who steer with their legs, and a young driver with no legs aspiring to compete in Formula 1. Remarkably, a racing driver who had all his limbs amputated competed in the 24 Hours of Le Mans, forming a racing team to make it happen.

Frédéric's journey to the 24 Hours of Le Mans was extraordinary. With support from friends and his own financial resources, he built a racing team around himself. In 2016, he qualified for the race in a specially adapted Morgan LM P2 car, prepared for him by Ligier Automotive.

The big day came on June 16, 2016, when he stood on the grid alongside Christophe Tinseau and Jean-Bernard Bouvet. A day later, Frédéric crossed the finish line—not as

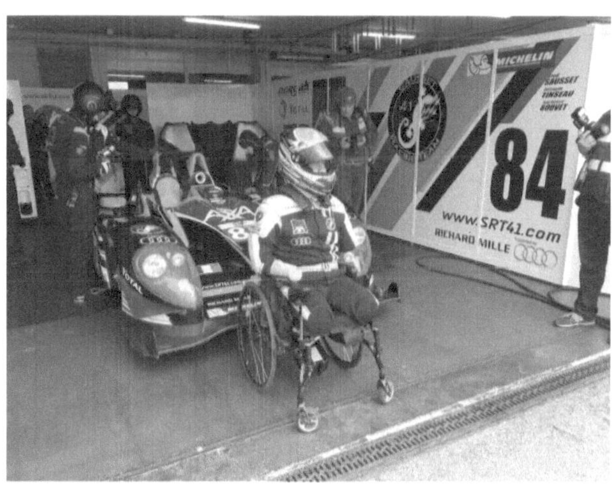

the race winner, but with a personal victory that highlighted the progress of inclusive motor racing. He became the first quadriplegic in history to not only place his car on the grid but also complete the race.

We were inspired by his story and interviewed him, with his PR manager, Mat Fernandez, assisting as a translator since Frédéric does not speak English.

You almost lost your life after the bacteriological infection. Did they amputate your limbs because the infection was progressing rapidly and needed to be stopped, or because there were no other treatment options?

In 2012, I innocently scratched my finger and contracted an unknown virus. Within 48 hours, an aggressive bacterium was attacking my body, and I fell into a coma. It took time for doctors to understand the infection. Amputating my limbs was necessary to save my life and prevent the infection from spreading further.

Have you tried artificial limbs, or do they not work in your case? Did you choose not to use them to see what you could accomplish without any prosthetics?

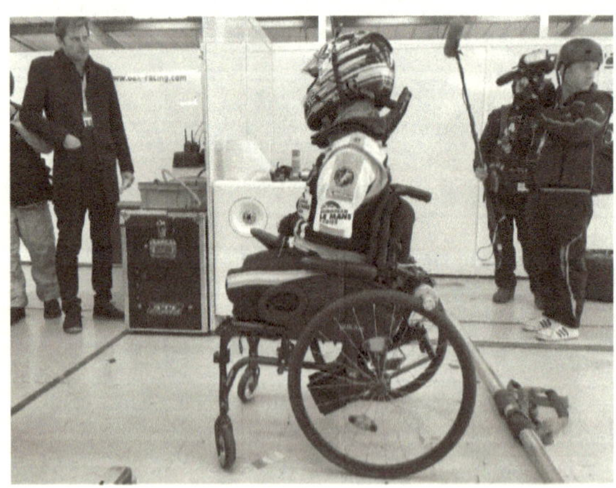

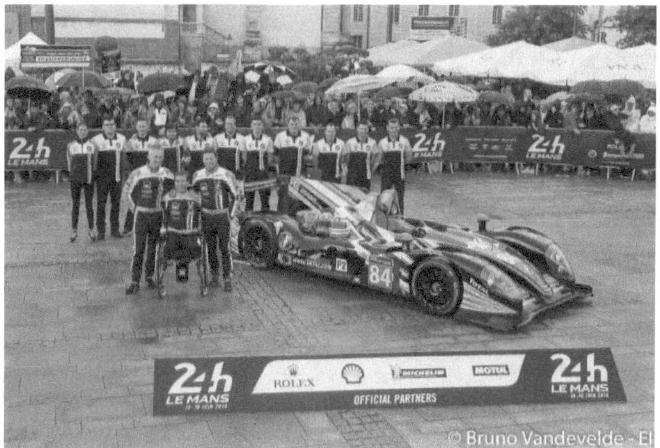

There are artificial legs on the market. I've tested a few, but they're painful and exhausting to use. Technology is improving, and I hope that in the future, they'll be less taxing. I do have an artificial hand that I use for tasks like signing autographs, but I don't wear it permanently.

How much did your life change after the amputations? Did you find a new purpose or dimension in your life?

The change was enormous in every aspect of my life. While recovering in the hospital, I set a goal: to compete in the 24 Hours of Le Mans. Finding a new purpose was vital for me—it was that or give up entirely.

You are a businessman. Do you still run your business, and has the publicity from Le Mans helped you?

Yes, I still run my clothing shop. I handle everything from delivering goods to management tasks. However, the publicity from Le Mans didn't directly impact my business.

Going from an ordinary driver to competing at Le Mans is a huge leap. Were you a motor racing fan before, and did you

fund your team solely to achieve this goal, or did you want a career in racing?

I established my own team specifically to compete at Le Mans. The team's focus is on enabling three disabled drivers to compete in the 24 Hours of Le Mans. We have Ben Moussa, a French driver without his left arm; Nigel Bailly, a Belgian paralyzed from the waist down; and Takuma Aoki, a Japanese driver also paralyzed from the waist down. To prepare them, I founded an academy called La Filière Frédéric Sausset.

Were there objections from the organizers or the FIA when you entered in 2016? Did they impose specific conditions on the car or require an FIA license?

We conducted extensive testing in collaboration with Ligier Automotive, adapting the car based on my feedback. There was plenty of preparation on both the technical and driver fronts. In 2015, I drove a specially adapted prototype during free practice at Le Mans.

Did your 2016 crew include three disabled drivers, or was that plan postponed? Did companies specializing in products for disabled people support you?

No, my two teammates in 2016 were not disabled. We didn't receive support from companies specializing in products for disabled people. The technology on the car was developed by me and my team.

What is the aim of La Filière Frédéric Sausset? Are you paving the way for other disabled drivers in motorsport?

The aim is to demonstrate that a disability isn't a barrier. Disabled drivers can perform as well as, or even better than, able-bodied drivers. I proved that in 2016.

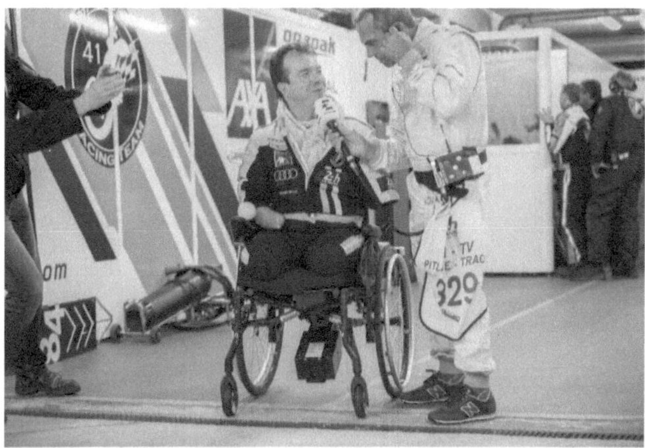

Was Le Mans a one-time goal, or do you plan to build on this experience to make driving more accessible for disabled people?

I intend to return to Le Mans as a driver. For now, my focus is on ensuring my team and its three drivers succeed.

How long did you train to compete at Le Mans? Were you driving at full speed, or was your goal simply to take part and finish?

It took two seasons to prepare for lower-class competitions. My goal wasn't to win but to prove I could compete alongside others.

Your car had special controls and an ejection seat. How did this work with your teammates? Did you test the ejection seat?

Our pit stops were longer because I needed assistance getting in and out of the car using a special device. The equipment and steering wheel had to be swapped during stops to accommodate my teammates.

How do you manage daily life without limbs? Do you require constant care?

I receive support from my wife and a caregiver, but I also have enough independence to drive, eat, and drink on my own.

2019

JAMIE ANDREW

All I need for my life I manage myself

Scottish mountain climber Jamie Andrew will never forget January 1999. That month, he and his friend Jamie Fisher left Chamonix to climb the north face of the 4,000-meter summit of Les Droites Mountain. Conditions initially seemed ideal, and they planned to be back within two days. Sadly, just 48 hours after reaching the summit, a severe storm trapped them on the snow for five harrowing days.

While Jamie Andrew suffered frostbite on his arms and legs, his friend Fisher succumbed to the brutal conditions. A daring helicopter pilot, flying under hazardous conditions, rescued Jamie on the brink of death, but tragically, Fisher could not be saved.

In the hospital in Chamonix, doctors did everything possible, but they couldn't save Jamie's frostbitten limbs, and all four had to be amputated. Despite this life-altering loss, Jamie didn't

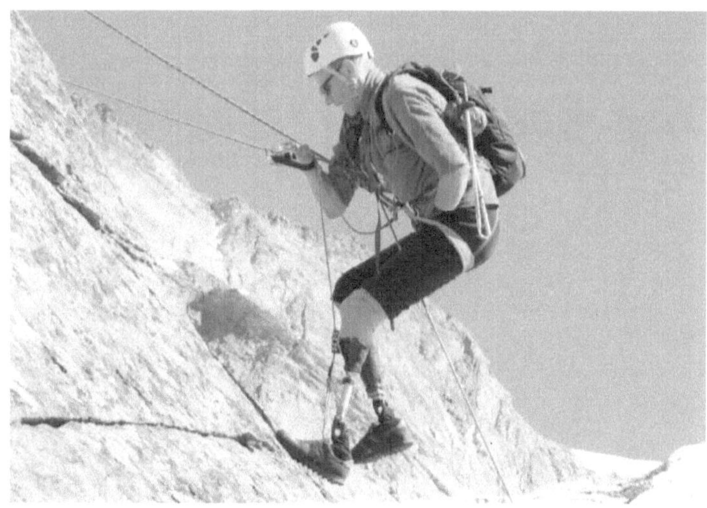

give up. He learned to walk again, wrote a book about his experience, and became a motivational speaker, traveling the world to share his story.

Amazingly, he returned to the mountains, skied, and even ran marathons. We reached out to Jamie in January 2017, and within a week, we conducted this interview via Skype.

What were you thinking about during those five days in the snow, with powerful storms surrounding you and no rescue or escape in sight? Was it hard not to break down and lose hope?

We didn't anticipate being there for five whole days, so we took it hour by hour, focusing on small tasks like keeping warm and staying positive.

We concentrated on survival—talking, keeping each other warm, and avoiding thoughts of our desperate situation. Resting was crucial, even though lying still in such conditions is tough on the body. We tried to sleep, but it was incredibly hard.

Having each other for support was vital. We even made jokes to keep our spirits up and to distract ourselves from the possibility that we might never make it home.

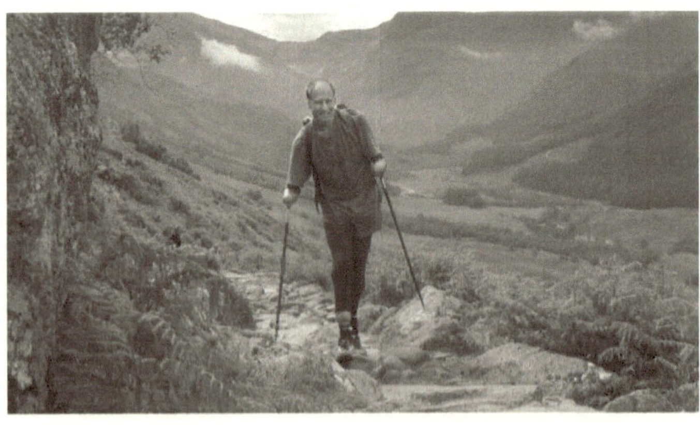

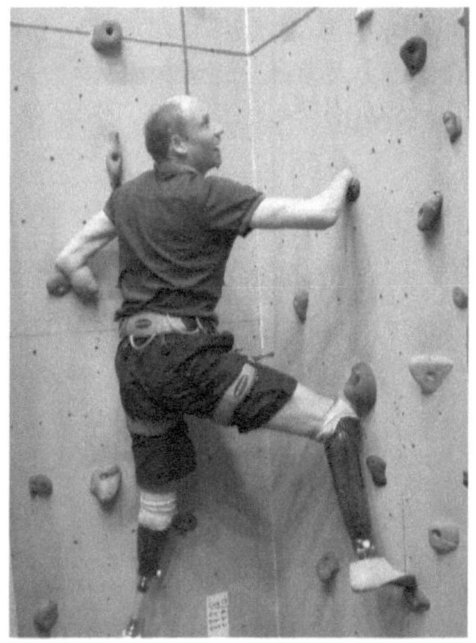

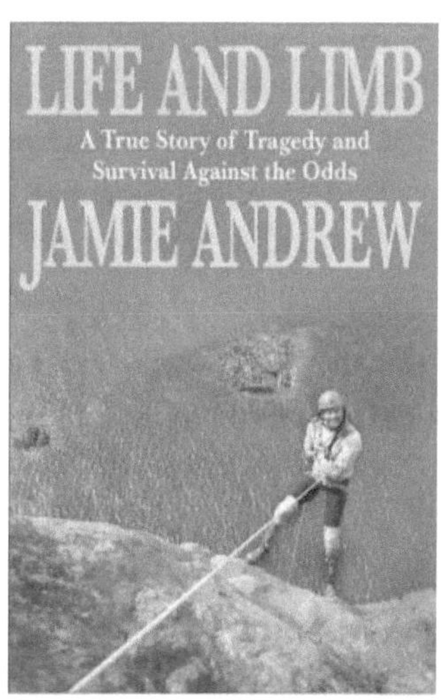

You planned to be back in two days, so you didn't bring much. Did you have enough food and drink?

We only had enough food for two days. After that, all we had left was a pack of biscuits.

Liquid was a bigger problem. By the time we reached the summit, we had none. Our camping stove didn't work for the first four days because of the wind. When we finally managed to make hot tea, it probably saved my life.

The conditions were unbelievably difficult.

When you were lying there with frozen limbs, essentially waiting for death, did you prepare yourself for the worst? Did you reflect on life or make resolutions for the future?

Yes, those thoughts crossed my mind.

When Jamie passed away, I realized my own end might be near. I thought about my life and the people I cared about—it was a deeply emotional experience.

It was also confusing because, when someone is freezing to death, they drift into dreams. I often felt like I was watching myself and Jamie from above. It was surreal.

I told myself that if I survived, I would be more grateful for life and the love and care I receive. But I didn't make any specific promises about things I would or wouldn't do.

Is it true that when someone is freezing to death, they feel warmth in their body at the end?

I can't say. That wasn't my experience. I couldn't feel my arms or legs because they were frozen, but my body was warm enough to keep me alive.

What were your first thoughts when you woke up in the hospital and realized you had no arms or legs?

At first, I didn't feel much because I was just out of surgery, and my limbs were bandaged.

I knew what had happened, but I didn't want to believe it. The idea that I'd lost my limbs for life was hard to accept.

I often wondered if it would have been better to die. I felt like a child again—completely dependent on others and unable to even feed myself.

Did you ever think, "Jamie is gone and at peace, but I have to live with this"?

No, I saw it differently. I told myself that Jamie was gone, but I was the lucky one who survived.

I was given a second chance, so I decided to make it count. It became a new challenge: to see what life with such a disability could bring, what I could achieve, and where I could go.

I even thought that if Jamie Fisher had survived, he would have handled it better than I did.

Does your brain work the same way as before, or did you have to teach it new things, like relearning to walk?

It was a challenge, but I approached it positively, solving

problems step by step.

Every day I learned something new, which was exciting and uplifting. First, I learned to grab things with my stumps, then to walk on artificial legs. It's all about facing and overcoming the challenges.

People often say tragedy changes their perspective on life. Was that true for you?

I've always appreciated what I have, but this experience made me realize just how lucky I am.

The support I received after the accident was overwhelming. Hundreds of people offered help, which was something I never expected.

With your involvement in extreme sports, have you become a guinea pig for companies developing aids for disabled athletes?

Not really. I'm quite unique—likely the only extreme sportsman in the world with no limbs. Because of that, there isn't a big market for the equipment I need.

Most of the aids I use are my own designs. When I have an idea, I ask someone to build it for me, but it's never mass-produced.

When you returned to the mountains after the accident, did you have flashbacks? Did you ask yourself why you were doing it again?

My return to the mountains was one of the first steps in reclaiming my life.

It wasn't impulsive; I was ready. I wanted to forgive the mountains and myself. Standing among them again, I felt the joy and desire to climb and ski. I couldn't force myself—it had to come from the heart.

You wrote a book about your experience. Was that your idea, or were you approached by a publisher?

It was my idea. I wanted to tell the true story, as the media often got things wrong or left out details.

I typed it myself on a regular keyboard with my stumps, and it took about ten months. It sold 50,000 copies in England, though it hasn't been translated yet.

Do you manage everything on your own now, or do you still need assistance?

For the most part, I manage everything I need by myself. However, there are tasks that take too long or are tedious, so I ask my wife to help with those. Occasionally, I might ask someone else for assistance, but generally, there aren't many things I can't do on my own.

Now you are a well-known motivational speaker. Do you feel the accident enriched your life, or do you sometimes wish you had your healthy limbs back?

It has been an extraordinary experience. The accident opened so many doors for me—doors I might never have approached otherwise.

The accident was one of the most significant events of my life, and I wouldn't undo it. I wouldn't even wish for my healthy limbs back.

You've said every problem can be solved and that it's all in our heads. Do you think there's a limit to what can be achieved, no matter how hard someone tries?

Generally, if we approach a problem believing it's unsolvable, we won't find a solution. I think the key is to try and believe we can manage it, even if it's hard and challenging.

Of course, humans have physical limitations, but our ability to innovate and adapt often surpasses expectations. Two centuries ago, no one believed humans could fly or communicate across the globe instantly, yet now these things are normal.

When faced with a challenge, the least we can do is believe we can overcome it.

You've run marathons, climbed mountains, and been part of a climbing team where all the members had artificial limbs. Do you pursue these activities out of love or to push boundaries, like Heyerdahl, Hillary, Messner, or Amundsen did?

I think I'm in a unique position to show the world what's possible. Since there are very few people without limbs doing these things, much of what I attempt is a first.

This lack of competition makes it easier for me to push boundaries. I believe everyone should embrace challenges, push limits, and live life to the fullest. I always try to take the next step forward in whatever I do.

Have you been approached by filmmakers to adapt your story into a movie?

Not yet. In recent years, we've made a documentary, but Spielberg or Eastwood hasn't called me—yet (laughs). If they do, I'd love for Brad Pitt to play me (laughs).

What do you do for a living now?

I used to work for a company that specialized in climbing high and hard-to-reach places in industrial areas. Now, I'm a full-time motivational speaker.

I travel the world sharing my story, encouraging people not to give up on life, and inspiring them to face challenges head-on.

2017

JAN POTMĚŠIL

The only real victim of the Velvet Revolution

At present, there is only one Czech actor who performs in a wheelchair: Jan Potměšil.

Born on March 31, 1966, Jan began acting at the age of eight and had several successful films under his belt by 1989. That same year, on November 17, the communist regime in Czechoslovakia began to crumble. During this period, actors traveled across the country to discuss the political situation with people in remote areas who were unaware of the unfolding events in Prague. Jan was one of these active participants.

On December 8, while returning from Ostrava, Jan's car was involved in a crash. At just 23 years old, he became paralyzed from the waist down.

Jan didn't give up. After undergoing rehabilitation, he returned to the stage and screen, eventually becoming an acclaimed actor. We met him at a theater café before one of his

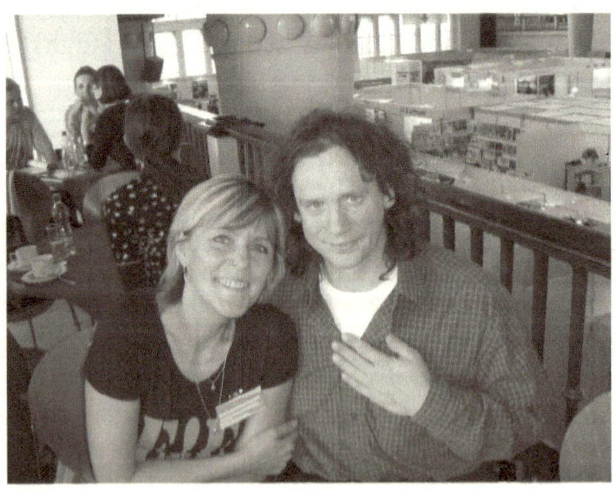

performances. What was supposed to be a 30-minute conversation turned into a two-hour discussion.

What sort of childhood did you have? Did your parents support you?

I have an older sister, Klára, who is five years older than me. My father, an avid sportsman, encouraged me to try everything from football to skiing, while my mother introduced me to the arts, taking me to the theater, opera, and cinema. My childhood was filled with activities, and my parents supported me in every way as long as I kept up with my schoolwork.

They drove me to both filming, sports and theater rehearsals, ensuring I had every opportunity to pursue my passions. During my first performance, I sat in the front row, played a judge, and joined the cast on stage for the final applause. That moment proved a return to the theater was possible. More roles followed, and I realized I could succeed—whether I was disabled or not simply didn't matter.

After your near-fatal accident, when did you decide to continue acting despite your disability? Did returning to the stage serve as a driving force in your recovery?

When I was lying in a hospital bed, completely paralyzed, the only thing I could do was wink my eye. Acting was the last thing on my mind. I spent three months in a coma, and after six months, I began rehabilitation. That was when I slowly became aware of my surroundings.

I had my diary with me, which reminded me of the performances I had been scheduled to give, and I missed that part of my life. But over time, I stopped dwelling on it. Small opportunities arose—brief chances to reconnect with my profession—but my focus was on intensive rehabilitation and regaining independence after two years in hospitals. More than acting, I was concerned with practical matters—how to drive a car, get in and out of it, and navigate daily life.

Then came an offer from the newly established Theatre Kašpar. It was a serious opportunity and a challenge. In my first performance, I sat in the front row, played a judge, and stepped on stage only for the final applause. That moment showed me a return to theater was possible. More roles followed, and I knew I could continue.

You excelled in plays like *Richard III* and *Flowers for Algernon*. How does acting in a wheelchair differ from acting without one? Are your expressive capabilities limited? Was it difficult to make the audience focus on your acting rather than your wheelchair?

That's a question better answered by the audience. I simply started acting, and over time, my wheelchair became irrelevant. Eventually, we incorporated my disability into performances. In Richard III, for example, we adapted the character's outsider status and childhood disability. I entered the stage in a wheelchair modified as a battle cart, holding a sword, which added a unique layer to the performance.

There's a big difference between appearing on stage in a wheelchair for a charity event and performing in recurring theatrical roles. After one show, where I transitioned between a sofa and a wheelchair, a spectator approached me backstage. When I wheeled up to him, he froze and asked, "Why didn't you get rid of the wheelchair?" He hadn't realized I was actually disabled. Now, the wheelchair is part of my life and craft. When I fully embody a role, the audience sees the performance, not the chair.

When we've met you, we've always felt love and positive energy from you. Do you try to be an example for others with disabilities, or is your optimism just part of who you are?

In life, you always have a choice: see yourself as a victim or embrace challenges as opportunities.

When I woke from a three-month coma, I felt overwhelming gratitude just to be alive. The fact that I could still hear, speak, and see felt like a gift—a second chance to embrace life. Each day, things improved little by little. Given the original prognosis, simply being here, even in a wheelchair, feels miraculous.

This mindset shapes how I engage with the world. The positivity I give out comes back to me. I have no regrets—everything in my life has had meaning. The accident only sharpened my focus and taught me to live more fully. Life can change in an instant, but I was doing what I believed was right, and I wouldn't change a thing.

When you perform Shakespeare or other great works, do you feel like a medium connecting historical heroes with today's audiences?

That's a beautifully put question. Even plays written 600 years ago remain relevant today. They resonate with timeless truths about human nature.

I remember performing shortly after 9/11. The theater was so silent you could hear a pin drop. The emotions were raw, and it felt as though we were at the epicenter of the tragedy in New York. That's the power of great theater—it transcends time and speaks directly to our hearts.

Sometimes, when everything aligns, the energy is so immense that I can't sleep afterward. Touring shows help in such cases; the return journeys allow me to decompress.

Once, while performing *Richard III*, I became so immersed in the role that I carried the character into my everyday life. It wasn't long before life "slapped me in the face" and reminded me to return to myself. That experience taught me a valuable lesson about balance.

2015

JASON BECKER

Composing an album takes me years

Jason Becker was a gifted and talented guitarist in the late '80s. Along with his buddy Marty Friedman, he established a metal band-duo called Cacophony, toured the U.S. and Europe, and released two albums. Then Marty left to join a band called Megadeth, and Jason launched a solo career. Just as he was about to start working with David Lee Roth and his band, he was diagnosed with Amyotrophic Lateral Sclerosis (ALS), which slowly forced him to quit gigging, then playing, and eventually robbed him of the ability to walk, play, and speak.

He can now only communicate with his eyes, but that hasn't stopped him. Not only does he communicate with his eyes, but he also composes music and records albums. His remarkable willpower, courage, and story led us to contact him. Since he was working on an album, his mother Pat was willing to help us out with an interview, as it would have been too exhausting for Jason alone. Thank you.

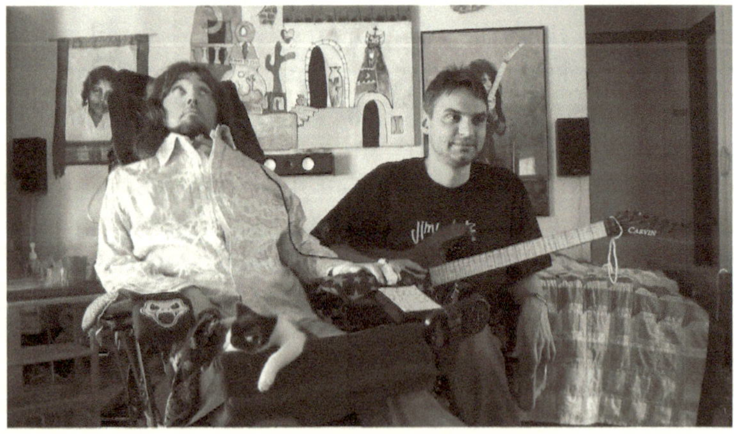

It is said that you studied Nicolo Paganini's work and performed it on guitar. Did you generally like classical music, or was it just Paganini that interested you enough to turn it into metal music and create something new and interesting?

Jason has always loved all kinds of music, including classical. He studied Paganini because he loved it. He listened to Mozart, Bach, Beethoven, Stravinsky, and Debussy because he loved their music. If you've seen his documentary (*Jason Becker: Not Dead Yet*), you hear his friend saying, "he was the guy listening to Bach on the radio, and you could tell he understood it."

He was very young and energetic and loved to play the guitar at lightning speed, so he was attracted to that as well. I think he just took that love of classical music and combined it with his energy, which resulted in some awesome music. I remember it was just fun for him, and I know he always wanted to create something new and interesting while finding his voice.

You were voted best new guitarist of 1990 and cited Bob Dylan, Jimi Hendrix, and Eric Clapton as your idols. What kind of music did you play with your duo Cacophony, and which countries in Europe did you play in?

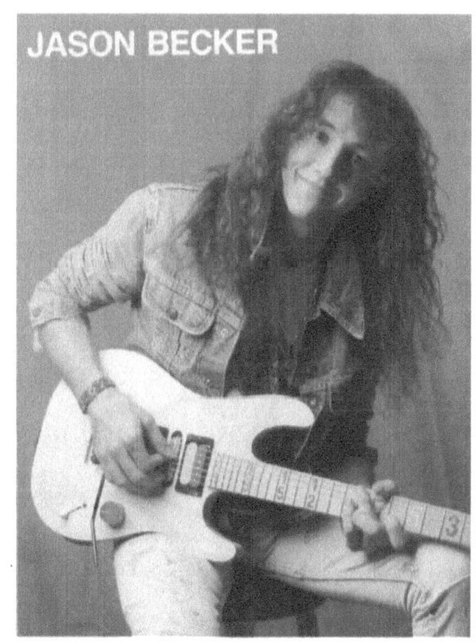

Jason's dad (Gary), uncle (Ron), and I all loved Dylan, so Jason heard it constantly and loved it too. He loved the melody, emotion, and meaning of the songs; he loved the stories. And he thought Dylan was cool. When the movie *The Last Waltz* came out (that story is also in the documentary), he discovered Eric Clapton and decided, at a very young age (around 12 years old), that he wanted to do what Clapton did—be a lead guitarist.

He also loved Robbie Robertson and the Band, whom the movie was about. We told Jason that we would get him the equipment he needed as he developed, and it was hard to keep up with him because he played the guitar tirelessly and kept us on our toes providing the guitars, amps, and recording devices he needed as his skills grew like crazy. I know he loves Jimi Hendrix, but I don't remember Hendrix being a huge influence in the beginning.

It's hard to describe what kind of music Cacophony played if you haven't listened to it, but I would say it was the best guitar-playing duo of its time. Jason and Marty Friedman were serious players and composers and very particular about their work; both were perfectionists in what they put out, and they loved and respected each other and what each brought to the band. The best way to understand it is to listen to their albums, *Speed Metal Symphony* and *Go Off!*

When you realized you had a 'lazy limp,' how did it happen? Once it started, did it progress quickly or did it come one day, stay longer, and worsen over time?

I know that Jason first noticed a sign of ALS on Mother's Day in May 1989. A limp developed slowly after that, and by October, the limping was pretty bad, with his right foot 'dropping' and causing him to fall frequently. He went to the doctor and was diagnosed in November of 1989, one week after being chosen as David Lee Roth's new lead guitarist.

Jason describes it as starting with a twitch in a muscle, which then becomes weak and eventually stops moving.

How long did it take from the first signs to the complete inability to use your hands and feet? Is there any treatment in

the early stages, or does it just keep progressing and getting worse?

That's hard to say, but it took a few years. It is different for everyone. The doctors give you three to five years to live, but there are people like Jason, Stephen Hawking, and others who have lived for decades.

You can find all that kind of information on www.jasonbecker.com. There are also galleries with photos, information on how he communicates, his discography, etc. It's a wealth of information about Jason.

Simon Fitzmaurice directed a film using the same device as you. How does it work when you compose music? Do you wink or blink your eyes to press certain keys and record the chords?

I don't know Simon Fitzmaurice or anything about a film or device, but if you mean a program called Logic, that is how Jason composes music. The communication system he uses was designed by his dad and is explained here: https://www.youtube.com/watch?v=rThFDRYKKZE&t=15s.

Jason thinks about what he wants to compose, and his caregiver hits the right buttons for the notes or instruments

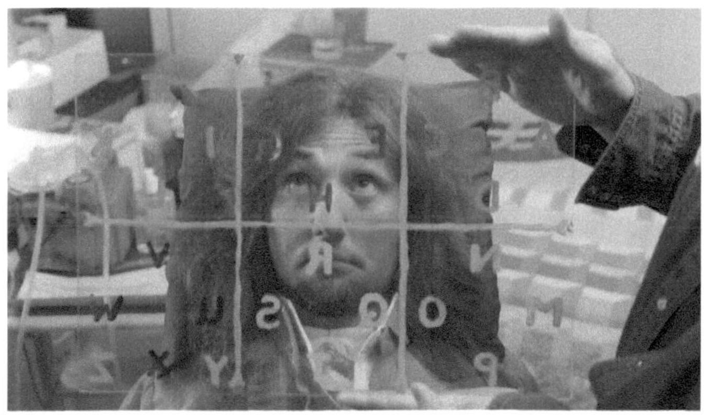

he wants. If he needs a guitarist to figure out what he wants, he usually asks his dad, since he plays guitar. He also has a producer who works with him to help create the final product.

It takes a lot of work and years for Jason to complete an album. It's unbelievable how much strength, talent, patience, and fortitude it takes, and we are all amazed watching him and hearing what he does. His next album is some of the most beautiful music I have ever heard, and I cannot wait until it is released.

Do you compose songs without lyrics, and is it only digital tones, or can you manage to get down what you have in mind?

Two of Jason's songs for the new album include vocals for which he wrote the lyrics. One tells his own story, and the other is a tribute to Prince, using his own guitar playing from back in the days when he played. He built the song around it.

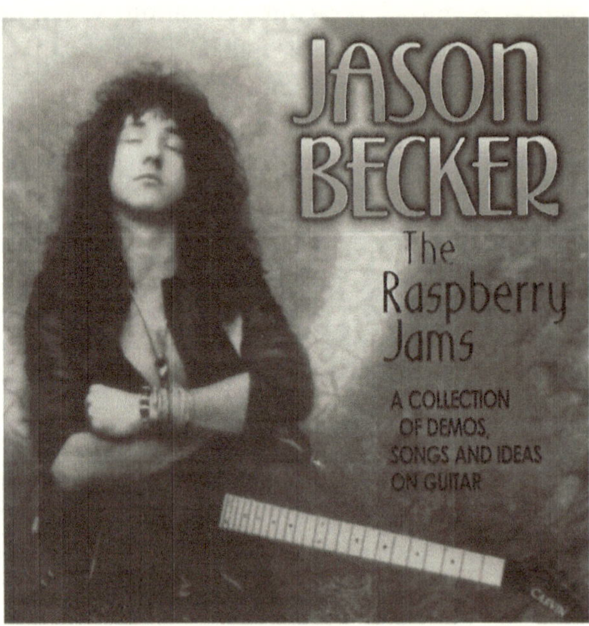

Both have beautiful melodies, and the words are pure poetry—and I'm not just saying that because I am his mother. You will get goosebumps when you hear this music. He has great sample libraries, so even his demos sound very real and emotional.

To release your new album, you set up a campaign that raised $100,000. How did you do it, and what was it all about? That's a lot of money for a DIY record.

Jason deeply appreciates everyone who contributed to his new album. He doesn't take that kind of generosity lightly. It's not easy for him to accept such help, but he is working hard to make it all worthwhile.

It is so much work to create five new classical pieces and get an orchestra to play them, or to write a Western-themed song that showcases eleven of the best guitarists around. He has also written two songs with lyrics and found singers, choruses, violin players, horn players, and so on.

It would be an overwhelming task for anyone, let alone someone who spends hours each day just getting up and going back to bed—with help. What he is doing is a miracle, and I think people recognize that and love and appreciate his music and his dedication to it. His supporters are giving him an incredibly meaningful gift, and I believe they are going to be very happy with the results.

You have friends who are musicians from bands like Van Halen or Megadeth. Do they contribute in any way, send money, or hold benefit gigs for you to keep your spirits up?

Musicians are generous people, and they do what they can for Jason. They have so much respect for him, and if they can do a benefit, they do. He truly appreciates their support. Eddie Van Halen has helped so much.

Jason sometimes feels down, like anyone else, but staying busy with his creative projects helps him remain mentally upbeat.

Do you stay at home with an assistant, or are you able to travel and maybe even go to some gigs?

Jason doesn't go out much because it's so complicated, but he can go out. He lives next door to us, and we see him every day. His uncle lives across the street, and his brother and his family live about an hour and a half away.

We spend evenings with Jason, watching movies or visiting with nurses, caregivers, or just among ourselves, and he has a lot of company from all over the world. If we do go out, it's usually to his spiritual retreat or an occasional movie or concert.

Is there any advice you would give to someone similarly affected, or is it individual?

I think Jason would say to remember that you are more than just your body; there is love and there are things to do. But he would also understand giving up and doesn't judge anyone for how they feel, good or bad. It is not easy or fun to be diagnosed with ALS, and he hasn't always been accepting and calm.

He has had rough times and has questioned the meaning of it all himself. But he has decided to live his life in the best way he can, to continue to make beautiful music, and to have fun with his family and friends. I could not be prouder of him and all that he does. It is astounding.

Here are some things that Jason says to people who ask for suggestions for ALS:

I would suggest getting tested for Lyme disease. It seems Lyme often mimics ALS. I know someone personally who was first diagnosed with ALS, but it was Lyme.

There is no pain with ALS, at least not in my case. I guess the most important thing is to have a lot of cool people helping you. Hopefully, you guys have that.

I tell everyone, even if they aren't having this problem, about the system I use to communicate since I lost my speech. It's the best system I know of, and my father invented it. It is called Vocal Eyes, doesn't use a computer, and here is a link to it: http://jasonbeckerguitar.com/eye_communication.html

I tried IV chelation therapy, and that made me a bit better for a while. I would recommend that.

Diet seems to help me. I am currently doing a diet recommended by Ray Peat. All of his suggestions give me more energy and even a couple of stronger muscles. I also haven't been sick in a while. I remember when I first got ALS, sugar seemed to make the muscles twitch and disappear faster.

I know someone who was helped by Edgar Cayce's Wet Cell therapy. That might be worth looking into.

2017

JENNIFER BRICKER

To be without legs is an honor and privilege for me since I can motivate millions of people around the world.

It was by chance that we stumbled upon this incredible story of a gutsy American lady. Jennifer was born in 1987 with no legs. However, that didn't stop her from dreaming of becoming a gymnast. She was abandoned by her biological parents and later adopted by Sharon and Gerald Bricker, who raised her alongside their three sons and placed no limits on her dreams.

Young Jennifer had a passion for tumbling and gymnastics and taught herself how to swim and roller-skate on her hands. At the age of seven, she started playing softball, and three years later, she began playing volleyball.

Her determination and effort soon turned her into an accomplished acrobat and aerialist. She competed in power tumbling for four years and qualified for the 1998 Junior Olympics, where she finished fourth. She became the only physically challenged person ever to compete professionally in power tumbling.

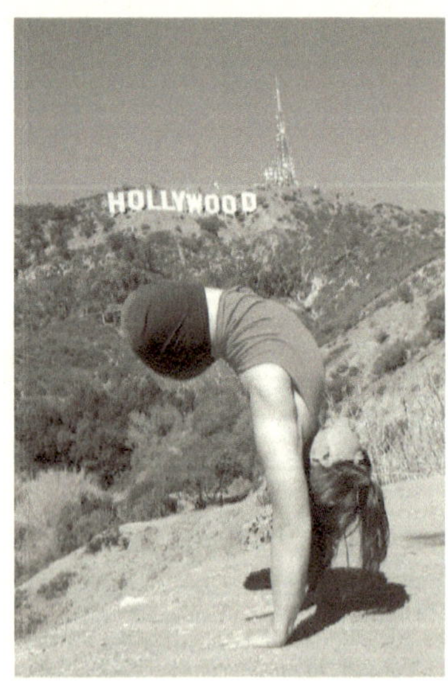

After graduating from high school, Nate Crawford began coaching her in aerial arts and refined her tumbling skills. She caught the eye of singer Britney Spears, who invited her to perform on her world tour. From a young age, Jennifer admired gymnastics champion Dominique Moceanu, who was part of the U.S. Olympic team that won the first-ever gold medal. Jennifer didn't know who her biological parents were until she was 16 years old and discovered that her idol, Dominique, was her biological sister. It took Jennifer four years to find and meet her sister. Later, she also met her biological mother without any hard feelings, though her father had already passed away. This unreal story deeply affected us, and we decided to contact Jennifer and interview her. We were assisted by her PR manager, Shannon Shade.

When you had no legs and started doing sports at the age of seven, was it because you loved sports and went for it, or because you wanted to show able-bodied people that you were equal or better than them and chose this way to demonstrate that?

Thankfully, I did not need to do sports to prove anyone wrong. I simply did the sports because I had a passion and love for them. I never participated in sports to try and prove anything to anyone. I was free to follow my passions, thanks to the way my parents raised me.

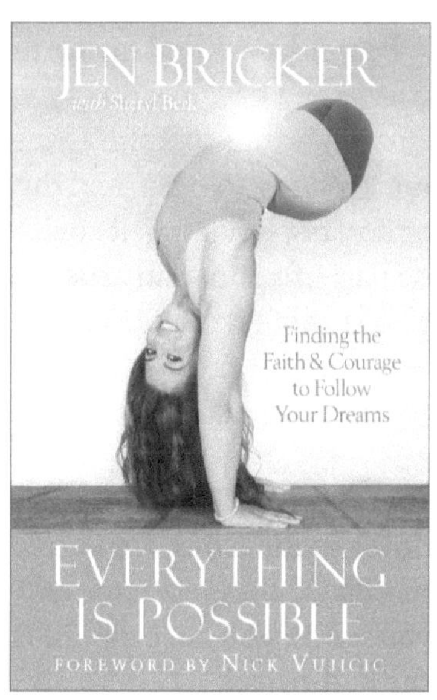

Did you experience any malice or disrespect from classmates or neighbors, which made you even stronger and more determined? What is harder: finding the power to motivate yourself or convincing those who don't believe in you?

My friends, teachers, and community were extremely supportive throughout my entire life. I was shaped by all the people around me who poured love and encouragement into me. I was never looked at as "the girl with no legs"—I was just known as Jen, strong, talkative, and athletic.

During acrobatic acts, able-bodied artists can grab partners by the hands or legs, but you can only be caught by your hands. Did you have to specially design your acts so your partner wouldn't miss the grip while you spun?

Every act is different, of course. When I used to do partner acts, we had to learn how to do some things differently because I didn't have legs. There was a lot of experimenting and practicing, of course. But that particular skill was done normally because it is common to grab at the arms for a partner spin. For the last six years, I have been performing as a solo aerialist.

How were your shows received around the world? Were they your own, or were they part of a circus or indoor program?

People have loved my performances in many different countries. They have been very well received! Each performance and job brings something unique. Typically, a company hires me to do my solo act, and they may also hire me to speak and/or do a book signing. It could just be a performance, or it could be part of a show, an artistic kind of show, or a venue where I also speak, like for a corporate company. My solo act is very versatile and can adapt to many different environments, such as corporate events, theater stages, or outdoor festivals.

You played volleyball, basketball, and softball, as well as doing gymnastics. Do you compete with able-bodied people in official competitions, and if so, are the rules the same for you, or do you have any advantages, like being able to touch the ball twice?

Yes, all of my sports were regular sports with able-bodied athletes. I had no special treatment or exceptions made. I wanted to ensure I had no extra advantages or special treatment over anyone.

When Britney Spears approached you, what did she want? Did she need a surreal stage act, or did she want to liven up her gigs with a sensation? When people applauded, did they cheer for your show or her songs? Was it a one-off deal?

They had me as a specialty act with my old partner. We did a duo trampoline act, touring with her and doing over 40 shows in North America and Australia. The audience went wild every single time—it was an absolute rush performing for up to 20,000 people! It was an experience I am very grateful for. Most people never get to experience that kind of moment in their entire life.

Do you treat your motivational talks as a job, or are they a mission while you look for other work? If it's the latter, what would your dream job be?

Yes, I have been a professional speaker for several years—it is my career, alongside performing and being an author.

Many disabled people give talks around the world, and thousands go to listen. Are those people just interested in hearing someone like you, or are they lost and desperate in their lives and in need of help? Aren't you afraid that you will tell them the same things as Nick Vujicic or others?

I find that the majority of people I speak to are not disabled. Everyone has something in their lives that they are dealing with—that's what makes us all the same. Everyone needs encouragement and healing, everyone. As far as Nick and I go, although we have similarities—and I love Nick; he is a great friend of mine—we are very different and have very different stories. So, there is no worry that we will say the same thing. Speaking is something we are both called to do, and there is room for both of us.

Being given away, adopted, and then finding out that your idol is your sister sounds like a Hollywood film. Have you been approached, or have you thought about writing a script for a biopic?

Yes, absolutely. There will definitely be a movie about my life one day. Whenever God has it planned, it will happen.

Given your unique experiences, do you think you have more in life and are richer than you would have been as an 'ordinary' person, able-bodied, one of many?

I am very grateful for the unique perspective that not having legs has given me. I do think it has made me a deeper and richer person. It was meant to be that I don't have legs—it was not an accident or a 'mistake.' God knew what He was doing, and I am here to reach millions of people around the world. It is an honor and a privilege.

2017

JIŘÍ KLÍCH

Jack of all trades in a wheelchair

Many people assume that life in a wheelchair means slowing down dramatically. But that is not the case with Jiří Klích; in fact, the opposite could be said. We met him at an airshow at the beginning of June. It took him seven weeks to find time to answer us. He was fishing, then he was at an archery competition, and then he was excavating the wreckage of a WWII German plane. Jiří is 33 years old, married with two children, and a metal cutter by trade. His near-fatal accident happened in 1989.

What actually happened then?

It was a freak accident. I was traveling as a passenger in a tractor, holding the handrail, which tore off, and I fell off. It was May 1989, and I ended up in a hospital in Novy Jicín, where I stayed for six weeks. Then rehabilitation followed for

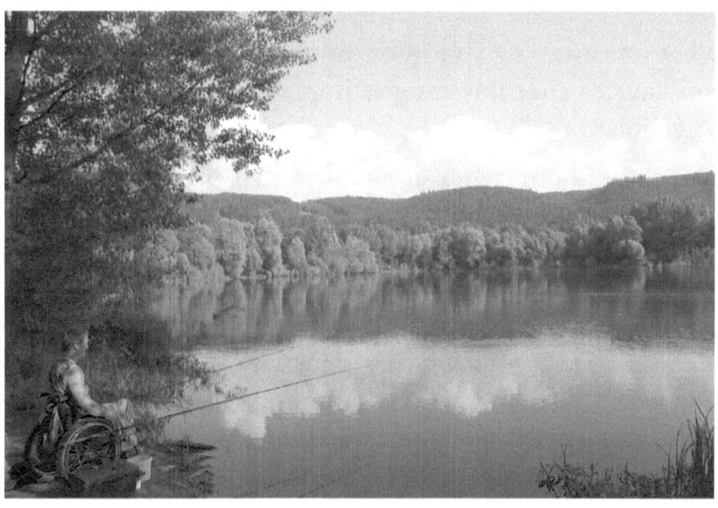

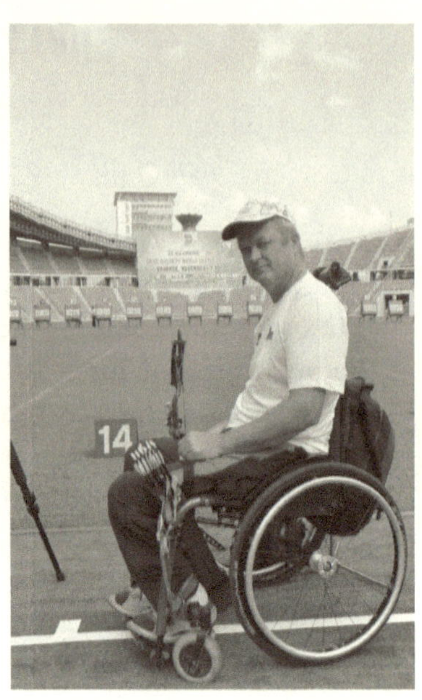

another eight months. I was in Hrabyne Rehabilitation Center. They treated me well since they knew what they were doing.

Did you have any mental blocks or were you shy about asking for anything, say, when you needed assistance in using the bathroom?

No, not really. They also paired a more experienced patient with a 'new' one. Since the 'old' one had some experience under their belt, the newcomer soon picked up what was needed—what they could do, how things worked, and what they were entitled to. They helped me after my return home by inviting me to some wheelchair events, which helped me transition back into regular life as a disabled person.

What was awaiting you upon your arrival back home? Did you have to alter anything at home to make it wheelchair accessible?

At the end of my stay at Hrabyne Rehabilitation Center, I used to go home on weekends. I was even at home for Christmas, so I slowly got used to everything, which helped a great deal. I live in a family house, so we had to add a ramp, alter the bathroom, and buy a lift for the stairs. It was interesting for both sides, as we had to adapt to new challenges and make significant adjustments to accommodate my needs. I made further adjustments when I returned home, according to my actual needs and ideas. My friends helped me a great deal too.

Before the accident, you were the 'head' of the family, the main breadwinner. When you returned home in a wheelchair, did you ever feel useless or afraid of being a nuisance?

No, not really. I had an idea that I would like to work with wood since I enjoyed it, so I built myself a workshop and bought machines that were accessible for someone in a wheelchair. So, I became a cabinetmaker. Obviously, not everything could be done from a wheelchair, so friends or family helped me bring in heavy pieces of wood, but I managed the rest by myself. With this work, I helped the family budget and felt like a very useful member of the family, not a nuisance. When the kids grew older and earning money wasn't as urgent, I switched my focus to making butts for historical weapons rather than window frames or doors. Thanks to this, I have more time for other activities.

After your return, did you go through a kind of depression that knocked you down, and then something came along that motivated you not to give up?

I think you should better ask my wife. I would say that the transition into ordinary life wasn't that dramatic, and I

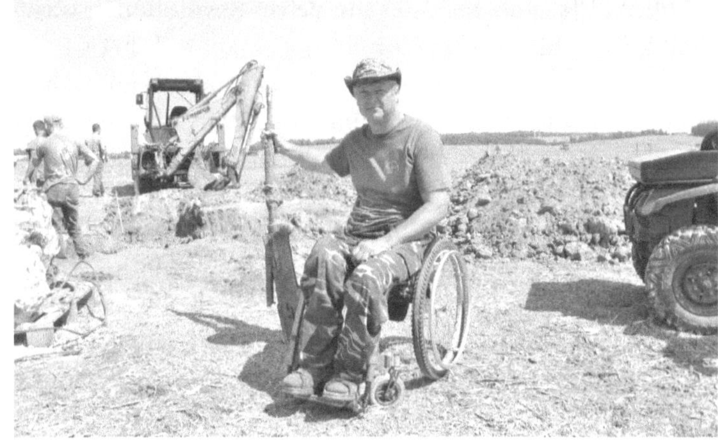

returned home pretty quickly. By no means was it easy—it was hard—but thanks to having friends among wheelchair users and having a place where I could ask for advice, it was much easier.

What are your experiences with the institutions and offices you had to deal with? Did you have to fight for what you were entitled to?

It was a nightmare. At that time, it was a complete disaster. If I didn't come with a sheet of paper stating which paragraph and which law entitled me to something, I had no chance of getting anything. I was just shown the door. My wife had to do everything, as there were only stairs, no ramps. Thankfully, I was insured, so I got the insurance money. One had to be unafraid and literally had to fight the offices. These days, it is much better, but I have heard stories of people being unfairly treated. Each office was different, but now it's a bit better.

When I met you at the airshow, you told us you competed in archery. Can you tell me more?

I always liked shooting. While in school, I liked shooting air guns or rimfire rifles. After my injury, we wanted to establish a Rimfire Rifle Club, but after the Velvet Revolution, it wasn't possible, as a disabled person with a weapon didn't sit well with many people. By pure luck, I heard about an archery club in East Bohemia, and I joined in 1993. I shot with a recurve bow for ten years, but I damaged my fingers, so I had to switch to shooting left-handed with a compound bow. In 1997, I started going abroad for international competitions—the European Championships, and World Championships—and I visited countries like New Zealand, South Korea, France, England, China, Australia, and Greece. I also competed in the Paralympic Games and always ended up in the world's top 10.

Is there any difference between disabled and able-bodied archers?

No, there isn't. We are members of the Czech Archery Federation and take part in their events, and vice versa. The rules are the same for both groups. Our events are part of the Czech Archery Federation calendar. In the Czech Republic, there are only two archery clubs for disabled people—one in the north in Teplice and one in East Bohemia, in Nové Mesto nad Metují. When I shot with a recurve bow, I represented the Ostrava team in the first league. I even won a Czech championship of able-bodied archers and represented the Czech Archery Federation at the World Championships in Leipzig. I'm still good enough to represent my country, but sometimes the traveling takes its toll, and I think they should give the duties to someone else.

Did the sport enrich you in some way? You've traveled and had the chance to get to know other countries, cultures, and people. Do you see differences in how disabled people are treated in other countries?

It's different everywhere; it depends on where we are. Europe is, of course, more developed since 1989. The Scandinavian countries are on a different level—they have everything for disabled people. The east is much worse, but Ukraine and Turkey are more advanced than the Czech Republic. The problem in the Czech Republic is the endless fight among federations, which is well documented publicly; it goes to court, and instead of finding good sponsors, it all goes downhill. I'm speaking from an archer's point of view. I don't have enough knowledge to judge each country as an ordinary tourist.

Could you tell us more about the excavation club you're a member of?

We have our own museum here in Suchdol nad Odrou, which contains all the sites our club has excavated in the area. We have to do all the necessary paperwork, find the site owner, pick up the tools, and off we go. When we find wreckage, we go to the archives and try to identify the plane, the pilot, and which base it operated from during WWII. What we find, we clean up and put into the exhibition. In August, we dug up an American Mustang fighter plane and found out the pilot had survived. It was Lincoln T. Hudson, a Black pilot from the famous 'Red Tails' 322nd Fighter Group. He died in 1987. Last year, we dug up two Russian bombers, and the whole crew was killed. The Russian Embassy was notified, and we will hold a ceremony for the crew. The grandson of one of the crew will arrive from Russia. So our 'job' is not just to dig out pieces of metal, but also to find details about the crew and, if possible, locate the family and get in touch with them.

What do you do on these missions? Don't tell us you work with a pickaxe from a wheelchair.

No, I drive the quad, pick up excavated pieces, take pictures, and shoot videos.

What else do you manage to do apart from the things we've talked about?

I go fishing, and I'm also a keen beekeeper. In my garden, I have 36 beehives. When I have time, I shoot guns. I'm not an idle man.

2014

KACEY MCCALLISTER

If you take a road with no obstacles, it probably leads nowhere

When Kacey McCallister was six years old, he ran into the road without looking. An oncoming truck hit him, tearing off his left leg and crushing the right one, which had to be amputated. When he was discharged from the hospital, someone advised his parents not to be soft and to let Kacey do everything his brothers and sisters did.

So, he did chores, cut the grass, washed the dishes, and did the laundry. At school, he decided to do wrestling, cross-country running, and athletics. He was so good at it that in 2011 he was included in the Wrestling Hall of Fame in Oregon. During a cross-country run, he met his future wife, Jennifer.

Kacey takes part in the very physically demanding Spartan race, where he competes with able-bodied athletes in various disciplines. He doesn't even mind crossing red-hot charcoal.

He does have artificial legs, but they are gathering dust in his garage, and he doesn't use them. Life is a challenge for him, and he earns his living as a motivational speaker. He and his wife Jennifer have four children of their own and have also adopted a six-year-old Ukrainian orphan with cerebral palsy. We have great respect for such a man.

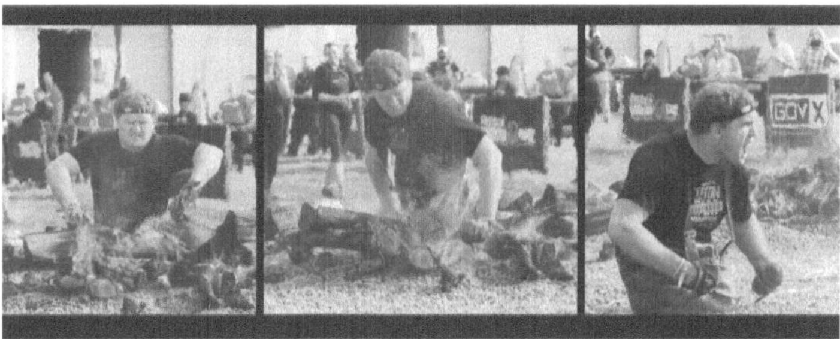

When you woke up in the hospital and found out your legs had been amputated, did you ask yourself why you had tried to cross the street without looking first? Did you think your life was all over? Did you get any insurance money?

When I woke up in the hospital after losing my legs, I looked down and saw that they were gone. With a shake of my head, I lay back down on the bed and went back to sleep. By the time I woke up again, I was ready to begin a life without legs.

I soon started learning how to live a normal life without legs. My parents never let me make excuses or come up with reasons I could not do something. They always made sure I knew that I could do whatever I wanted to do. I did get some compensation from the accident, but I have always believed that I need to work. I have had a job since I was a little boy—delivering newspapers when I was young, and now I work as a motivational speaker.

What sort of childhood and school years did you have? Were you ever abused or bullied by classmates, or were you popular

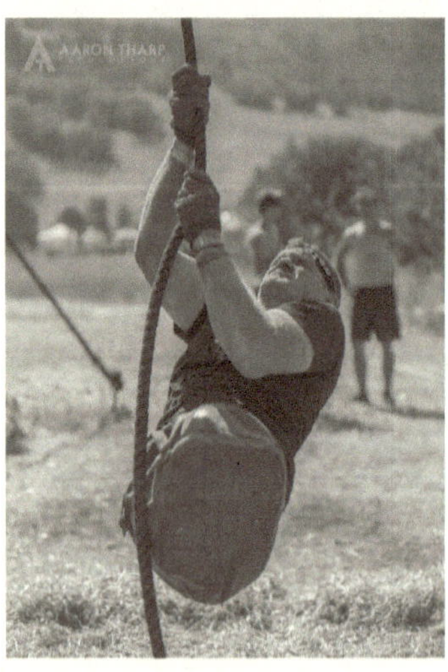

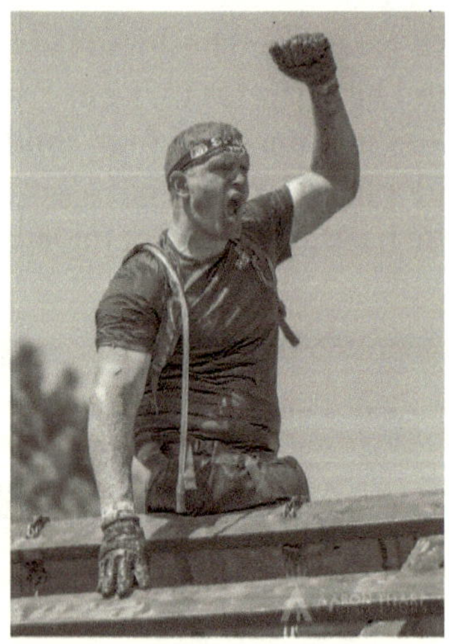

because you were doing the same things but looked funny and determined?

I always loved going to school. I loved learning and participating with the other children. Like any child, there were times when I felt left out and unwanted. There was a time when I felt like I would never have anybody to be friends with. However, I eventually found friends and a sense of belonging. But like everything else in life, that did not last forever, and soon I was involved in sports and making friends by participating in all types of athletics.

Did you have or ever try to get a nine-to-five job to make money but were rejected by bosses for not looking right, or have you always been a pro sportsman, so you made money from that?

I never had any issues getting a job because I was in a wheelchair. I was very determined to show people that I was willing and able to accomplish whatever I set my mind to. I would often show up for a job without the boss ever knowing I didn't have legs. They might be unsure at first, but soon they would see that I was more than able to do anything that was required of me. I have yet to earn much money from being an elite athlete. Hopefully, one day that will happen for me, but until then I will continue to work.

Do you just try any sport or other crazy activities because you like to try new things, or do you test your ability and how far you can go in order to pave the way for other amputees? Do you approach it with the motto 'It's not winning that matters but taking part and having fun'? Did you play American football in an ordinary league, and if so, for how long?

I am always looking for a new challenge. I cannot just sit back and let things happen. I feel the need to get out there and make them happen. I want to see just how far I can go and what is truly possible.

There have been times when I have not been able to accomplish a task the first time I tried it, but that doesn't stop me from doing it again and again until I find a way to do it. I hope other disabled athletes and others as well are able to see what I can do and realize that it is possible regardless of their situation. I am out there to do the best I possibly can do. If that means I win, then great, but regardless, I will push myself and be better because of that. I did do one season of American football in grade school with my school.

Tell us about that Spartan race—did you have to train specially for that, or did you just go for it and use your muscles and fitness to handle various disciplines?

The hardest thing in the Spartan races is the distance that I have to travel. Because the terrain is unfriendly to wheelchairs, I have to complete it mostly on my hands. This is very difficult and energy-intensive, so I train as much as possible to do the races as fast as possible. I do train for the obstacles, but more to keep my strength up.

Do you cooperate with any footwear company to test the boots you wear? Do you have only one, or do you have—say—a leather one for athletics and a Kevlar one for the Spartan race, so you just change them like people change shoes?

Since no expert has come forward, I've had to make my own equipment, continually improving the boots I use on the race course. I will continue to make them better as I go along. Every race, I find a better way to make the boot.

You also swim (how do you manage to keep your balance and not get drowned?), throw the spear, and also jump over fire.

Did you ever get into any situation where you realized it was a close shave and that was your limit?

I have been swimming since I was a child. I have even done triathlons. The more I train for it, the better I do. The spear throw is my most challenging obstacle, requiring the most practice. The fire jump seems pretty scary. Even now, when I have to do it, it always makes me pause before going over it. But I have my boot and my gloves, so I don't get hurt. I haven't found my limit. There are things I have done that are very hard. Some, in fact, are difficult enough to make me quit. But I take those times as a challenge and come back better the next time.

When you got into wrestling, did you fight under ordinary rules, or were they somehow adapted to be fair to both sides? Your rival had to lift only half the weight, and you couldn't use your legs to maintain stability and fight back. Do you take every sport as far as you can go, e.g., the Paralympics, or do you just try it, enjoy it, and then go on to something else?

When I wrestled, it was with regular people. The rules were the same, and we both figured it out as we went along. Sometimes my opponent would have a tough time trying to figure out how to wrestle me. By the time I had left school, I had made it to the state tournament and took second place.

Do you drive a car (specially adapted hand-drive)? If so, do you intend to be a pioneer in motorsport and drive, say, the 24 Hours of Daytona with a disabled crew?

I do drive a car. It would be a blast to be on a crew for a team like that. It hasn't been one of my goals yet, but who knows? I might get into it someday.

Did your disability teach you something about yourself you didn't know, and now you bless the truck driver who hit you back then?

Because I have lost my legs, I have been able to find out things about myself that I might not have been able to learn if that had not happened. I am tough, and I am strong, but more than that, I am able to overcome challenges that are placed in front of me because I know that I can. I have done hard things in life; some little annoyances can't really be that bad because I have done something much harder.

The man who hit me in his truck may not have known it, but he gave me the greatest blessing in my life. I wouldn't change what happened that day for anything.

How do you train for a 24-hour race or Ironman? Running on residual limbs must put a lot of strain on both them, as well as your hands and shoulders. Do you have some physio who tells you that you are still doing okay, or now you are hurting your body more than you should and will face problems?

I am training totally differently than I have been doing for the last few years. I am now trying to find ways to help me cover the course faster as well as be able to compete for a long time. Running on my hands is extremely energy-intensive. I run through my energy reserves very quickly. If I can find a better system, it will hopefully help me not use as much energy to cover the same amount of ground. One of my greatest concerns is how long I will be able to continue. I have been working with a physical therapist to figure it out.

2019

KATEŘINA MOROZOVÁ

I see my future in front of the camera rather than behind it

Always smiling, young Czech woman Kateřina Morozová (1994) was born with knuckles fused together and dysfunctional muscles, which meant she would never walk, and movement in her hands was very limited. She gets around in a wheelchair, and at home, she crawls and rolls on the carpet, doing most things with her mouth.

Despite her limited abilities, she decided to fulfill her dream of becoming a film editor. The Miroslav Ondříček Film Academy in Písek (Miroslav Ondříček was the cinematographer for most of Miloš Forman's movies), or rather its director and owner, Miroslav Terc, not only offered her the chance to study at this university but even sponsored her.

This woman's story aroused our interest, and we decided to interview her. Everything happened incredibly fast. On Wednesday morning, we asked the Film Academy for her contact details and got them within three minutes.

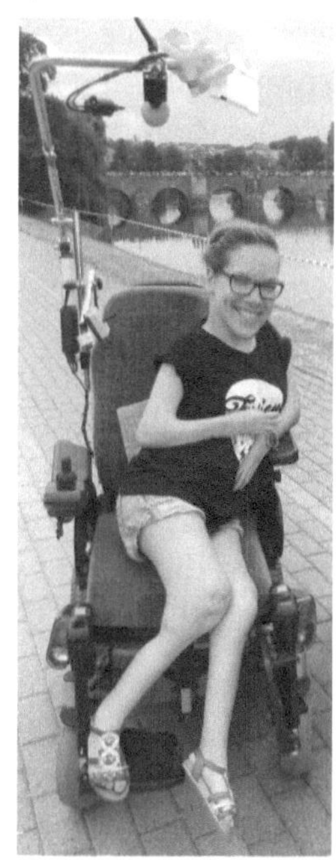

We wrote to Kateřina Morozová and asked if she would like to contact us by telephone, Skype, or PC. She replied immediately and chose to communicate via email. We worked out the questions, sent them to her, and the next day we received her answers. Incredible.

What is the illness that you were born with? We read that you were adopted

from an orphanage. What were your childhood school years like?

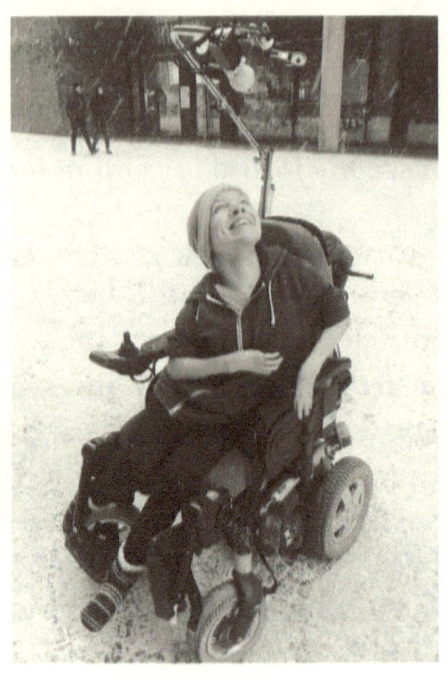

My illness is called arthrogryposis multiplex congenita, which roughly means stiffness of limb joints. Yes, I am an orphan. After my birth and a short stay in the hospital, I was placed in an orphanage, where I stayed until the age of four. Then I was taken in by a foster mother and father, and I grew up among "healthy" kids. I was raised the same as my siblings, and I am very, very grateful for that. I am pleased they didn't treat me as something less, with some exceptions and extra allowances. Of course, I always had—and still have—things that are more difficult for me than for others, but I was always surrounded by people who supported me, which gradually enabled me to fend for myself. As for my childhood, I don't regret anything. It was great—sometimes mad, sometimes sad, as happens in big families.

You graduated from the socio-legal school of the Jedlička Institute, also known as the Prague Institute for Blind and Disabled Children. Did you have a clear idea that you would like to help or defend people, but then your interest changed to film editing, and you arrived at a crossroads and pondered which to choose?

When I entered the Jedlička Institute, I had no idea what I wanted to do. In fourth grade, I started to take an interest in film editing, and I've followed that ever since. So, at the moment, I'm not at a crossroads—I know what I want to do. I work at a company called Newton Technologies in client support, and when I have time, I edit films, which suits me perfectly.

Irish film director Simon Fitzmaurice can communicate only with his eyes but still directed the movie *My Name is Emily*. Is film editing the final stage in the film business for you, or would you like to progress to directing, too?

In the film business, I want to move forward, but more in front of the camera—some acting, if that makes sense. We'll see how it goes, since I have no acting education. So, at the moment, I try small parts—bigger than cameo appearances, and similar roles. As for devoting my time to directing instead of editing? No chance.

What was it like at the Miroslav Ondříček Film Academy? Did you feel at home there, or did you realize it was different from what you expected?

I didn't have big expectations. It was a priceless experience for me. This institute opened doors for me that I never, ever dreamed would open.

Do you intend to search actively for deals with film companies, or do you hope that somebody will call you, give you a job, and fulfill your dream that way?

I monitor the Konkurz.cz (Audition.cz) Facebook page and actively look for small roles. I'm registered with many casting agencies, and from time to time, they write to me that they are looking for a person with a disability in a wheelchair. So, I think I'm active in this direction, and editing is slowly lagging behind that right now.

You are very much involved in theater. Do you have hidden talent, or are you just happy among other people, and this is one way you fulfill that?

I don't know if I can say I have talent or not, but I rehearse and take each new performance as a challenge. Even with each rehearsal, I leave my comfort zone, and it pushes me forward. Of course, I am happy among other people, but that is not the primary reason why I try to act.

You used to live in Písek, but you wanted to make yourself independent and live in Prague, for which you need a good job and an excellent salary. Do you have any timetable or plan for how to manage such a difficult change comfortably by yourself, step by step?

At present, I already live in Prague. I made myself independent, and I do have a job, but the journey to independence was very difficult. After graduating from university, I found myself living in a house for people with disabilities. There, I set myself the goal of living alone, independently. I lived there during the vacations and at the same time organized accommodation at the Jedlička Institute, which offers a one-room apartment during the school year as part of a program called Independent Living. During those months, I also actively searched for a job, and with the help of my family and the Jedlička Institute, I managed to get one.

Do you have any experience, positive or negative, with getting a job and accommodation for yourself as a physically person with a disability who wants to live life independently and to the fullest?

I was looking for living quarters and a job mainly on the internet. Most of the time—nine times out of ten—they told me that either the job or the apartment was not wheelchair accessible. But I didn't give up and kept going.

I told my friends I was looking for a job, and it paid off since my friend from the Jedlička Institute put me in touch with Mrs. Dita Horochovská, a career counselor who helped guide me. The first meeting was about a voice computer control program. Although it wasn't the right job for me, I remained open to further cooperation. We talked about many other things, and out of the blue, she referred me to Petr Herian, a contact she introduced me to, who—after trying hard for several months—found me an ideal position.

As for accommodation, at the Jedlička Institute, a small group of people with disabilities got together with one aim—to find suitable accommodation. With some help, we got access to the media and told the public about our aims and needs.

We pointed out the problem of barrier-free living and set up a website called www.bezbabyty.cz. We organized an event with overnight accommodation in tents. TV made footage of it, which was broadcast on the news, and we asked people, if they had flats and wanted to rent them out with reconstruction, to get in touch with us. We got a response, and thanks to that, I have a place to stay now.

You are full of positive energy. What recharges your batteries and makes you happy?

I am happy when the people around me are happy. I think I complain about something every day, but I overcome it with my optimism.

With an instructor, you have been on a bobsleigh and on skis. Do you have any ultimate dream you are slowly aiming for?

I have lots of dreams that I want to fulfill. My biggest dream is to visit America.

You enjoy traveling. How does it work in the Czech Republic? Does a helper drive your car, or do you ask your parents? And do you also travel abroad and to the coast?

I have to organize assistance well ahead. Then we have to plan the journey and everything around it. Mostly, we travel by train or bus.

Thanks to your positive attitude and approach, you are often mentioned in the media. Do you mind publicity, or does it help you open doors that would otherwise stay shut for you?

I don't mind publicity. I take it with gratitude and modesty, but I also want to show people that I can live a full life with a disability.

2019

KYLE MAYNARD

The obstacles put in front of us and the way we deal with them form our personality

Many people take for granted having been born with both arms and legs, assuming that's just the way it is. However, some individuals are born with congenital disabilities. Kyle Maynard was born in Washington in 1986 with a rare genetic condition called Congenital Amputation, resulting in residual limbs ending at the forearms and above the knees. Most people might choose to avoid challenges and take a less demanding approach to life, but not Kyle.

At the age of 11, he began playing football but soon shifted his interest to martial arts, wrestling, and Jiu-Jitsu. For wrestling and martial arts, he needed a high level of fitness, so he started to exercise and power-lift. Soon, he became the strongest teenager in the world when he bench-pressed a 120 kg bar 23 times. In 2014, with chains attached to his limbs, he lifted an incredible 210 kg above his head. In 2012, he also became the first disabled person to climb Mt. Kilimanjaro, which is 5,895

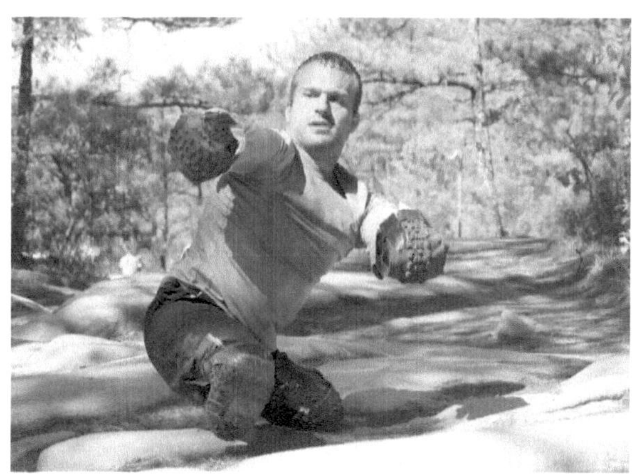

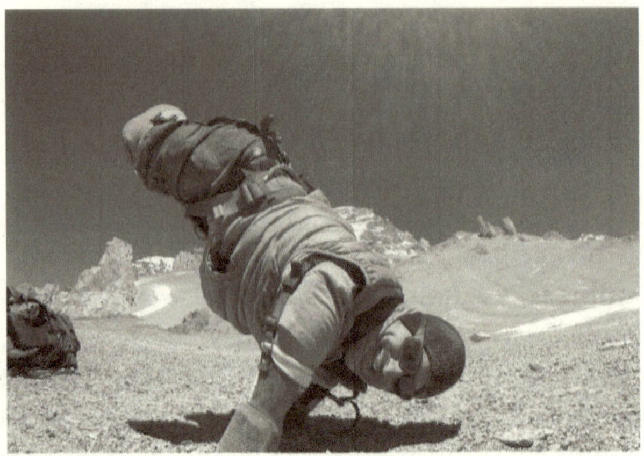

meters high. Not long after, he bettered this achievement by climbing Aconcagua, the highest peak in the Americas at 6,962 meters, in Argentina.

Now, Kyle travels around the world, speaking at universities and to major companies like Coca-Cola and Microsoft, sharing his story of overcoming physical limitations and motivating others to pursue their goals despite obstacles. He also devotes significant time to supporting wounded American veterans. He has appeared on major talk shows with Larry King and Oprah Winfrey and even caught the eye of action star Arnold Schwarzenegger.

Kyle put his story into a book titled 'No Excuses,' which became a bestseller. He can make 50 keystrokes a minute on a keyboard and drives a car, allowing him to maintain his independence. He also fulfilled one of his life dreams by opening a gym called No Excuses CrossFit.

We were fascinated by Kyle and requested an interview. His business partner, Joe Leonard, responded within two days and helped arrange the interview.

Did you have a traumatic childhood before you realized you were different from other kids?

I was born as the first of four kids; I have three sisters, who are healthy. My parents gave me lots of love and treated me as an equal, normal member of the family. Since they never looked at me as something different, I learned to treat myself the same way.

So even at school, you were not the target of malice or bullying from your classmates?

I used to go to school with others on the school bus. Sometimes I was angry and asked myself why it had to be me, but then I realized I was as normal as the others, just more noticeable because of my physical differences.

So, you never regretted that you had no arms or legs?

Sometimes, especially in sports. I got hooked on wrestling, where I missed my arms because I couldn't hold my rival the way I wanted to, but I had to develop unique techniques and leverage my strengths differently. In the beginning, it was very hard, and I lost all my wrestling matches in the first and second seasons. But my parents stood by me and didn't allow me to give up, so I worked hard and eventually won all my wrestling matches against adults in my third season.

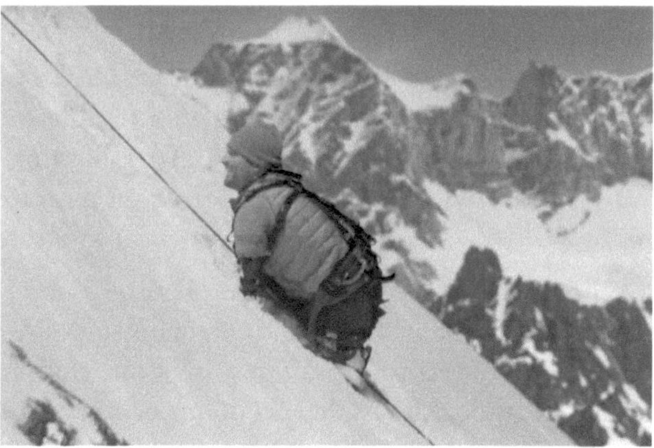

Why did you take up sports with your disability?

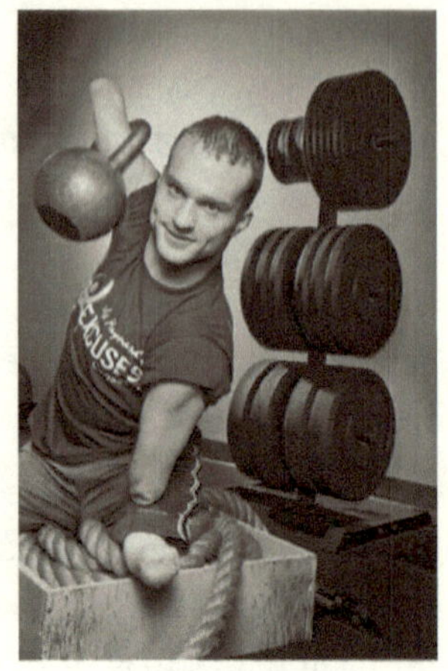

I was just an ordinary boy, just a little bit smaller. I liked sports from my childhood, whether it was baseball, basketball, or hockey. Later on, I played American football, and eventually, I got really hooked on wrestling.

American football is a very tough game. Didn't you have problems with it?

In the beginning, my rivals didn't take me seriously, but when I knocked them down and they hit the deck hard, they realized I meant business, and they had to take me seriously too. In wrestling, I had a similar advantage: the element of surprise. When my rival was on his back after ten seconds, he realized I was a serious opponent who really wanted to win.

You also did martial arts, is that true?

I became the first man without legs and arms to compete in the mixed martial arts ring. Now I am studying the Brazilian version of Jiu-Jitsu for the seventh season.

Climbing Kilimanjaro is no small feat for an able-bodied person. Why did you choose this particular mountain, and did you receive advice and preparation from a mountain climber?

Mt. Kilimanjaro has been a dream of mine since I first climbed Stone Mountain, a small mountain outside of Atlanta, GA. It took a lot of training and the help of our close friend and mountain guide, Kevin Cherilla, to make it happen.

Was it as you expected, or were there times when you thought you had had enough? Were you on the verge of giving up? Do you plan on any higher mountains, or after Mount Aconcagua, have you decided that's enough?

On Mt. Kilimanjaro, day four was extremely hard for me. We were climbing for four straight days, and we skipped our rest day to try to make better time. My limbs were swelling up, and everything hurt. When I got to camp that night, I was lying in my tent and could hear my friends laughing and joking outside, which made me angry that they were having fun while I was suffering. It seemed unfair. Then I thought about what was really unfair—that Corey Johnson, the soldier whose ashes our team was carrying to the summit, would never get the chance to climb this mountain. The pain didn't go away, but my perspective changed.

You do climbing, wrestling, Jiu-Jitsu, play American football, write books, make speeches, and travel a lot. How do you fit it all in? Do you dedicate blocks of time to each activity, or do you switch from one to another?

Like anything in life, there are different goals or things that get more focus at some times than others. Speaking engagements have always been more frequent during certain periods, and we've structured our business to allow for more free time to follow some of my other goals. Most of the companies approach Joey and me for speeches or other requests.

Since 2008, you have had your own gym. Is it like other gyms, or do you offer something different?

I actually sold my CrossFit gym earlier this year to a close friend of mine. People used to exercise there who wanted to develop a more positive mindset and commit to living a healthy lifestyle. Community-minded people gathered there too.

Do you live an ordinary life and take it as it comes, or do you set goals and follow a yearly plan?

If I'm at home or with friends and not giving a speech, I don't think about the disability, so I think it's a pretty ordinary life that doesn't look much different from yours.

2018

LOUISE HUNT

Tennis champion on wheels

Louise Hunt is the daughter of former British speedway rider Tim Hunt. She was born with Spina Bifida, which meant she never walked. Thanks to significant support from her family, she became one of the best disabled tennis players, not only in the UK but also in the world.

You were born with a condition that prevented you from walking. When did you realize you wouldn't be able to walk, and that you would be different from your classmates? Was it a hard pill to swallow, and did your world fall apart?

I have always been fully aware of my situation regarding being in a wheelchair. I am very fortunate to have supportive parents who have always been honest with me about my disability and what my body limits are. I have lived a full

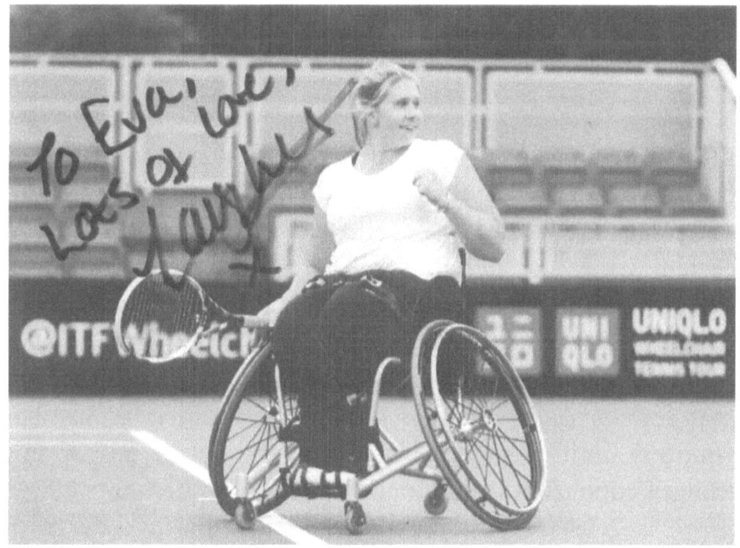

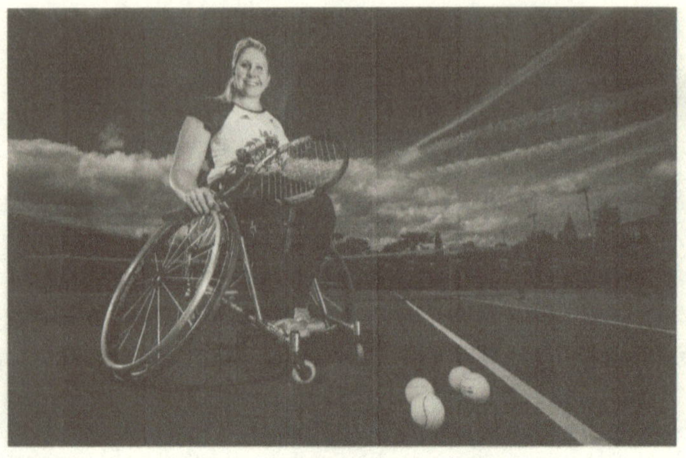

Hi Vitek and Eva,

Thought you might like this one too
An official photo from the Rio 2016
paralympic games.

Louise

p.s. Thank you so much as always for your
support and friendship
x

life, not feeling that I have missed out on much. However, the only time I remember it hitting me was when I went to secondary school and wasn't allowed or couldn't join in with certain games and activities in P.E. lessons. As I have always loved sports, it came as a bit of a shock to me and was quite upsetting.

I never wanted to miss out on anything, but I had to accept that perhaps rugby on a playing field was something just beyond my limits. I soon realized that there were only a few things I couldn't do, and I made up for it in other areas of my life.

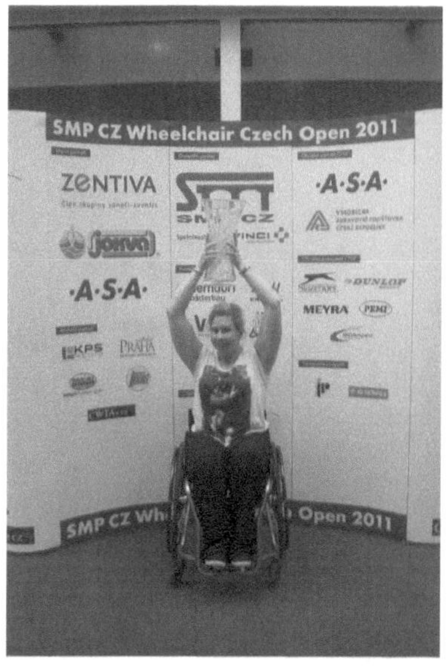

When you are young and dependent on the help of family and others, does a feeling of dependency and shame build inside you, which persuades you to gain independence?

I have always felt well-supported in my life, both physically and emotionally. However, I am very independent and like to prove to myself and the world that I don't need help with anything. Unfortunately, from time to time, I do need some help and still don't like to ask for it, but I am learning to accept that it's okay because everybody needs a little extra help from time to time. This certainly makes me more determined to achieve unexpected things.

Have you ever received a look of disdain or been made to feel inferior because you are disabled?

Like many disabled people, I have experienced a lot of prejudice and discrimination. I was bullied at school, but I overcame this by eventually confronting the bullies, and from that day, it never happened again. I was respected by my fellow pupils for being Louise, not just 'that girl in the wheelchair.' My sporting success at school helped, as I was seen as someone achieving things. For example, if I had won something or met a celebrity, everybody was interested in what I was doing.

However, I have to say my schools, college, and university were always very supportive and understanding of my life as a wheelchair user. It has gotten much better now, but

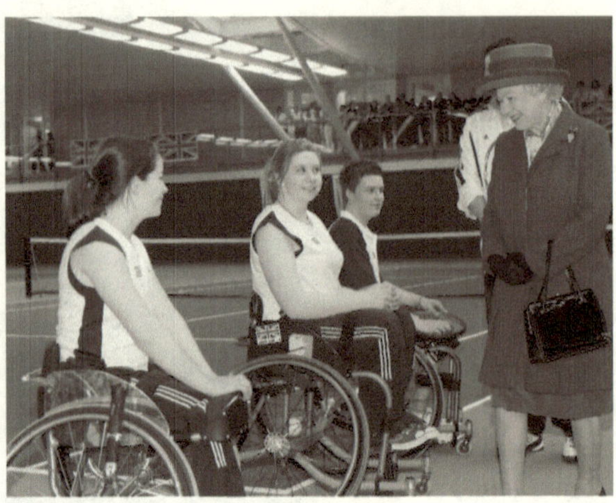

shops, cinemas, and airports used to make me feel unwelcome. A typical example of this is when I go to use a disabled bathroom—they are often being used as storerooms. When I ask for things to be moved, I am sometimes perceived as a nuisance, as it isn't always clear what needs to be moved.

Have you ever tried to join a community of disabled people because you didn't feel comfortable among able-bodied people and wanted a world closer to your own?

I have never felt like I needed to find a disabled community as such. However, when I found disability sports and began spending a lot of time with other disabled people, it gave me a real feeling of comfort, as everybody has a basic understanding of each other's needs and no explanations are ever needed. We all accept each other for who we are.

When people helped you in different situations, did you sense that they did it out of pity, and in reality, they would rather you weren't there?

Yes, I do get a sense that when certain people help me, it's from a sympathetic perspective, but I am now a good judge of character and simply steer clear of these people. My life is amazing, and I am extremely happy, so there is no need for anybody to feel sorry for me.

Why did you choose tennis? Did you want to do something extraordinary in sports or maybe find a way of earning a living from it? Have you ever thought about a nine-to-five job, or was tennis the hardest sport, so you tested your stamina and endurance?

I tried many sports when I was younger because I love a physical challenge, but I chose tennis because it was the hardest, and I enjoyed it the most. When I first started tennis, it was because I had a passion for it, and as I got better, I realized the potential to make a career out of it. I consider myself lucky to have my greatest passion as my career, but this has only come about through a lot of hard work and determination. I have the ambition to do other things after tennis, but right now, I am living my dream.

It was probably no mean feat to learn to play tennis in a wheelchair. Have you ever thought you made the wrong decision and wanted to give up?

Like any athlete, I have good days and bad days. On the bad days, maybe I've had a terrible match or a bad training session, and I've had moments where I've wondered if it's all worth it. But it doesn't take me long to remind myself that it's minor in the grand scheme of things, and tomorrow will be a better day.

Do you think that 'thanks' to your disability, you have seen more countries, met more people, and gained more than you would have normally? Has your condition enriched you in a way?

There are times when my disability has restricted me, but due to my determination and ambition, I have used my disability to my advantage. This has come through a lot of hard work, but it has been totally worth it. Being an elite athlete is amazing because I get to do the thing I love the most every day. I have also traveled the world competing, met many inspiring people, and had experiences that will live with me forever.

I now work in the government to help other disabled people fulfill their potential. I love that I can use my experience as a disabled person to encourage and support others in their journey. I don't know what I would be doing if I were able-bodied—maybe my life wouldn't be as good. But what I do know is that my life is heading in a direction I am happy with, and for all the little things I miss out on, I feel I gain a thousand others.

Could you tell us more about your accolades in tennis and your career?

I have been playing wheelchair tennis since I was five years old (I am 22 now). I have been playing at an elite level for six years and last year qualified for the Paralympic Games in London, ranked World number 18, my greatest achievement so far. I am the number-three ranked woman in Great Britain. I play on average 15 to 20 tournaments a year located all over the world.

Last year, my tournaments were in Australia, Germany, the USA, Brazil, South Africa, Japan, Korea, Israel, Belgium, and Poland. To date, I have won over 30 world doubles titles, 15 world singles titles, and four team titles. I have been fortunate enough to meet many famous people, including sports stars (Andy Murray, Lennox Lewis, the England Rugby team, and many more) and TV personalities (Stephen Fry, Cliff Richard, among others). But the highlight for me has to be being invited to Buckingham Palace for a garden party this year by the Queen, where I got to meet the Royal Family.

Your parents had to sacrifice a lot for you. Did you have moments when you knew they were proud of you and you felt you paid them back for that?

In my opinion, everything I have achieved has been a team effort. By this, I mean my parents, family, and friends have supported me from day one in all my dreams and ambitions. Although I am fully independent now (I travel alone and support myself financially), I never forget that without my mum taking me to training sessions and tournaments, my dad helping with my wheelchair and equipment, and the general emotional support from my brother and loved ones, none of my achievements would have been possible. I know they are proud of me, and I am of them, but we keep each other grounded and in touch with reality.

What would you like to do in your life in the future, and what would you advise young people who are wheelchair users?

For now, I am still competing, and I wish to continue my current work with the government, charity work, motivational speaking, and appearances. My ambition is to inspire others, helping them fulfill their potential and be the best they can be.

My advice to other young disabled people is that you are going to face many barriers and hurdles in your life, both physical and emotional. Sometimes things are out of your control, which will be hard, but try to accept it and know that you can cope with whatever life throws at you. Focus on controlling what is within your reach. Once in a while, accept help; there's no shame in accepting that you need a hand from time to time.

The world is scary, and that won't change, but sometimes doing something to push you outside of your comfort zone will open your mind to a whole new world. Ignore negativity; you're not weird or any other of the random names they come up with for you. You are simply unique, and that is such a rare thing nowadays—embrace it!

There will be sad times that feel like they will never end, but I promise you can get through them. Take it as character-building, which shapes you as a person today; in the long run, it only benefits you. As they say, "What doesn't kill you makes you stronger," and it's true! You have to experience the bad days to appreciate the good ones; life is just a series of moments.

You have traveled around the world. Did you find any differences in attitudes toward disabled people in different places?

I have traveled to many different countries, and the attitudes and services towards disabled people vary drastically. Countries such as China and the USA are extremely helpful and efficient. They always ensure that my needs are met, treat me respectfully, handle my wheelchair safely, and listen to my requirements.

However, this is not always the case. Many other countries I have visited see me as an inconvenience, refusing to listen to my needs and mishandling my equipment, as well as treating me as though I am incapable of making my own decisions. This is always a frustrating experience.

2013

LANDON WEEKS

I can either cry or laugh at my state, I chose the latter

We were looking for a story about a disabled musician and were eager to find a pianist. Luckily, we came across Landon Weeks, who was born with a rare condition called phocomelia, which means he has no forearms and only three fingers on each hand. He fell in love with playing the piano during childhood and now performs across the USA. His brother, manager, agent, and sidekick, Abram, was very helpful in organizing an interview for us.

How rare is phocomelia?

It is an extremely rare disorder. In some cases, like mine, a spontaneous genetic defect may cause phocomelia.

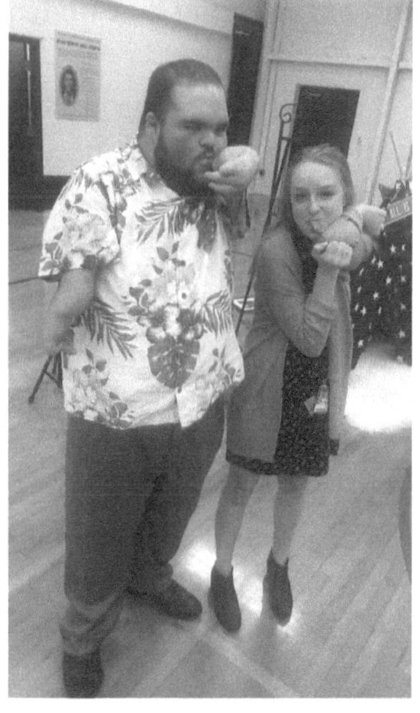

What kind of childhood did you have? Were you treated well by schoolmates, and did you attend an ordinary school or a special one?

I had a pretty normal childhood. There were times when I was bullied, but I ultimately overcame it and tried to fit in. Schoolmates laughed at me when I rode a bicycle with a helmet on and fell off often. I told them I had met aliens and that if they didn't stop laughing at

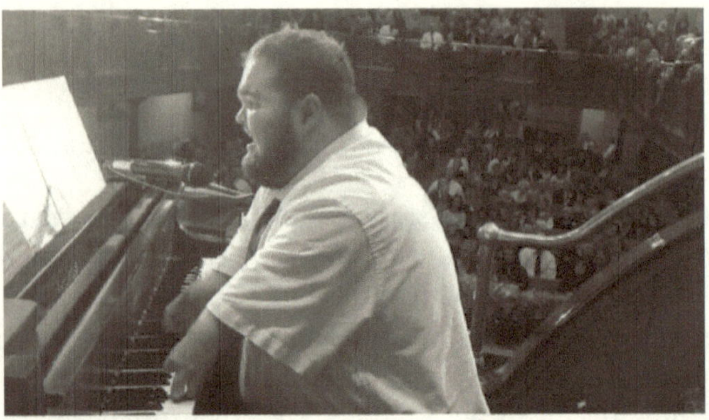

me, I would ask the aliens to do something with their hands too. I attended a regular school.

You started playing the piano at six after seeing your brothers play. Did you like the music and instrument, or did you want to match your brothers, making it your first life challenge without realizing how difficult it would be? Also, how old are you?

I wanted to play the piano because all of my brothers were taking lessons, and I wanted to learn as well. It was definitely hard, but I learned the best I could. I was born on a leap year, on February 29, 1996, so I am six years old. But in normal counting, I am 24. I have three brothers, and we are each two years apart.

Ordinary pianists use ten fingers—Jerry Lee Lewis even used a leg—you have only six. Were you taught any tricks to level that disadvantage, or do you play faster to match the tempo?

I learned to adapt the chords of the music so I only play three of the notes in each chord at most. It still sounds the same, but it took a while for me to discover the technique that I use.

Your parents had trouble finding a teacher for you and ended

up with a paralyzed lady who had only two fingers. Were the "normal" teachers just not interested, or were they scared that it might be too difficult to teach you? Is it really that hard to teach a disabled pianist and "feel" their way of playing?

It did take a while for my parents to find a teacher for me. Most teachers felt like they couldn't teach me because they had never taught someone like me, but my teacher had faith in me, and she helped me become the musician I am today.

Our teacher was a concert pianist who later suffered a paralyzing injury, leaving her with only two fingers on one hand. She said, "If I can still play the piano with my two fingers, then I can teach Landon to play with the fingers he has." It just so happened that she lived less than a mile from our house and taught our entire family to play piano—all my brothers and even our parents. It all lined up too perfectly to be just a coinci-

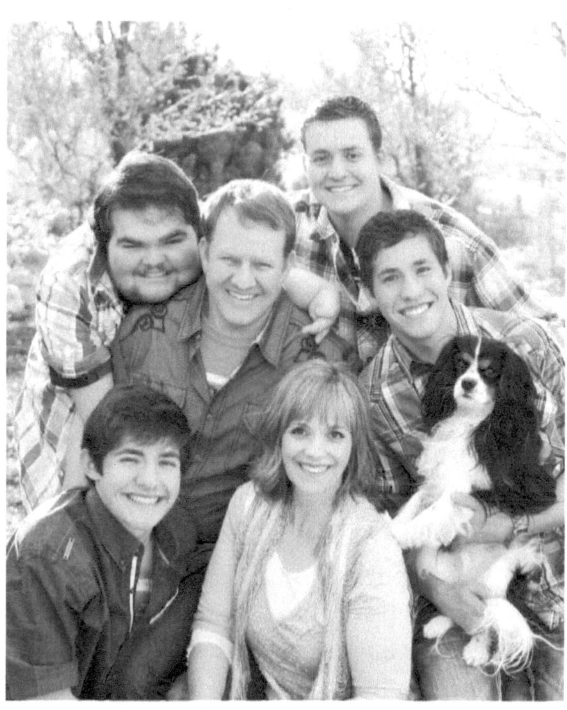

dence. It was a literal miracle for our family. I struggled with confidence until I learned to play the piano. My talent, which I worked hard on, gave me the confidence I needed to pursue a successful life.

Have you ever thought about, or were you told to try, a different, less complicated instrument, such as drums or the trumpet, and to give up the piano?

I actually played percussion in my junior high band for about three years. I still play the piano. I wish I would have played the trumpet or French horn in junior high as well, because I think that would have been fun to learn.

How often did you practice per day, and when were you told you were good enough to play publicly with confidence and without embarrassment?

When I was learning, I practiced around three hours per day. Now, I don't have as much time, so I practice less often. I do performances all the time. I still get nervous, but I enjoy performing.

Can you play anything now that you've mastered the skill, or are there certain styles, like ragtime or rock and roll, that you can't play? Can you read music, or do you play by ear?

I play pretty much any kind of music, and I learned to read sheet music. I can't play by ear.

Do you work, or is playing just a hobby? Do you intend to play for a living, and has it fulfilled your life dream?

I've done tours around the United States, mostly in local schools, but it would be cool to do a tour in Europe someday. I'm currently getting a master's degree in school and mental health counseling, so maybe I will be able to do a European tour after that. I've been working full-time at this company for the past six years. The company is Utah Behavioral Services , where I monitor kids diagnosed with autism. I create treatment plans for them while encouraging appropriate behavior and helping them learn how to function in society.

Have you been asked to record a CD, or do you intend to do so in the future? Do you use your disability to attract interest and gain an audience, like Jerry "Tiger" Lewis or perhaps Landon "Fingers" Weeks?

I've recorded videos of my performances, but I don't have CDs. Maybe someday I'll do that.

If you were to accompany an orchestra, would you need to make special arrangements with the musicians and conductor, or could you play like any other pianist?

I've never accompanied an orchestra before, but that would be a great opportunity someday.

Do you tour America, and would you travel to Europe if there was a chance? What is the fee for one of your gigs?

We would absolutely love to do a European tour. As far as the fee for a gig, it really depends. For school assemblies, most schools have a budget for assemblies, so we work with each school to make it reasonable for both the school and us. The price also depends on how much time and travel are required to get to the venue. For example, we usually charge about $500 plus travel costs for schools in Utah. Out-of-state performances can range from $1,000 to $5,000, depending on whether or not we're able to schedule multiple performances during the same trip.

Most of the time, it's relatively easy to get Landon booked once people realize how talented he is and hear the amazing message that he shares. I wish we had more people calling and asking him to come perform, but he isn't well-known outside of Utah. That might be why.

Your brother Abram is your sidekick. How did the cooperation between you and him start? Does he do everything for you because you're closer to him, or is it because no one else in your family wants to do it?

The whole talent competition started our assembly tour. Abram was the senior class president, and it was announced in our student government class that KSL, a local news station, was doing a statewide high school talent competition. They were looking for candidates, and Abram immediately volunteered me. I ended up winning the competition and won $1,000. With that money, we bought a portable keyboard, an amp, and everything else I might need to perform in various places.

That was back in 2012, and since then, we've done hundreds of assemblies across the U.S. He just happened to be in a position to volunteer me. He had never run for student government before his senior year, and looking back, it all seems like fate.

Abram is my manager, agent, stage crew, scheduler, and driver. He handles everything—from getting me a gig, driving there, doing the performance, cleaning up, and then writing a thank-you note. It's a lot of work, but it's worth it. We've been very close since childhood, and he has always helped me, so it was natural to team up.

Do you intend to make a video as a guide for other disabled would-be musicians who would like to follow you but don't know how to start?

I have never really thought of doing that before. I think it would be awesome to make YouTube videos for other disabled people to learn the piano. It would definitely be difficult, but it would also be a great learning experience. 2020

MARIAM PARÉ

When I was injured, all my friends left me. It was just me and my father, with no support.

We found some very interesting and beautiful paintings on the internet, and when we learned they were made by a mouth-painting artist who had been shot and paralyzed by a criminal on the street—and yet became an even better artist than before—we became intrigued. We reached out to this lady, and she kindly and honestly answered our questions.

Your father was an American Marine who went to Morocco after fighting in the Vietnam War. So, you are half American and half Moroccan, right?

Who do you think you inherited your artistic gift from?

Yes, I was born in Morocco. Although my father was a

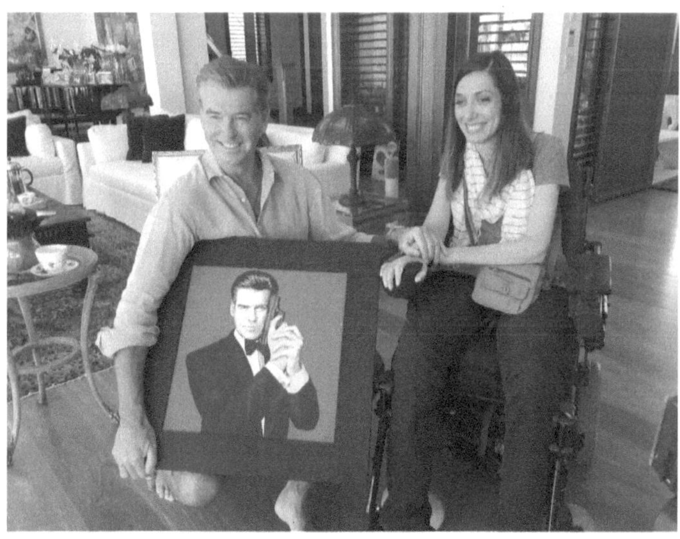

Marine, he was also very creative and took wonderful pictures of our family and my childhood. My mom was creative as well—she cooked beautifully. I think both of my parents used their hands to create something nice, which inspired me greatly. That's where I think I inherited that spirit.

When you were accidentally shot and left paralyzed, how long did rehabilitation last? Did you stay at home and go for exercises and rehab, or did you live in a center during that time while your parents adapted the house with ramps and other facilities for wheelchair access?

It was very complicated at that time. I was 20 years old, living in San Francisco, and visiting a friend in Richmond when the injury happened. I was driving their car when I got hurt. My parents were divorced—my father lived in Chicago, and my mother lived in Arizona. My father flew to Richmond to be by my bedside while I was in the Intensive Care Unit. I stayed there for three months because I was badly hurt and had many complications.

When I was stable enough, my father wanted to take me

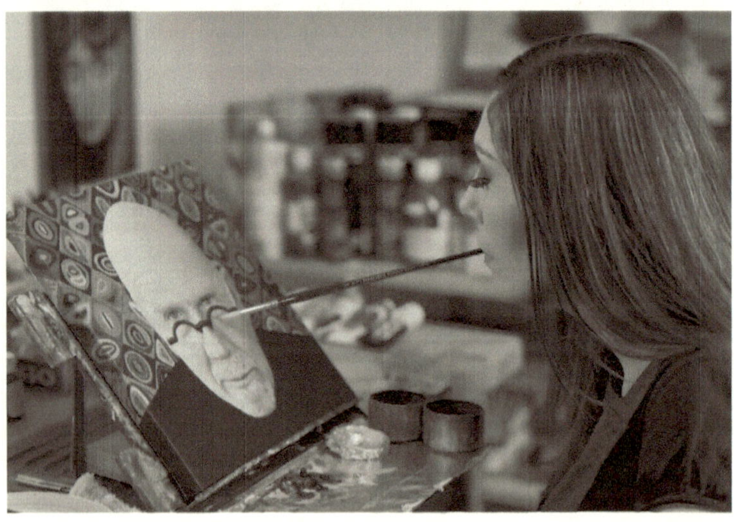

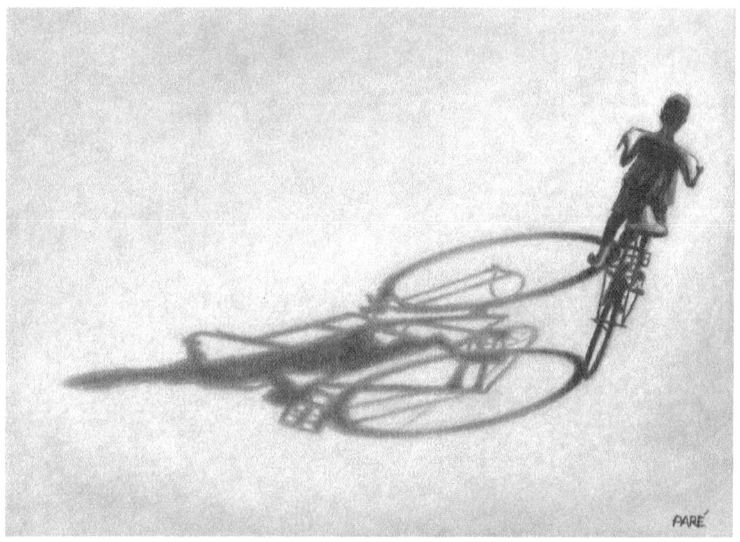

to his home in Chicago, which happened to be near one of the best rehabilitation centers for spinal cord injuries in the world. When they told me I was paralyzed and would never walk again, my father insisted I stay in Chicago to attend that center. I had previously lived and graduated in Chicago before moving to San Francisco, so it felt like coming back. I was taken to Chicago by air ambulance and spent five months at the rehab center. They taught me how to use my body, how it would react, and basic skills like brushing my teeth and using the bathroom—it was long therapy.

That was in 1996, and it was also the first time I experienced mouth painting. When I was discharged, I had nowhere to go because my father lived in an apartment with stairs, and my mother had been out of the picture since my teens. My father tried really hard to find an accessible apartment for me, but it was incredibly difficult. I almost ended up living in a nursing home, which made me very depressed. Eventually, my father found me an apartment in a suburb of Chicago, where I could live independently with assistance. I've lived there on my own

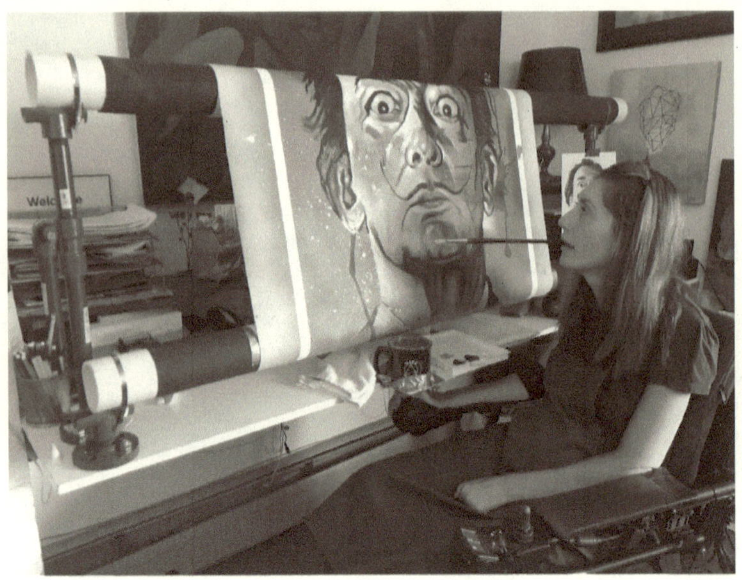

for the past 22 years.

Although the shooter wasn't found, did you manage to get financial compensation from the state or an insurance company? Or were you left completely on your own? Did you receive a wheelchair for free, or did you have to buy everything yourself?

I was 20 in 1996, and the laws in the USA were slightly different back then. Since I was considered an adult, I wasn't covered under my parents' insurance plan, so I didn't receive financial coverage for the accident. Also, because I was so young, I hadn't worked long enough to qualify for Social Security benefits. Here in the USA, you only get a disability pension if you've worked enough to pay into the social insurance system.

I was completely destitute—I had no money to live on and no way to pay the enormous hospital bills, which amounted to one million dollars. I relied on public aid, but that didn't help my situation much. I couldn't afford to make the house accessible or buy a wheelchair. It's a very difficult time in your life when you're young, have no money, and no one to take care of you. It's easy to slip into alcohol or drugs, but thankfully, I had my dad.

The shooter wasn't found, and I didn't receive any money from the state, as they didn't feel they owed me anything. I was essentially left alone to navigate my way out of that terrible situation. Public aid provided me with the lowest level of welfare, which barely covered my apartment. I was very grateful for that, though, and determined to get employed, support myself, and get off welfare.

When I was injured, all my friends disappeared—not because they were mean, but because they didn't know how to deal with the situation. They realized they couldn't hang out with me because I was in a wheelchair. It was a very lonely period, but it taught me who truly cared. It was just me and my father, and I am forever grateful for what he did.

Public aid gave me a used wheelchair, and since beggars can't

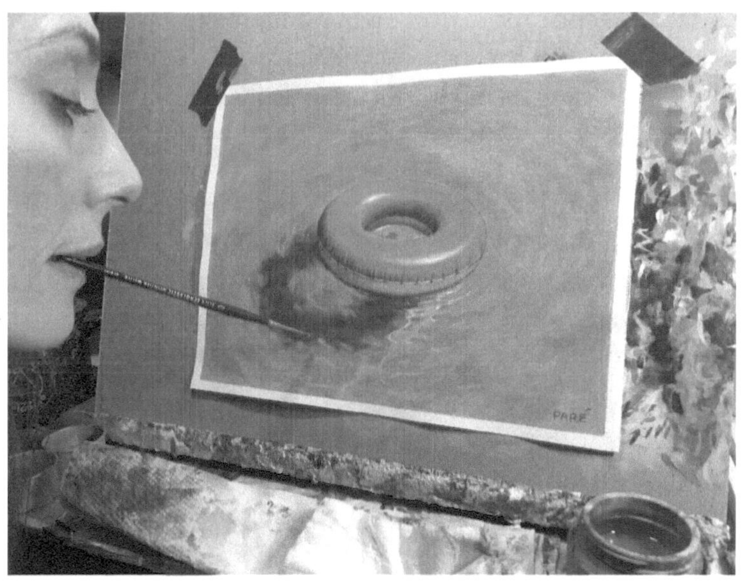

be choosers, I had to accept secondhand equipment. But it's better to have something than nothing at all.

You were on your way to becoming an artist before the accident. Did you consider any other possibilities to fulfill your altered life, or was painting always on your mind, and it was just a matter of adapting the technique and finding a way to do it?

After the accident, I initially thought my life was over. I couldn't do anything—not even move the hair from my face. But doctors and therapists encouraged me in different ways, and I celebrated small victories, like learning to use a fork to feed myself.

While at the rehabilitation center, a therapist asked me to try writing my name by holding a pen in my mouth. That's when I realized I could use my mouth for other things, and maybe even painting. I always had an artistic heart, and I knew that even if I was physically disabled, the drive to create was still inside me.

It took a long time to figure out how to make it work. At the beginning, I wasn't very good at it, but I didn't give up. I saw the potential and knew that if I kept practicing, I could be just as good as I was before the paralysis. That was my goal.

A painter transfers their emotions and feelings from their heart onto the canvas by hand. How did you manage that when you started mouth painting? Obviously, it's not natural, so were there times when your early paintings weren't what you wanted them to be? Did you ever feel frustrated?

When I painted with my hands, I was very, very good. Starting to paint with my mouth felt like being a child all over again. But creativity was always in my heart, and the knowledge was in my mind. It was just a matter of finding a way to transfer that onto the canvas.

It took a long time, and I had to practice relentlessly. I knew the quality was within me, and with each painting, I got a little bit better. I wanted people to like my work because it was artistic, not childish. I didn't want them to just say, "Oh, how nice." I wanted respect for my talent, and I wanted to back up my work with the skills I knew I had. That determination kept me moving forward. I wanted to communicate with the world through my art and show people what was inside me.

We admire the clean, precise, and beautiful painting you do. Could you walk us through the process, from a blank canvas to the final signature? How long does it roughly take? Do you paint from your imagination, images you see, or anything that inspires you?

I've been an artist for the past 22 years, even before my injury, so art has always been a big part of my life. Painting with my mouth has become second nature, and I barely remember what it was like to paint with my hands. I do it so often now that I don't even question it.

At home, I have a room that serves as my studio, with a table that I can wheel up to in my chair. I can't squeeze out the paint myself, so at the beginning of each week, I ask my assistant to squeeze out a bunch of paint onto the palette so I'm ready to go whenever I feel inspired. I usually think about the subject for a few days before I start painting.

I paint a variety of subjects. I don't limit myself or stick to one thing for too long—I love challenging myself. I particularly enjoy painting portraits, which are very challenging and can take me up to a month, working eight hours a day. Other paintings take just a day, depending on how complex they are. I'm slower than most painters because I can't be too vigorous; I have to be careful with my back and mouth. I take my time, but my approach is also simpler.

You have a degree in Fine Arts and Web Design. Does that mean you could apply for a job in those fields in the future, or is painting your true passion, with the degree as a safety net?

About five years after my injury, I started working as a graphic designer for a year and then freelanced as a web designer for about five years. I had bills to pay and needed to make money, so I worked with a cosmetics firm in Singapore and did packaging design.

When I went to college, I was eager for information and took many courses—I figured they couldn't hurt, and I've always liked technology, so I pursued that as well. But now, I make my living as an artist, and I don't do as much graphic design as I used to. Painting is both my passion and my job now.

You're a member of many organizations. Is that to keep yourself socially connected, be part of a community, spread knowledge, exchange experiences, or help encourage others with similar disabilities?

As I've gotten older, I've found it important to have camaraderie with others who are disabled. We share experiences and stay in contact—not just through the internet. I'm a member of many organizations for disabled people, and I've also taught children, both disabled and able-bodied, how to paint with their mouths, which was a lot of fun. I like to be involved in programs that connect me with others in similar situations.

How did it happen that Pierce Brosnan invited you to his Malibu residence? Did he see your paintings and ask you to paint him? What was he like?

I get that question a lot. Meeting him was definitely one of the highlights of my life. He's genuinely very nice and down-to-earth, and not many people know that he's also an artist—he paints too.

It was in 2013 when I painted Pierce Brosnan because I liked James Bond and found him interesting. I posted my work online and even made a video of me painting. I honestly didn't think he would ever hear about me. He saw my paintings, and as an artist, he got interested and asked about me through the Association of Mouth and Foot Painting Artists, which I'm a member of.

When I heard he'd asked about me, I was so honored that I wanted to give him one of my paintings. The next thing I knew, the association told me he had invited me to California to give it to him personally. So I went with my assistant, and there he was, welcoming a girl in a wheelchair to his house.

He came barefoot, wearing shorts and a shirt, his dogs running around, and he even kissed me on the cheek. We parked our rental van in his garage, right next to his Aston Martin. He invited me into his living room, and we talked all afternoon about painting and art. It was very emotional—he shared that he's quite lonely on set when away from his family. He told me he paints to cope with that loneliness.

He showed me a portrait of his daughter, who he lost to cancer, along with his ex-wife. He painted it to show how much he misses her. Like me, he likes to use bright colors, reflecting the happiness he had with them. He sent me a lithograph of one of his paintings—a man crying with tears in his eyes—and signed it, "Mariam, live your life. Love, Pierce." I still have that, and I am very proud of it.

Do you think, in a way, your accident was a blessing that led to a better painting career, allowing you to meet interesting people and become better known than you might have been as an able-bodied artist? Would you change your life if you could?

It's an interesting question, and I've often asked myself that too. I went to art school because I wanted to be an artist, and it's such a competitive world that unless I had been really, really,

really good, I would've ended up as a commercial painter, not an artist like I am now.

I think I'm competitive with other artists, but I wouldn't have been able to make the kind of art I create now for myself. My disability allowed me to approach painting differently. When I learned to paint with my mouth, I didn't think of it as a job—I painted because I loved it. If I hadn't been disabled, I would've had to turn painting into a profession and I wouldn't have had the time to pursue it fully.

So it might sound strange, but my disability has been a kind of blessing because it allowed me the lifestyle to paint more. Since painting is such a competitive field, perhaps because I paint with my mouth, it gives me an edge. People are fascinated by how I paint, but I'd rather they appreciate the quality of the work itself—if it's provocative or moving—rather than how it was made.

Of course, I'd love to be able-bodied. Who wouldn't? It's incredibly challenging to rely on someone else for everything. If I could be able-bodied, I think I'd sacrifice being an artist, knowing I could do other things in my life and keep painting as a hobby.

Do exhibition centers contact you to showcase your work, or do you need to reach out to them and offer your portfolio? Have you had exhibitions abroad, or are they mostly local?

I've been painting for 22 years, but I've only had real success in the last three or four years, especially around the Chicago area. My name is known enough now that galleries call me and invite me to exhibit. I don't have trouble getting exhibitions anymore.

Things really took off after I met Pierce Brosnan and got media attention. I've had exhibitions in Europe too, because our Mouth and Foot Painters' Association is based in Liechtenstein. Most of my artworks are currently in Europe. Last year, we had a big exhibition in Barcelona, and this year, we're planning one in Rome. I'd love to come to Prague too.

2017

MARIANNA MACHALOVÁ-JÁNOŠIKOVÁ

I only illustrate ordinary feelings that we all have

Sculptor Marianna Machalová was born in the Slovakian town of Michalovce in 1972. When she was 15, she started to have problems with her eyesight as a result of rheumatism. At the age of 18, she graduated from school, and four years later, she became completely blind. To be able to fend for herself, she attended a course at a special center in the Slovakian town of Levoca. Not only did she manage to look after herself, but she also got married, raised a child, and taught blind children, using molding clay as a means of communication and expression. From there, it was just a small step to sculpture. Today, she not only has her own studio but also makes a living from sculpture and organizes her own exhibitions.

At the age of 15, you started to have problems with your

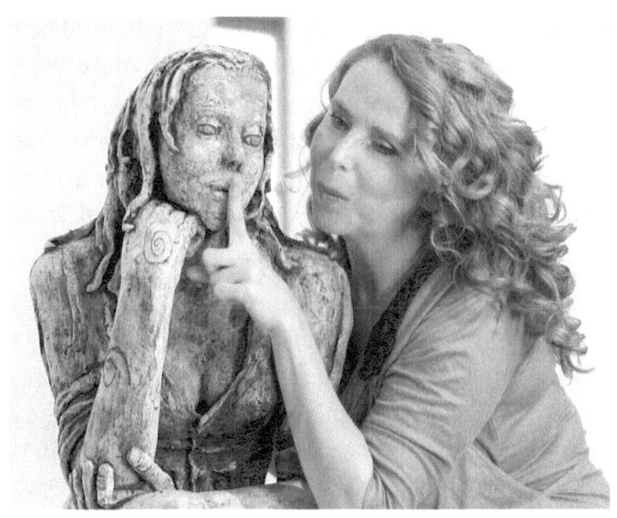

eyesight due to previous rheumatism. Did you have plans for what you wanted to do in your future life and did you have to change your mind when you became blind?

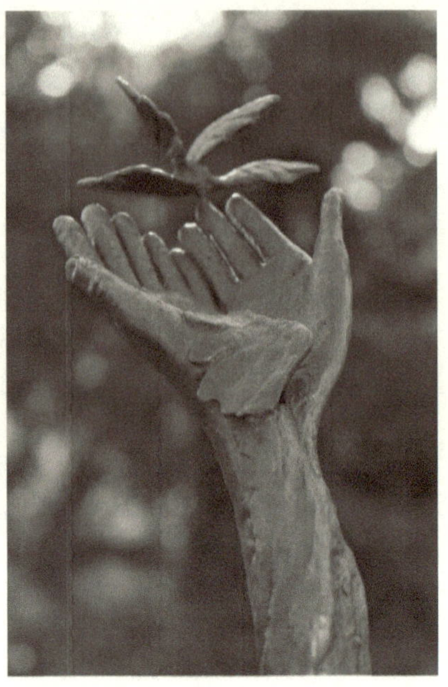

I attended agricultural school, and my idea was to be a vet. We had many animals in our family; my grandfather bred horses, so I wanted to keep the family tradition alive and care for animals. That was my dream, but when I was losing my eyesight, I realized I would never be able to do that, so I dropped that idea.

What did you do when the doctors told you that you would lose your eyesight and there was nothing that could be done? Did you try to put into your mind as many pictures, colors, feelings, experiences, and perceptions as possible to store them for the future, or did you slowly prepare yourself for blindness and shut your eyes and try to learn to understand the world with your hands, which is what awaited you in the not-too-distant future?

I started to do all things by touch, and I slowly started to rely on touch and hearing rather than sight. I didn't try to use magnifying glasses, but I thought ahead about what was waiting for me. I was a very attentive child and up until the age of 20, I paid attention to a wide range of details, mainly in nature, so I had stored a lot of things in my mind. I also observed the anatomy of animals and their muscles. I studied various encyclopedias. So now, when I go to the zoo with my daughter and she tells me the name of an animal, I can describe in detail how it looks and what color it is. My husband always confirms that I am right. I have everything in my mind, but I don't know if all blind people have it like that.

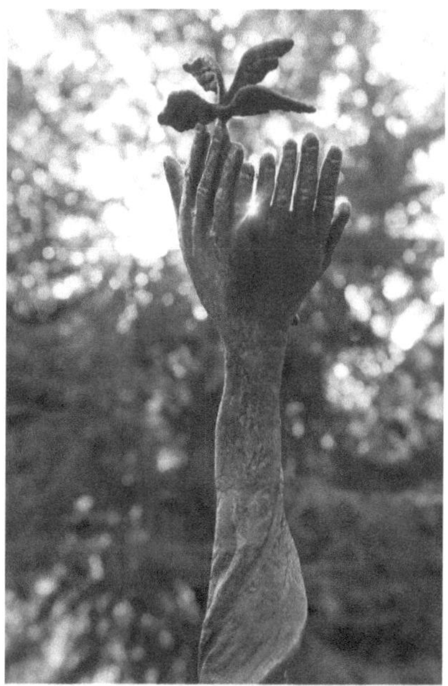

Can you somehow describe the feeling when you know that in a week you will never see the sunrise again, or the faces of your family? Is it desperation, sadness, or fear, or can you handle it better because it happens gradually rather than losing your sight suddenly overnight?

I think it is much better when it goes slowly. I didn't take it so tragically because I have a gift: I enjoy looking ahead. When I knew I wouldn't see, I told myself that I must learn how to be independent, so I could manage shopping, cooking, and cleaning the house by myself. I was worried that I wouldn't manage that before I went blind since I didn't want to be dependent. I am a very practical woman, so I wanted to master things myself. I didn't know what I would do or what my job would be. Before I went blind, I wanted to go to art school, but I wasn't accepted because they could not imagine how it could work. So, I always set myself a target of what I wanted to learn the next day. I think that is a kind of natural defense of a human being when he thinks he won't see from tomorrow onwards. I was very upset that I wouldn't see colors and nature, but I wasn't sorry, and I am still not sorry today, that I don't see people. My only regret is that I don't see my daughter. I miss the sun the most, but I have it stored in my mind. So, it wasn't that I told myself, "So, tomorrow is the last day I can see this or that." Instead, I told myself I had seen enough. At a school for parents who were preparing for loss of sight, there were girls who were born blind, and I explained colors and shapes to them that they had never had a chance to see.

How long did it take you to become 'functional' in your new life situation? How did you learn how to do this or that without getting injured, hitting something, getting scalded, or falling? Do you have only darkness in your mind as if the lights have been switched off? How do you know what time it is, or if it's getting dark outside?

In my daughter's room, which I arranged and which I cleaned, I know exactly where everything is. So, when I get there, the plan of that room automatically opens in my head, and with the help of sound, I know where the door is, where the table is, the chair, where the corner for teddy bears is, and my brain creates a whole picture of that room. I don't have complete darkness in my head; it looks like golden light. My day starts with the alarm clock, which is a talking mobile. My computer also talks, and I listen to the news, so if anybody suddenly walks in, they won't know I am blind. I clean the house, cook, and help my daughter get dressed. I recognize clothing by feeling for long and short sleeves. I put everything in its place, so when I need to find something, I know where to go.

Does your husband sometimes place things somewhere other than where you are used to having them because it's his world too? Do you then have trouble finding things in

your world?

No, it's not a problem for us since he has his corner where I don't go, and he doesn't enter my corner or my daughter's cupboard, so there is no chaos. When I iron, I put his things in his corner—that's all.

You iron? That's really impressive!

Of course, I iron. I do everything except drive a car—I can't do that. When I iron, I remember which T-shirt has which picture, so I turn it inside-out to avoid touching it with a hot iron. I like ironing because the clothes are crumpled at the beginning but after ironing they're nice and flat. I also check for any holes that need to be sewn.

How do you do the sewing?

I do everything by touch; I know where to put the needle. When I thread a needle, I find the 'eye' with my tongue and know where to put it through. When you do something every day for twenty years, you get used to it. Most often, I sew teddy bears, so I organize an 'operational day.' My daughter only has to tell me what color they are for me to find the right thread.

What is better—being born blind or losing your sight later in life? Someone blind from birth might have superior touch or hearing. Can a person who becomes blind acquire these skills?

I think you can train yourself well. The brain itself evaluates how I should move in a different environment. Problems arise when some change is made. Not long ago, I hit a door that my daughter didn't shut because I wrongly evaluated the space. I also use sound for orientation. When I play with my daughter in the garden, I hear which side the dog is barking from, I hear the tree in the wind, etc. Since I don't want anyone to guide me, it is important to be careful when walking on the street.

Before your blindness, did you have any particular inclination towards the visual arts? When teaching kids, did you use molding clay to express your feelings? Did you discover not only the children but also yourself and your abilities?

When I was losing my sight, I was scared of being around kids because sometimes their innocent questions can hurt you. But I always liked drawing and painting, mainly faces and stories, and working with kids was a real challenge for me.

Because you've seen things, you have a certain idea of what they look like. How does it work when you want to show an expression in a sculpture, but you have no control over whether you created what you really wanted and felt? Is it depressing? Your husband can hardly help you because he has different feelings, can he?

Recently, I have been using my daughter Eliška—she will be seven years old soon—and she tells me clearly whether the sculpture is sad, happy, or thoughtful. I used to rely on my husband for evaluation, who would tell me if it was straight or crooked, and whether I should place an eye lower or higher since I don't recognize millimeter differences. The face is nice as it is symmetrical, but small differences escape my perception. My husband tells me to adjust something higher or lower, but the expression on the face is my own business—my feelings—and I don't let anyone influence that. I normally leave the sculpture covered for the whole day, then I come back to it, take the cover off, touch it, and feel it. I touch the mouth and wrinkles, and my brain creates the feeling. My brain evaluates the expression of the face and determines whether it is angry, joyful, or just playing a game. Sometimes, I remove the head and make another one. It happened recently with a female sculpture—I created ten different heads.

Do you tell your husband what you want to create in advance, or does he only see the finished piece?

He has no chance to see the sculpture in progress because I made it from the bottom—from the legs—and shaped it as I wanted. When my husband watches me work, he only sees some pipes and has no idea what I intend to make. I put bars inside the sculpture to hold it together, so it looks more like a beehive. When it hardens, I add more clay piece by piece, step by step, until it takes its final shape. The pieces that are waiting to dry stay uncovered, and those I have already dried are covered in blue cloth. I remember precisely what the next step is. My husband doesn't see this process; he only sees the final product and then gives me feedback, like "The shoulder is too high; put it lower" or "The arm is too long; shorten it." It's good to make it according to my feelings because I can measure that, but of course, I can be wrong. This is the only time I let my husband comment on what I have done. In other cases, he doesn't see the piece for a month. Sometimes I get angry if things don't work my way, so he leaves me alone.

In 1994, you made your first sculpture, and a year later, you opened your studio. Does that mean you were so successful and intrepid that it happened quickly? How did people respond?

Well, at the beginning, I created the studio only for myself. I set up one room where I could experiment. For many years, I worked eight to ten hours a day to understand clay, what I could do with it, and what it allowed me to create. It was a never-ending process of building and tearing down my work because I am a perfectionist and don't stop until it's exactly the way I want it. It took almost ten years before I was more or less forced to hold my first exhibition. I was 28 years old, and my friend told me I would have a chance to exhibit in one of the museums in eastern Slovakia. They had pictures of Czech painters on the walls and made the empty space in front of the pictures available for my sculptures. If there had been no pictures, I wouldn't have had the courage to exhibit just by myself.

You have an idea for a sculpture in your head and then transfer that into the clay. How long does it take for a sculpture to take form in line with your idea? Since you make sculptures for a living, do you feel pressured to work quickly to sell more and earn more money?

When I get a commission, it doesn't work that way, since I feel responsible and worry about whether everything will meet the customer's expectations. I don't like working that way. It is much better when people come who already know about me, understand what I do, and have their own ideas—which I respect but do in my own way. Sometimes, I keep ideas in my head for many years, and some ripen quicker than others. I often think about my ideas in the car when my husband is driving, and there is silence—which suits me. Creating one sculpture takes me about a month, working eight hours a day. When I get up, I tell myself that today I will make either a head or a hand. Sometimes it doesn't work smoothly, and I have to knock it down and start all over again. Then my daughter comes home from school, and I turn into a housewife and have to interrupt my creative work.

Has it ever happened that you worked on a sculpture for, say, two weeks and then realized it was not what you had in mind, and you had to stop, knock it down, and start over?

Yes, it has happened, and it was a bummer. I was furious that I wasted two weeks of labor, and I could have done something else instead.

Do you buy the clay, or do you make it yourself from raw materials?

They bring it to us, but my husband mixes it to my exact requirements. With regular clay, I can make sculptures up to half a meter or a meter tall. When I mix the clay with paper and cardboard, the sculpture can be much larger; it keeps its shape well and doesn't break.

So your husband mixes the clay in your workshop, and you're in the kitchen mixing him chili, and then you sit around the table and evaluate who did better, right?

You got it spot on (laughs). He tells me, "It tastes good today," and I reply, "Hmm, but you made it too thin—put more cardboard in."

We like your creations called 'D.N.A' and 'Barrier.' How does it work in exhibitions when you can't see your own work or the reaction of visitors? Do you know whether they are truly appreciating your work, or are they just being polite?

Those who don't like it won't come to me anyway. It is obvious that not everyone has to like my work, but usually, people who were touched by my sculptures come to me. They tell me what my work gave them, how the sculpture reminds them of something from their own life, and sometimes they even cry. Once, about ten visitors cried on my shoulder, and my husband didn't know what to think about that. I wasn't sure if it was right or wrong, but I have gotten used to the fact that my sculptures bring both happiness and tears.

Has people's interest exceeded your expectations? Have you ever been rejected or received negative comments?

I didn't expect anything, and I didn't feel like showing my work to anyone initially. In the beginning, it was a kind of therapy for me. I lost my sight and needed to get the images out of my head, create them, and preserve them. After I accepted the fact that blindness would be part of my life forever, I enjoyed showing people the nice moments we have around us, which they should notice too. I only depict real human stories or feelings that every one of us has. It wasn't easy at first because galleries didn't know what to expect from me, and they weren't ready for it. Usually, I approached them and felt pity from them, but when I showed them pictures of my work, they became interested, and we made a deal in the end. After that, an article was written about me, and galleries started to show interest. I also experienced my first insult when the head of one gallery told me I was "nobody," and he wasn't interested in my sculptures because he only exhibited "A-class artists" and that I had no pedigree. He asked what I could create if I was blind and didn't even look at the pictures I showed him.

Do you know if there are any other blind sculptors living and working in Europe, and are there workshops or competitions for them?

In the Czech Republic, there is a 'touch workshop' where they teach blind people a craft using some mathematical system. I was invited there, and it was very interesting. They taught people how to make utensils from clay. But I didn't like the system; I worked using my feelings, not mathematics. I took part in an exhibition in Prague with various disabled people, but I was the only blind one. There were competitors from 32 countries, and we were given a task to make a sculpture in front of the board, which consisted of Japanese people, and they had no idea I was blind. I was very pleased because I was always hesitant about whether people really liked my sculptures or whether they were just being polite. I finished second, which was a small victory for me since it showed they truly liked my work without knowing about my disability. If I am correct, there is a blind sculptor in Italy, but I have never met him, and we are not in contact. In Slovakia, I have a female friend who makes utensils, and she is also blind.

How is the situation with the pain in your knuckles? Are they managing to treat it, or is it getting worse, so that within ten years, you may not be able to work at all?

The knuckles were my primary illness, and blindness was a side-effect of it. I have the best possible treatment in Prague, and I am getting something to stop it. They are healing to some extent, but I have days when the pain is so great I can't do anything at all. It may slowly lead to the fact that I won't be able to do anything, and I am starting to prepare myself for that.

2017

MIKE WOOD

I liked the challenge of finding a way to do things

We were looking for an interesting disabled person to interview and ran into Mike Wood, who had done so many things that he became our prime candidate. He responded immediately, and what he said was both interesting and shocking at the same time.

Could you tell us more about your accident? How old were you, what happened, whose fault was it, and what were your injuries?

It was October 28, 1978. I was 33 years old, and the last thing I remember was driving into a place called Norton on my Honda motorcycle on my way to work. *Honda – Norton*, any motorcyclist will see the irony in that. I have two vague memories of my accident. The back of a truck came off and knocked me off my motorcycle, sending me into the mud in the road that had spilled off the lorry. Whatever happened, I went over the top of my bike, landed headfirst, and crushed a bone in my neck. There are eight bones in your neck, and between them, the nerves spread out to control the parts of your body that are close by. My injury was between C6/C7. I am paralyzed from the chest down with partial use of my hands and arms. I would soon learn just how lucky I was. I never found out the names of the people who saved my life: the postman who called the ambulance, the ambulance crew that got me to the emergency room, and the nurses and doctors who got me through the first few weeks. I remember a doctor saying, "Mike, you've broken your neck, injured your spine. You won't be able to walk again." I can't remember what my thoughts were at the time. I remember terrible pain and nurses taking great care of me. I vaguely remember my girlfriend and other people visiting me. One vivid memory was a doctor saying he had to drill a little hole in each side of my skull to allow a kind of pincer arrangement to grip my head and keep my neck stretched while the bones healed. He said, "The drilling shouldn't be a problem, but the anesthetic may make you sick." To this day, I can't decide whether it was the needle, the drug, or the sight of the doctor holding an ordinary workshop hand drill in his hand that made me sick, but, oh, was I sick! I couldn't move, and it just seemed to go straight up in the air and then down all over me. So here I am, flat on my back, with a hook in my head and about 4 kilos of lead on a string hanging over the top of the bed, lying on special

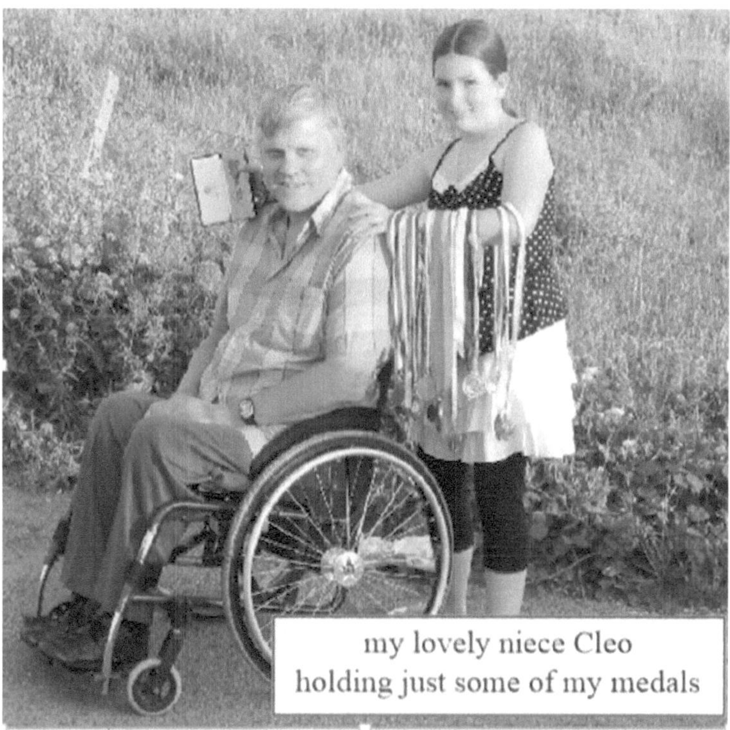

my lovely niece Cleo
holding just some of my medals

pillows to prevent skin pressure sores, and being turned side to side every three hours, day and night, by a team of four nurses.

Were you a sports-oriented person before that, or was it rehabilitation that got you into it? What did you want to do in life before your accident, and then after that?

Before the accident, I sold motorcycles for a living, so I had motorcycles to play with. I was also a mechanic for an endurance motorcycle racing team and got to travel all over Europe with them. I was the leader of our local Boy Scout group and organized regular camping weekends, so I had a pretty carefree lifestyle, enjoying myself. I was 33, divorced from my first wife, Mary. Carol, my girlfriend/partner of about four years at that time, had had enough of me. I wasn't that ambitious, hardly put any money into the home, and was a bit of a waster. Carol wanted better things in life—she had a good job, and it was getting better. She told me she wanted me to leave. I should explain that although I was upset, the parting had nothing to do with my accident. But after my accident, there had to be a

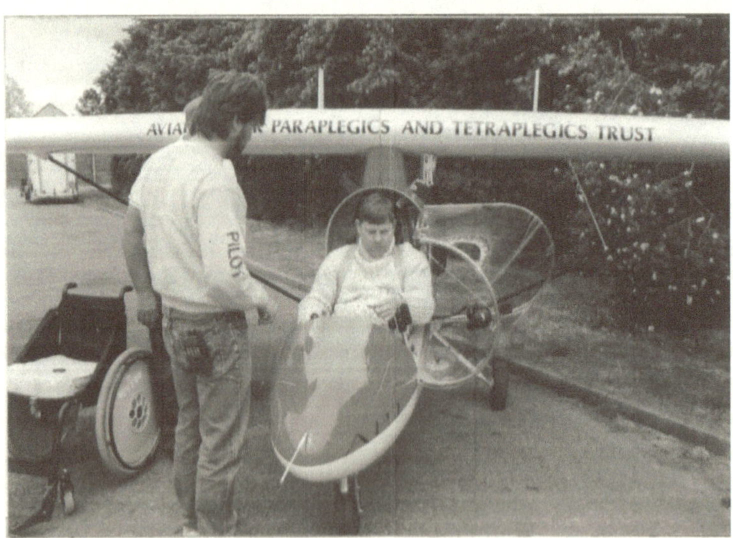

parting because Carol couldn't cope with two wheelchair users. She used to visit me in the hospital, but within a few months, she found a new boyfriend.

You had a hand in many activities and charities. Did it start gradually? You became an athlete, and after winning whatever you could, you realized there were other activities to do, so you established the Gloucestershire Disabled Anglers Association, then dinghy sailing, yachts, hand carts, and the like. Did you choose these because you liked the sport or because you heard people needed help there?

I'm an active and determined person. Introduced to sport for rehabilitation, I became the National Archery Champion and represented Great Britain in shot put, discus, javelin, and triathlon, winning many international gold medals. I retired as the British record holder in all these events. I also played wheelchair rugby at the national level and learned to sail, ski, and fly airplanes. Being an active disabled person

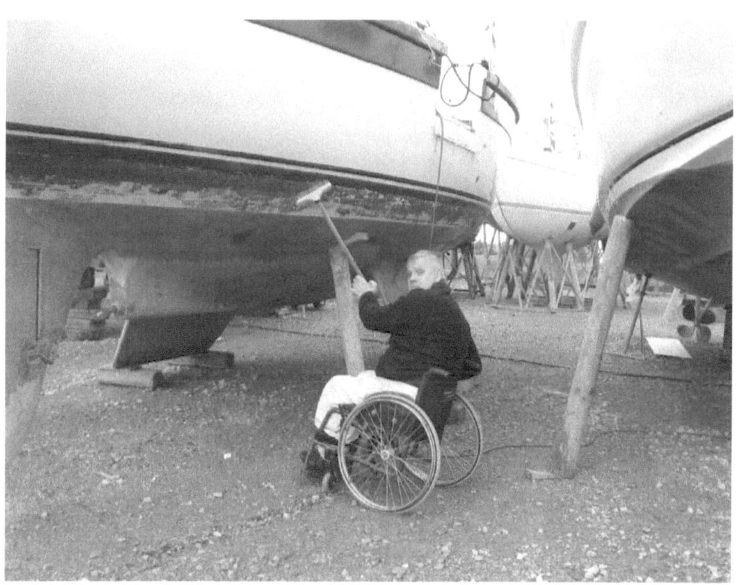

sometimes opened doors to opportunity. There are still some able-bodied people who find it difficult to deal with a disabled person, but I usually find a way around them. I studied the rules and laws and used them to achieve the things I wanted. I had a nice house, sports cars, holidays… a good life, and I found it fun to organize all sorts of activities for disabled people. At first, it was a selfish motive so I could "have a go." This all changed when I started seeing the impact my activities had on my peers and those less fortunate than myself. Even after 30 years, there's a huge buzz, a tear in my eye, or a lump in my throat when I see a severely disabled person using facilities I've been involved in providing. You can see the increase in their self-esteem, confidence, and pride when they realize they can do things they may have never dreamed of. I can't explain the emotion involved for me—smug satisfaction, a sense of achievement—I don't know what it is, but I like it. Seeing the results of doing something good for someone else is an addictive drug.

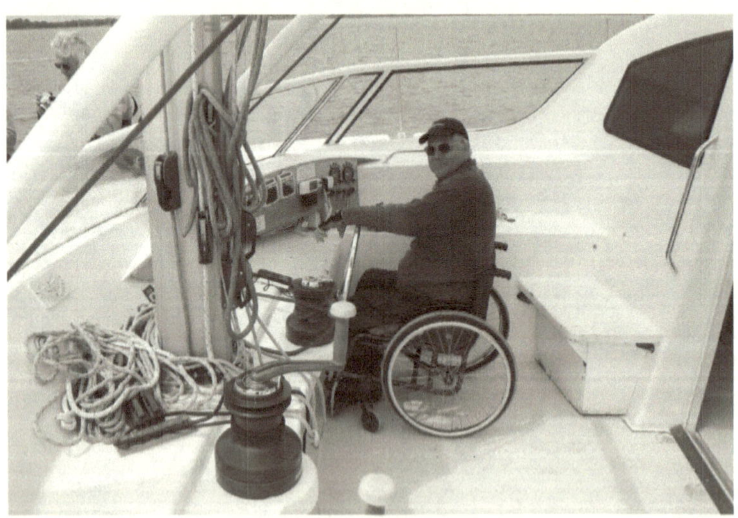

What was the hardest task in establishing various associations—getting money, or going through red tape? Roughly, how long did it take you to get the Disabled Anglers Association going, from the start to full swing?

Public perception is the hardest thing to deal with, as well as reputations. If the public believes something is already happening, you're seen as a troublemaker if you highlight the problems. Fundraising is difficult because organizations are not honest or are misleading in their statements, but no one seems to care. I have much documentary evidence of this.

How did you manage to fulfill so many different roles and still apply yourself fully to the various activities? Once you set one successfully into motion, did you hand over the project to somebody else to take it further?

I found that I wasn't so much interested in the day-to-day running of things; I liked the challenge of finding a way to do it. I didn't like meetings or committees, so once things were running smoothly, I let other people take over and run things, and I found another challenge.

Did you have any previous experience with the sailing business? Was it the reluctance of Jubilee Sailing Trust that annoyed you and sparked a will to do something about sailing for the disabled?

I was introduced to sailing when an international sport meeting was canceled because it was too hot, and someone offered me a chance to try sailing a dinghy. My first lesson consisted of, "Pull this to make it go, let it go to stop, and steer with this. Just bring it back when you get tired." At one time, I was alone in a Sunbird, in thick fog, out of sight of land and anyone else, with just a compass and silence. I can't explain how I felt—the clarity of mind. If you're not seriously disabled, you won't understand what 'alone' really means. It was a turning point in my life. As it does for many, you either love or hate sailing. If you love it, you can't put into words the emotions the sea brings out in you. I set up the Thomas Morley Trust, now more commonly known as the Disabled Sailors Association (DSA), in 1993 after continually being refused help with sailing by the RYA, the Jubilee Sailing Trust, the London Sailing Project, and the Ocean Youth Club. No one except the Jubilee Sailing Trust had wheelchair-accessible facilities, but Jubilee wouldn't take wheelchairs on certain voyages, wouldn't take electric wheelchair users at all, and seemed to exclude many people with intellectual disabilities. Despite organizations publicly stating they provide for all disabilities, they continually refused me and a number of my peers. So, I researched the need, obtained a mandate from my peers, set up a charity, raised funds from grant-making trusts, designed and built accessible yachts and dinghies, and have quietly been providing facilities for those left out for 25 years. Sadly, although it appears about £100,000,000 of lottery funding has been given to the sport of sailing, none of it has come to the DSA boats. It's much the same story today. The evidence shows that wheelchair users and severely disabled people don't have access to good facilities for sailing, except for the facilities the DSA has designed and built. The DSA has always been refused by the National Lottery/Sport England. We were informed there was no demand and that we were too ambitious, or our applications were ignored despite the fact that the DSA provides four times as many sailing places as the Jubilee Sailing Trust, which the National Lottery has funded with over £12,000,000. The DSA currently runs at near capacity, providing over 2,000 sailing places a year, and uniquely, it can and does accept any disability. I personally meet with our clients on a day-to-day basis, discussing their needs, ambitions, and dreams. I understand them because I am one of them. With the help of a respected group of Vice-Patrons, I then fundraise with UK grant-making trusts, design, build, and provide facilities to meet the ambitions and needs of my peers. I have personally raised and spent £5 million on our various very successful projects. No other individual, and certainly no other organization in the world, has this level of knowledge and experience of sailing for disabled people. The UK's "people in charge" of sailing for disabled people do not seem amenable to change. They do not support the very successful DSA activities, to the point that the DSA had to set up its major dinghy sailing activities in Europe.

The Thomas Morley Trust Disabled Sailors Association (DSA) has provided sailing for disabled people in its purpose-designed wheelchair-accessible cruising yachts since 1995 and in its special dinghies since 2003.

Over the last 25 years, the DSA has completed several in-depth research projects for dinghy sailing for disabled people, including:

- Visiting and sailing at more than 400 different sailing clubs in nine countries.
- Interviewing over 2,000 disabled sailors.
- Producing a detailed test report on all the main dinghies in use by disabled people.
- Purchasing dinghies and loaning them to clubs and individuals to use and develop.
- Organizing national and international regattas.
- Modifying and refining existing dinghies.
- Designing and building new types of dinghies.
- Producing national magazines and newsletters about sailing for disabled people.

Full reports of our work on all the yachts and dinghies in popular use by disabled people are available on our websites: www.disabledsailing.org and www.sailabilityinternational.

org. Videos of some of our activities and testing can be seen on the DSA website: www.disabledsailing.org/videos.

How does it work in sailing? Must a disabled person be accompanied by an able-bodied person just in case of an accident or capsizing, or can both be in wheelchairs, doing all the rope and canvas business and safely getting back to the harbor and rolling onto the beach?

All disabilities are different, and we take each case as it comes with safety first, allowing the disabled person to do as much, or as little, as they can or wish to.

You've built two specially constructed yachts for wheelchairs. Did you raise the money and find a company to do it, or was it built with the help of friends to show to others?

I raised all the money myself, but had a very good plan taught to me by a girl who has helped me many times. Getting funds is about credibility and funders being able to see the results, and we used respected people, whom we call Vice-Patrons, to support our letters, newsletters, and videos to show our funders what we've achieved.

How did you get Princess Anne to attend the launch of your yacht? It's quite an achievement.

You made me smile here… If you're not British by birth and haven't lived here all your life, you'll never understand the culture or why Britain is so successful for its size and position. If you understand how things work, the royalty in the UK can be very, very powerful indeed. If you saw the diary and workload of the main six royals, you'd be shocked and embarrassed that you don't work as hard. They also give their money but ask not to be named. I've received funding from all the main royals. The lesser royalty may not always seem as good, but some are. Princess Anne was easy to get. While I was building my first yacht, another yacht, Verity K, was being built next to it. The owner of the other yacht was a very scruffy woman, and we often met and talked about how our yachts were being built and became quite friendly. One day, a policeman came into the workshop and said, "Do you know who that lady is?" and explained that she liked to be in public but not be recognized. So, the next time I saw her, I apologized for not recognizing her and asked her to launch the yacht, and she agreed.

Could you tell us more about your yacht club in Spain? Do you own the harbor, or just anchor your two yachts, which can be rented by anyone in the world who is in a wheelchair?

In Spain, we just rent space in the marina, but the marina owner is a sailor and likes to use our boats for himself and his friends, allowing us to do what we like. We don't charge to use the boats in Spain.

Can you and do you take part in any yacht regattas, or are there some regattas for disabled sailors?

We take part in many disabled regattas in the UK, Spain, and around the world. Many clubs allow us to race in regular club racing.

If the sea gets really rough and the waves are big, do the disabled people have any 'anchors' or belts to keep their chairs in place? Do they have to stay on the deck all the time, or are there accessible places inside the yachts?

Our experience is that it is dangerous to strap people in, and it is very rare to need to tie a wheelchair down.

Since you are a kind of guinea pig in various respects, is it you who sets the standards, or do you have to meet health and safety criteria and pass them before it can go into mass production?

We use the standard Marine Coast Guard "code of practice" rules and EU legislation as the basis. Where we cannot meet these rules, we document how we achieve a superior position of safety on those issues.

Have you ever come across an organization that claims to be accessible to disabled people in order to have a better image and charge more, but simply lied and didn't care about disabled people at all? Are there many liars and hypocrites in that business?

Would you like a list and documentary evidence? It runs to many pages.

Who helped you raise five million pounds – ordinary working people or companies connected with disabled people's needs?

This is mainly from grant-making charities in the UK, and one company, the Scott Bader Resin Company, who help a great deal, along with five other companies that give small funds now and then.

2020

PAVEL HEJHAL

Even a mouth painter has his own handwriting

This interview happened purely by accident. For Christmas, we received an envelope from UMÚN, a Czech organization for mouth and foot painting artists, which contained some Christmas cards drawn by their clients. We liked some of the cards very much, so we Googled the artist and discovered it was Pavel Hejhal. We decided to reach out and ask him for his story.

He was born in the town of Písek in 1983 and studied at a technical college focusing on furniture making. His life took a dramatic turn on December 15, 2002, when he was involved in a car crash that left him paralyzed from the neck down. Since that time, he has been connected to a mechanical lung ventilator, as even his diaphragm is paralyzed. A year after the accident, he began painting by mouth.

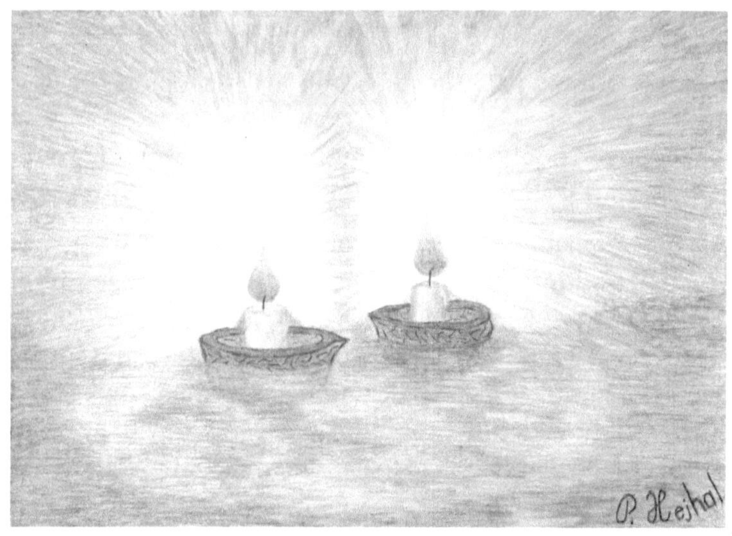

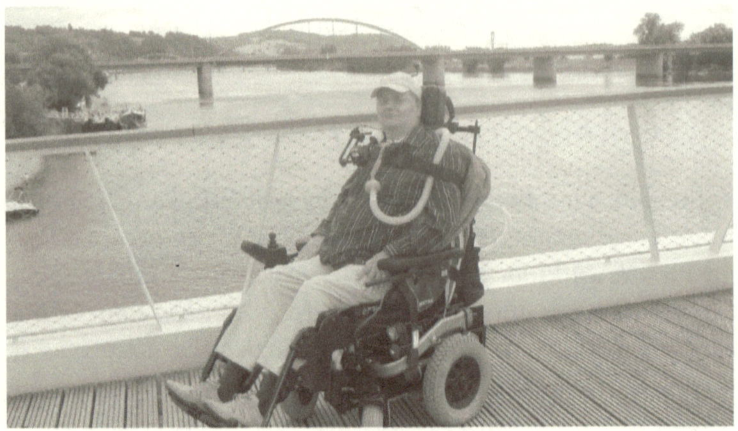

Eleven years ago, you started mouth painting. Did you have any connection with painting before, or did you become interested in it after, say, a rehabilitation nurse told you about it?

Before the accident, I didn't have much interest in art. In elementary school, my teacher gave us a solid foundation in drawing, which came in handy at technical college where we had to do a lot of technical drawings. After the accident, with more free time and the opportunity to explore art, I developed a keen interest in painting, especially artistic topics.

What got you hooked on painting? Was it the way you could express your feelings? Was it a form of self-realization?

When a rehabilitation nurse told me that there are people who paint with their mouths and suggested I give it a try, I thought she was crazy. "Mouth painting? I can never manage that," I thought. But she insisted I try, so I gave in and gave it a go. It was very hard at the beginning—learning how to hold the pencil, how to move it on the paper in a way that would express what I wanted. I had to figure all that out. But the good thing was that I got hooked very early on. I became interested in how far and how quickly I could progress. I was curious about what was inside me, what I was capable of learning, and what I could paint. At first, it was more of a curiosity, a way to pass the time during my long stay in the hospital. Now, it's about expressing my inner feelings, my mood, and creating something based on my own ideas. The most satisfying thing is that what I've done so far is well-liked and appreciated by others. That really uplifts my spirit.

Every painter has their own 'handwriting,' which is like their trademark and makes them easily recognizable. Can anything like that be said about a mouth painter after a longer time?

Yes, I think so. When a painter masters their technique, their 'handwriting' can become apparent. I mean, they develop certain unique characteristics or signs that are specific to them. Just as an interesting observation, when I sign my name now, I notice some similarity to my handwriting before the accident. This shows that I'm still controlled by the same brain, which governs everything. It's the same with the dominant side of my body—now I hold the wooden extension for pencils or brushes on the right side of my mouth, just like I used to write

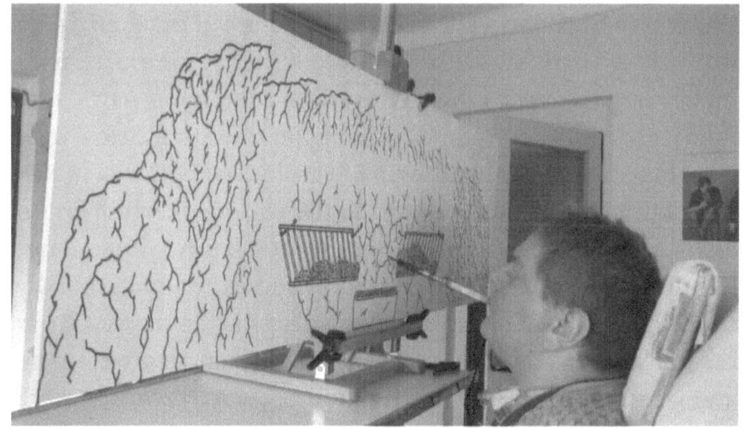

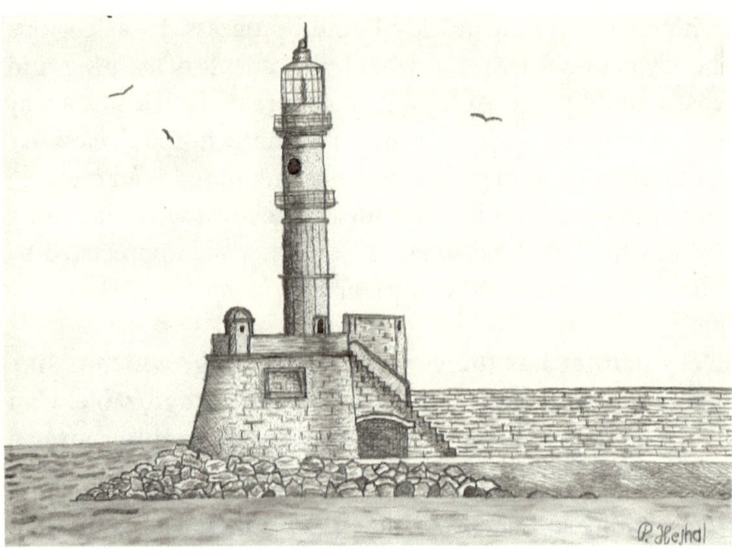

right-handed. I tried to paint with the left side of my mouth, but it was like trying to write left-handed. I didn't get very far.

Could you describe what mouth painting looks like and how long it takes to paint a picture?

It varies. When I draw something like a church from a postcard, I first try to establish the shapes and get the proportions right, testing their placement on the paper. It's difficult because I can't step back and view the whole picture at once, so doing it up close is tricky. Once I've managed the proportions, I make rough sketches, lightly outlining the main parts, and then start adding color and focusing on the details. How long it takes depends on the drawing technique and how complex the picture is. The time also varies depending on whether I'm using a pencil or a pen. My picture of a church took about 15 hours. When I draw from my own imagination, I usually carry the idea in my head for a long time, trying to work it out mentally. When I feel ready, I take a pencil and start drawing, and it usually takes about seven hours.

When you master your craft and become a skilled mouth painter, does it become easier to transfer your emotions and vision onto the drawings, the same way able-bodied artists do? Or is there a disconnect where your mind wants to do something but your body doesn't quite cooperate?

Personally, I believe that once you master a pencil, brush, or pen, there's not much difference whether you're drawing by mouth or hand. An able-bodied artist can place their hand on the table for greater stability, which I obviously can't do. But now, I don't think about how to hold the pencil or where to place it in my mouth—it's automatic, just like an able-bodied artist. The only limitation is the size and format of the picture. I can't set up a 1x1-meter drawing board on an easel and paint. But I've realized that drawing also has a beneficial side effect for me—it serves as part of my rehabilitation. The movements I make when drawing help to improve my physical stability. As I gain more control over my body, I can tackle larger formats, so the two things go hand in hand.

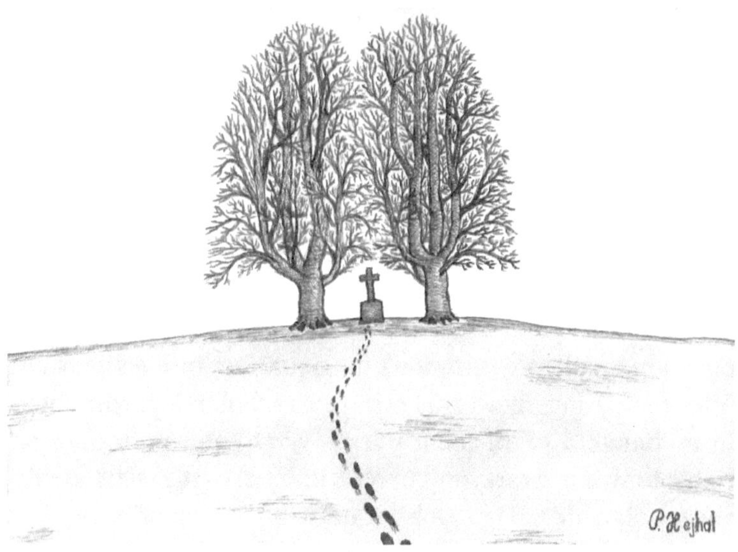

You mainly paint flowers. Is that because you love them most, and maybe portraits wouldn't have the same appeal, or is there another reason?

The truth is, I love nature—flowers, meadows, trees. Painting flowers has another advantage: if my pencil doesn't go exactly where I want it, I can simply shift a leaf or bloom a little bit elsewhere, and no one will notice. Try doing the same with portraits, though, and you'd end up with the left eye much lower than the right one, ha ha. I would love to try portraits, but I'm not confident enough to start just yet.

Do you draw spontaneously, or is it just part of your everyday life?

It depends. Painting and drawing are not part of my regular daily routine. Sometimes I paint or draw every day; other times, I don't touch a pencil for a week. It depends not only on my mood and will but also on my body—whether it allows me to do that. Sometimes I overdo it and paint for too long, and the next day, I end up with a neck ache, so I have to rest for a day or two.

Tell us about your scholarship from UMÚN. What are the criteria for receiving it? How do you make use of it? Is it only related to painting or drawing, and do you need to show finished work?

After I worked on and improved my mouth painting, my sister approached UMÚN Publishing. I sent them my pictures for assessment. Since they liked them, they forwarded my application to the organization's headquarters in Liechtenstein. After evaluating my work, I received a scholarship from them. In exchange, I grant them the copyright and reproduction rights for my artwork, and in return, I receive the scholarship. The scholarship covers tools for drawing and painting, as well as an assistant or even a teacher. I send them my pictures every year, and every three years, their committee evaluates each member's work. The board includes both disabled and able-bodied artists, who are at different levels. They assess whether the painter is making progress and moving forward. The scholarship is renewed based on their evaluation.

Are you in touch with other mouth painters around the world, and do you exhibit your work anywhere?

Yes, I've had many exhibitions on my own, but I prefer to exhibit under the UMÚN umbrella. They organize exhibitions throughout the Czech Republic, and that's where I meet most of my mouth-painting friends. These get-togethers are a great way to inspire each other.

You won the „Internet and My Disability" literary competition. Have you ever considered writing your own book, maybe including your illustrations? Do you think you could make a living from that?

Yes, I did win the competition. I don't think I stood out for my literary quality, but I think the content earned me the points. I wrote about how the internet opened the door for me to connect with the world from my hospital bed, and how I was able to finish my studies at a higher technical school thanks to the internet. I'm not sure if I'm good enough to write my own book, but I'd be lying if I said the idea wasn't tempting. I think a fairytale story for kids, illustrated with my drawings, would be a good option. We'll see.

2015

PETR ŠRÁMEK

It doesn´t matter how you create things, the important thing is the final result

Czech artist Petr Šrámek is an interesting man. Born in 1954, he has been physically disabled his entire life. He has paralyzed arms and partially paralyzed legs, and he is also unable to speak. Since the age of 15 (since 1969), he has lived at an activity center in Hodkovice nad Mohelkou. Through dedication and determination, he has learned to paint using his feet. He started with basic works, copying postcards, then progressed to reproducing paintings by various established artists. He began with illustrations of Czech geniuses Josef Lada and Jiří Trnka, then made a huge leap to copying the masters, including Vincent van Gogh. In 1993, Petr's work was noticed by people from UMÚN, a Czech association for people who paint with their mouths or feet. This organization introduced him to representatives from the World Association of People Painting by Mouth and Foot, based in Liechtenstein. They were impressed by Petr's work, and he received a scholarship from them. This financial support allowed him to buy brushes and paints, as well as books to educate himself in the history and techniques of painting. The scholarship also enabled him to recuperate by the seaside and at a spa. Today, Petr no longer copies famous masters; he has developed his own unique style, which has impressed visitors to his exhibitions both at home and abroad.

We thought this man was worth an interview, but the challenge was how to find out from a man who cannot speak what he feels, enjoys, or perceives. To learn more, we reached out to sculptor Ivan Kolman, who has been Petr's assistant for 15 years and is the person closest to him.

When you were asked 15 years ago to take care of Petr Šrámek, what made you accept the offer, knowing how severely disabled he is and, above all, that he can't speak?

Throughout my life, I have seen many exhibitions of paintings and graphic art created by people with mental disorders. They were always very powerful works, so I was interested in Petr's paintings.

How does your collaboration with Petr work? Do you teach him how to paint, or do you simply observe him and give advice that he takes in but doesn't reply to?

The first step was reviewing his paintings. He had a collection of copies of various famous painters. His copies of Josef Lada and Jiří Trnka were perfect, and his work inspired by Vincent van Gogh was top-notch. I realized that when he chose to paint using the scumble technique (a method of applying layers of paint in a way that allows for corrections), it was a logical step, as this style allows for corrections and the artist can return to a previously painted area. This is not possible with watercolor painting, which requires more dexterity and quickness. We had to consider that the wrist is more flexible than the ankle. Among Petr's works, I found portraits of staff and clients from the center, and their quality was very high. That was the beginning of our program. You may not believe it, but those paintings also expressed Petr's humor, which I welcomed and supported.

Was it difficult for you to imagine what he is capable of and what his limits are? How did you know what to expect from him and what was beyond his abilities?

Petr found his own unique technique thanks to the hundreds of paintings he had created, so I knew what he was capable of. As for boundaries? They don't exist. The founder of the UMŮN organization, Mr. Stegman, who is paralyzed himself, took a chisel in his mouth and started doing woodwork.

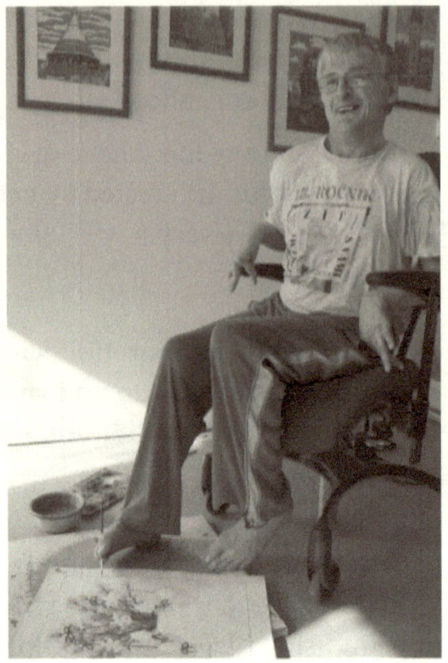

The UMŮN organization's motto is 'It's not the hand, but the soul that paints.' How can you tell if a foot painter has talent? We can't imagine how it works to take a brush between the toes and paint.

Talent in mouth or foot painting? It doesn't matter how you create things; the important thing is the final result. You can see many paintings of daisies—most are bad kitsch or poor realism. But then, someone comes along who elevates that daisy to something beyond words.

You can't see into Petr's soul, and he can't speak. How do you know what he feels, what is inside him, what he would like, what his limits are, and what he can't handle?

It's very, very difficult for me to communicate with Petr. I try to speak in the simplest way possible and help myself with mime. Petr communicates through simple drawings or symbols, almost like pictograms. If I want to show him that I would choose a darker color, I point to that area and scowl. If I open my eyes wide and smile, it means I would use a brighter color, and so on.

Petr has lived at the Activity Center in Hodkovice nad Mohelkou since 1969. Now at 61, he has outlived some nurses, and the political system has changed. What is he like? What has his life been like? Does he fully understand the reality of life, since his brain works perfectly despite his physical disability?

He is a very sensitive man, and it was very difficult for him to break free from the prison of his body into the world around him. It's strange that, through his difficult circumstances, he has humor and good spirit, which is reflected in most of his paintings. He did have a dark period in his life when he wanted a life partner, but it wasn't to be. At that time, he was very unhappy, and this is reflected in his paintings.

Can someone create their own style while painting by mouth or foot, or are they content merely to take a brush and apply color to canvas?

Yes, you can create your own style using your mouth or foot. If you have the will, determination, and effort, and if you want to express something, you can do it, even with your nose.

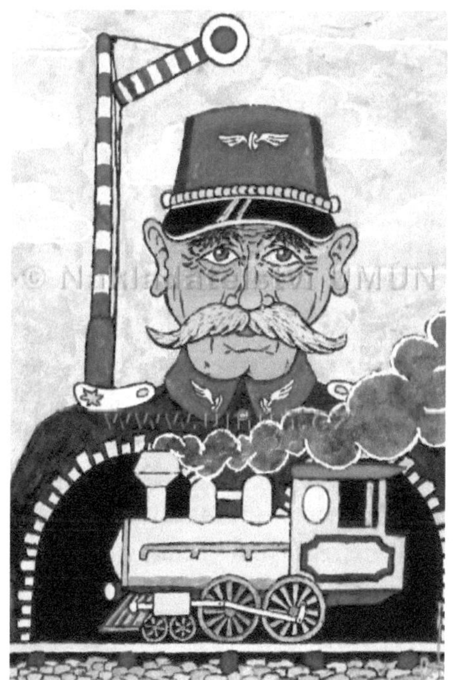

How can you, as an able-bodied

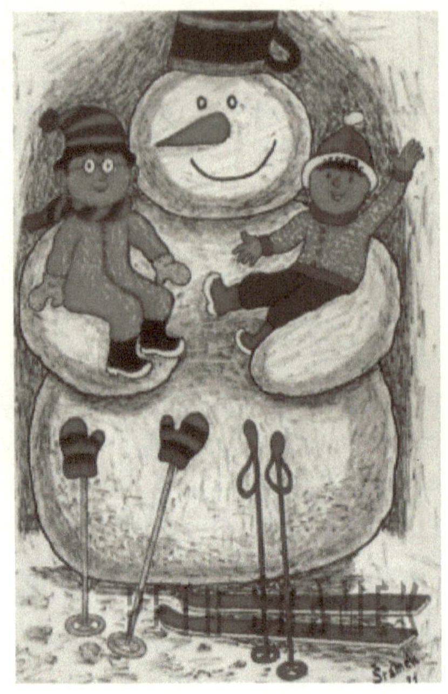

person, advise a disabled person with very limited abilities? Do you teach him more about art or about feelings and perception? What does Petr most like to paint? Did he find his own way, or did you give him tasks, like painting a face one day, an animal the next, and a landscape another time?

As an able-bodied person, I can't advise Petr much. Once, I showed him a technique that he used with joy. The empirical style played a huge role in Petr's case. His knowledge of underpainting (the preliminary layers of paint applied to a canvas before the final layers) is astonishing to me. Was it just intuition or acquired experience? I have no idea, but the important thing is that he works with it. For many years, Petr painted heads, skulls, and faces that carried a story. In recent years, he has preferred painting architecture, and I'm happy to help him by providing books where he can study details, color, and dimensions.

Do you teach him individually, or is he one of many clients? Can you tell whether his work has reached its peak and won't progress any further? If so, what can you advise him then?

We work individually with Petr. Other clients try small artworks with wax or clay in protected workshops. You asked if there could be any further progress in his work. Petr can

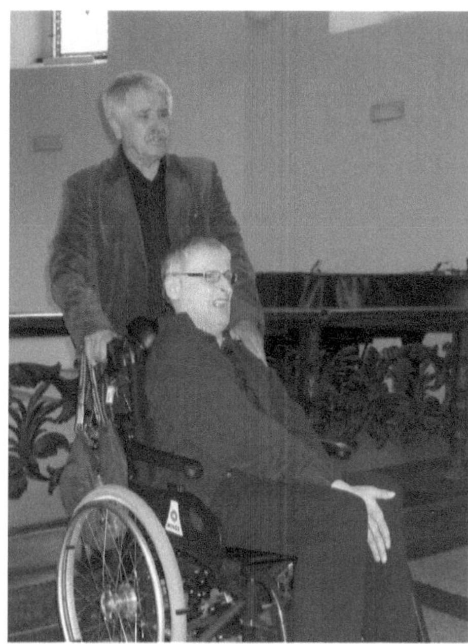

observe the world around him with his eyes. New things could capture his imagination and inspire him. Picasso had many different periods, but that probably won't happen in Petr's case. He lives inside his own closed world, but who knows? He likes browsing the internet, and maybe something will inspire him.

Is it true that some people have written letters to UMÚN claiming that someone ghost-paints for disabled people and that it is all a scam to make money? What drives such people to make these accusations?

There are people who don't believe that disabled people can work and create. They feel the need to belittle them. Thankfully, Petr wasn't affected by such behavior, but those who knew about the issue were very upset by such ugly accusations.

P.S. Sadly, Petr Šrámek passed away a few months later, making this his last interview. 2015

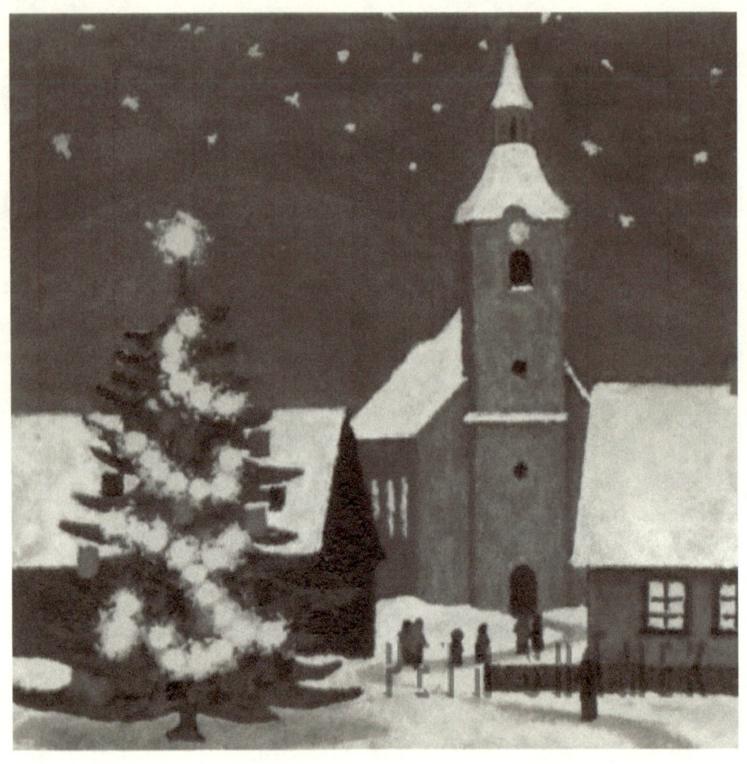

ROB JONES

I want to show other war vets what is possible to achieve regardless of sustained injuries

We had never done an interview with an American Marine who had lost both legs during the war in Afghanistan. What really persuaded us to contact him was the fact that he ran 31 marathons in 31 days on his prosthetic leg, which is something that even the famous Czech Olympic champion Emil Zátopek would take his hat off to. Rob Jones studied at Virginia Tech and joined the Marine Corps in 2007. He was deployed to Afghanistan in 2008 and 2010 as a specialist in finding hidden Improvised Explosive Devices (IEDs). During one mission, he stepped on an IED, and following the explosion, he had both legs amputated above the knee. In 2011, he was discharged with full military honors and took up rowing. After five months of intensive training, he qualified for the Paralympic Games in London, where he won a bronze medal. In 2013, he came fourth in the World Rowing Championships and also embarked on the challenge of cycling across America. Over 181 days, he rode 5,180 miles, raising $126,000 through sponsorship, which he donated to three war vet charities. In 2016, although he didn't qualify for the Paralympics, he achieved another ambitious goal: running 31 marathons in 31 days.

What made you voluntarily join the Marine Corps?

I joined the Marine Corps because I felt like I was missing something during my junior year of college. I couldn't tell what it was until I read the book *Brotherhood of Heroes*, about the Battle of Peleliu. It was from reading the stories of the Marines there that I discovered what my life needed: purpose, discipline, courage, altruism, and brotherhood. So, I joined the Marine Corps the next day.

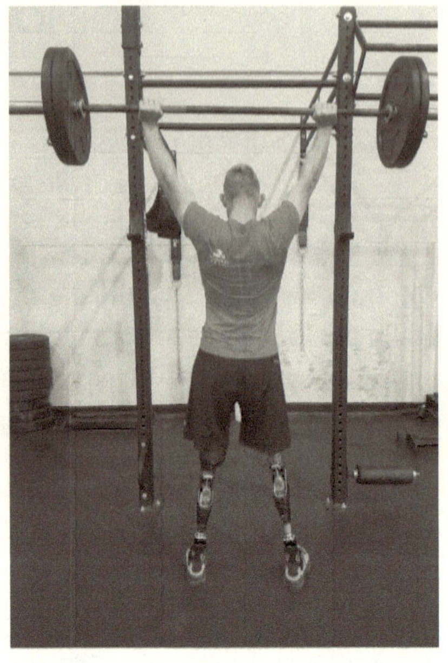

Did you go through a similar boot camp to the one in Kubrick's movie *Full Metal Jacket* or don't sergeants humiliate rookies anymore these days?

Boot camp is similar to *Full Metal Jacket*, with the screaming, insults, and punishment through exercise, but drill instructors are no longer allowed to strike recruits. I go into more depth about boot camp in this journal entry from my website: : http://www.robjonesjourney.com/journal/?offset=1456528162826.

The Second World War engulfed the whole world, but what was it like for you to leave your peaceful home for the war zone in Afghanistan, where bullets were raining and you were facing death every day?

Going from home to a combat zone certainly is a shock to the system. However, up to that point, we had done so much live fire training that the combat was not alien to us, so we adapted quite quickly to it. Our minds had been prepared before it started, so that made it much easier for us to hit the ground running.

How much do you remember from the moment you stepped onto the IED and realized you had lost both of your legs?

When you step on an explosive device, do you actually know about it, and do you have milliseconds to make a decision?

My memories of the day I was wounded can be found in these two journal entries: The first entry is from the day leading up to my injury: http://www.robjonesjourney.com/journal/?offset=1446757504931, and the second is what I remember afterward: http://www.robjonesjourney.com/journal/?offset=1434397144975

What happened afterward? Were you conscious when you were taken to the hospital, or did you wake up and realize you had lost your legs?

I was unconscious once I was put into the CASEVAC (Casualty Evacuation) tank up until I arrived at the hospital. I have written about my first week in the hospital in this journal entry: http://www.robjonesjourney.com/journal/?offset=1427477930050.

Did the army pay for your prosthetic legs and the entire rehabilitation process, or were you discharged as surplus to

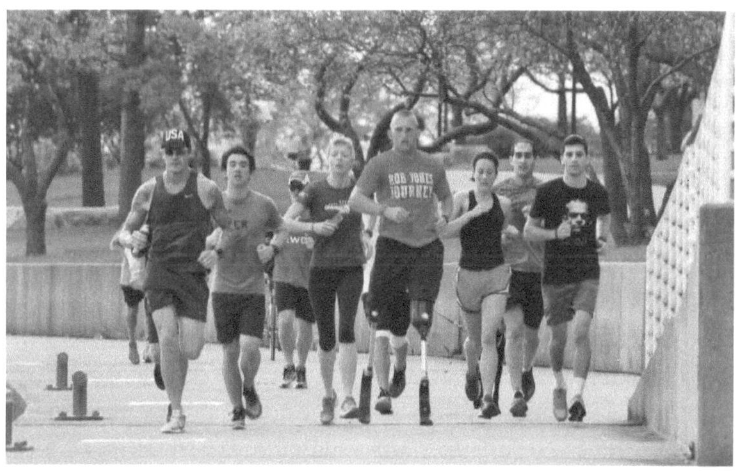

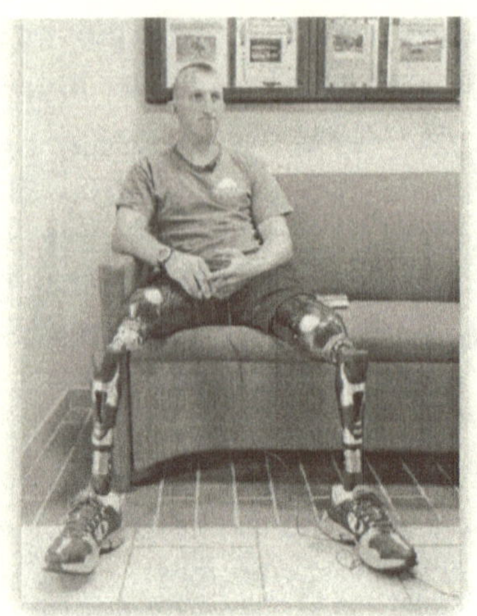

requirements and left to fend for yourself? Were you offered a job in the army, or did you ask to be discharged?

The military rehabilitated me fully and provided prosthetic legs and complete medical care until I retired. After that, I receive care from the Department of Veterans Affairs. I get all of my health care for free, and all of my prosthetics and other health care needs are paid for by the VA. I could have elected to stay in the Marine Corps if I had wanted to, but I would have had to stay in with a different specialty, as I was no longer fit to be a combat engineer. I elected instead to retire.

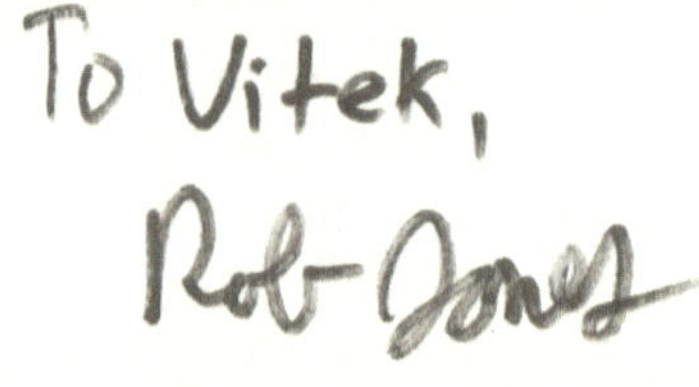

We have read about British soldiers who also lost limbs in Afghanistan, and the National Health Service left them in the lurch, and they had to beg various charities to contribute to artificial limbs. How is the situation in the United States?

The United States takes incredible care of its veterans overall. There are a few cases in which paperwork, bureaucracy, or mistakes lead to some veterans receiving less-than-ideal care. However, this is the minority, and in my experience, the military and the VA do great work to take care of veterans. Also, American citizens go above and beyond what they need to do to make sure veterans feel appreciated and are taken care of.

There are over 40,000 charities in the USA devoted to taking care of veterans, and I personally get thanked almost every day for my sacrifice.

Running one marathon is incredible. Running 31 marathons in as many days is something unheard of, and to do it on prosthetic limbs is just truly incredible. What led you to do this? Were you motivated by the fact that no one had ever done it before, or because it was the hardest way for you, so it took the greatest effort but also got the biggest publicity?

I decided to take on the 31 marathon task in order to show other veterans that it is possible to experience a traumatic injury and come back stronger than ever, regardless of whether your injury is mental, physical, or psychological. I made it as difficult as possible so that the completion of the challenge would have the most impact on what I was trying to prove.

When people run a marathon, often their legs fail them or the muscles cause problems; very seldom do they give up because of their lungs. How does it work when you have prosthetic legs? Do you feel any pain or exhaustion, or could you run three times as far without a problem?

Running with prosthetics is not much different from normal running. My residual limbs still get tired, just like anyone's normal limbs. My back and other parts of my body also became fatigued. I get blisters on my stumps much like people get blisters on their feet.

How long did it take you first to get your prosthetic limbs on, then to walk and to run? Do your stumps hurt?

I was walking in prosthetics after six weeks post-injury. I was running about a year post-injury. I didn't run my first marathon until five years after my injury, but that was simply because I hadn't decided to do it earlier. Yes, the stumps get sore and start to hurt during the race, just like anyone's feet or knees might.

You also rode a bike from shore to shore and won a medal in the Paralympics. Do you take these things as challenges and a new way of life, or just as a pure demonstration of your dedication and determination to motivate as many people as possible?

Yes, I took on these two challenges for much the same reason as my marathon challenge. I was seeking to show what was possible for an injured veteran.

Disabled people sometimes write books about their journeys and how they returned to life, and sometimes these books are turned into films. Some of these people become motivational speakers. Do you intend to do something similar?

I have been doing speaking engagements, yes. I try to think of unique perspectives on common thoughts. I am writing a book, but it is not an autobiography; it's a fiction novel about veterans. There have also been several short documentaries made about me at robjonesjourney.com/documentaries.

2018

PARVINDER CHAWLA

Globetrotter in a wheelchair

Parvinder Chawla was born in Ludhiana, India. At the age of 15, she was diagnosed with Rheumatoid Arthritis (RA). She recalls that even when she was in diapers, her mom would feed her and ask her to open her mouth wider. Parvinder insisted that it was already as wide as she could manage. Her mom took her to a homeopathic doctor who warned her that her condition could worsen as she grew older. But Parvinder was always a bubbly character who loved dancing, swimming, partying, and being carefree. After a while, she stopped taking medications when she thought her symptoms had improved. When her sister got married and they were getting ready to dance, Parvinder realized she couldn't crouch down and had to leave the stage. It was then that she realized her problems were serious.

She had to give up her active lifestyle, her knees failed, and she had to stay in bed for almost five years. Then, her brother-in-law gave her a fully automatic wheelchair, which changed her life, and she decided to travel. Parvinder is now 51, has strong faith in God, and is fearless, believing that "angels for the day" are all around and will help her. She was pleased with the interest from the Czech Republic and hopes to visit the country one day soon.

This is an 'IF' question. Do you think that if you had followed the advice of the doctors when they discovered RA, it could have been stopped and healed, and that you would be walking today?

I suffer from rheumatoid arthritis, which is an autoimmune disease, so I was always told there was no cure for it. However, they mentioned that it could possibly stabilize. I tried alternate medicine because, at that time, the doctors would only prescribe painkillers.

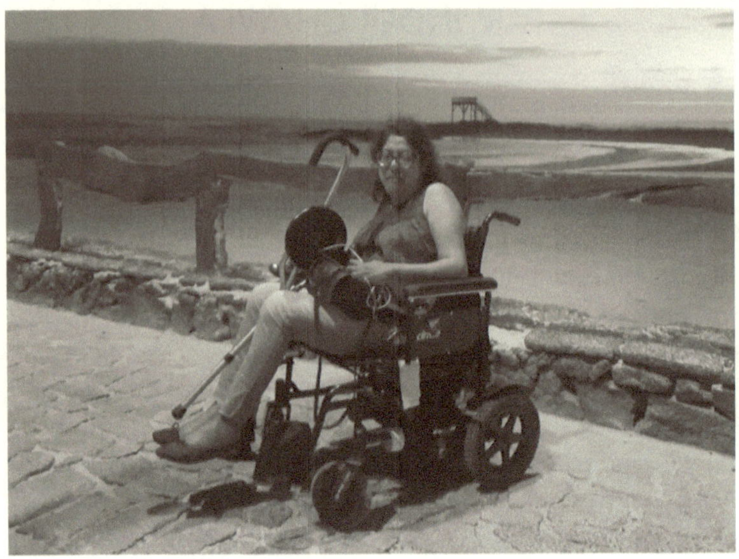

When you tried to find a job, were you rejected because you were in a wheelchair? Did you try anything that would pay for your traveling and give you freedom and independence?

I worked for BPOs (Business Process Outsourcing), where I was required to sit and take calls. I wish and pray I could get a job that would pay for my traveling and give me freedom and independence. I am still looking for an opportunity, even though I'm 52 years old. But as they say, it's never too late. :)

What were your first steps when you started traveling? Did you just choose a country, find a friendly assistant, and basically jump in at the deep end and try to swim, so to speak? And after coming home, did you analyze the trip, finding positive things and mistakes to make the next trip much better?

You're right in a way, but it was a little different in the beginning. Traveling out of India was a little expensive, so I tried traveling to nearby Asian countries that I could afford. Still, the big question was money. Traveling on a budget while in a wheelchair is very tough. My first solo trip was to Bali. I stayed at Tune Hotel, where there was no intercom service, and flew with AirAsia, the cheapest airline. To this day, I travel by cheap airlines, even if it means long connections and spending time at the airport just to save that money. I only travel by buses and metros.

If you're not positive, you can't make these trips—especially the solo ones. You have to be fearless, and I was because my faith in the Almighty is very strong. I've had so many incidents where, if someone else were in my place, they would have thought twice about traveling again. :)

How do you choose which countries to travel to? Do you choose as an ordinary tourist because you like historical monuments and places, and discovering wheelchair accessibility is a secondary task, an added bonus?

I'm not much of a historical monument person. I'm more of a nature person and love adventures—even being in a wheelchair. Initially, I would choose countries with accessibility, but since my dream is to travel to all 216 countries, I can't keep doing that. Traveling to more accessible countries and then

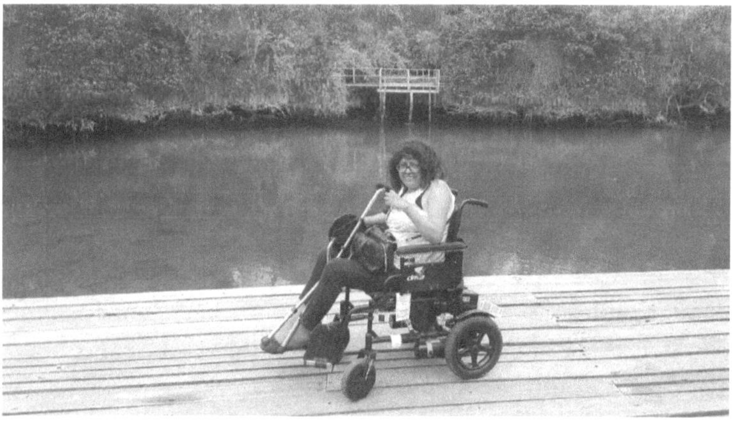

some Asian countries has made me confident. Now, I choose countries with good offers, easy access to visas, and connecting countries I haven't been to. A lot of time gets wasted because I can't just go to any country at any time—I need to plan, get a visa, and book tickets. I also have to research hostels, because I stay in them. What if I don't get a visa? That becomes a tough job. I wish I had a passport that allowed me access to any country at any time—it would be so much easier. :)

When you prepare for a trip, could you tell us the steps you take for planning, calculating the budget, finding places to stay, getting ready for the trip, and avoiding disappointment?

A lot of things are considered when I plan my trips—weather conditions, offers, visas, and deals. For example, it happened that I was planning to go to China and suddenly found a good deal for another country in my research. So, my plan shifted because I have to stick to a budget. Due to financial constraints, I stay in hostels and travel by buses and metros. When you're traveling alone and in a wheelchair, you can never prepare for everything. It all has to be an adventure with on-the-go solutions.

For my Italy trip, when I landed in Rome, I had not booked anywhere. I wanted to check out a hostel but wasn't sure if it was wheelchair-friendly. By the time I reached it, it was raining, and it was difficult for me to get in. They refused to let me stay, saying it wouldn't be good for their other clients. I ended up on the street until midnight trying to find accommodation. That day was one I'll never forget.

The world is a strange place these days, full of violence. Don't you feel vulnerable and defenseless in a wheelchair in some countries? Has it ever happened to you that you were robbed, attacked, or bullied on your travels?

The first thing is that you have to be fearless when you decide to travel solo, especially when you're in a wheelchair. I've been robbed many times, and I have many stories to tell. While in Rome, I was robbed of 400 euros by a roommate in a hostel.

You rent your apartment out through Airbnb and help your brother in his restaurant business. Does that mean you only live to travel, and once you earn enough money, you find a place to go and take a trip? How many trips do you go on per year, and do you only fly and take local buses and trains, or do you also rent a car and drive thousands of miles inland?

Yes, I rent my apartment out on Airbnb. I used to help my father in the restaurant business, but now my brother takes care of it, and I look for opportunities where I can make some good money. I make money to travel and live my dreams. Traveling to all 216 countries is one of them, and I have many other dreams. I've also started doing ramp walks—or should I say, being on the ramp in my wheelchair. :) I need income to fulfill my dreams, and due to the pandemic, the Airbnb business is difficult, so I'm looking for other opportunities. I will be launching a new business as a partnership soon.

Since there's so little time and so much to do, I'd take a trip almost every month. But for two years, because of the pandemic, I couldn't travel the world. So, I decided to travel around India, driving on my own. I've covered a lot of Indian cities and a few states, which I'll be visiting soon. When I was in England, they charged me a fortune for taking me to their lakes, but I can see lakes ten times nicer in my own country. In foreign countries, they always charge a lot for entrance fees to exotic places, so I prefer enjoying nature in places where it's more accessible.

I really wish I could get some sponsors to help me with my travels. Then, I wouldn't have to wait to collect the money. I'd really appreciate it if you could connect me with companies that might sponsor my trips so I can live my dream of traveling. :)

Do you take pictures, make documentaries, or write reports from your travels so other disabled people can find out what it's like there, kind of being a guinea pig for them? Do you connect with people from all over the world who invite you to visit their country and inform you about accessibility?

I've recently become very active on Instagram, posting stories and reels. I've connected with a lot of people through social media, and nice people like you write about my stories. It makes me happy that through these stories, I can inspire others.

And as I said, I'd love it if people around the world would invite me to their countries.

Are you asked by other disabled people or even travel agencies to find out about some places so they can use it for their own traveling, or would you see that as a less enjoyable task than your free schedule, so you don't do it?

Yes, I do have people who get in touch with me to ask about the wheelchair I use and to inquire about traveling. Many of them don't have the confidence to travel. So, I guide them and tell them about the places I've been and how easy it is to travel to those places. There's one person who contacted me because she wanted to travel to India, so I told her to visit Agra first. It's a beautiful city with wheelchair-friendly monuments. She went there, and when she came back, she was so happy and gained the confidence to travel more. I was glad I could help someone.

Has it ever happened that you planned a trip, and it turned sour? You found yourself stuck alone in a place where you couldn't move and had to beg for help to get out of there?

Yes, there are many stories about these kinds of situations. I went to China, which isn't very wheelchair-friendly. I traveled with a travel agency but didn't buy the tourist package due to my tight budget. When I arrived, I found out the hotel I had booked was demolished. A local person helped me find a taxi to a hostel. But due to a change in climate, I got a fever and couldn't communicate with the receptionist since Google is banned there. My condition worsened, so I had to return home. The flight had delays, and when I tried to walk with the help of my cane, I fell and suffered a concussion. That trip could have discouraged me from traveling, but it didn't.

You've visited 59 countries so far. Does that mean you've been to Antarctica with your wheelchair? Which countries in Africa have you visited? Which was the best equipped for wheelchairs, and which was the worst?

Yes, I've visited 59 countries, with Egypt being the last one before the lockdown. On the same trip, I was supposed to visit Lebanon but had to return to India. I haven't been to Antarctica yet, but I have plans to. I've been to Mauritius and a few other African countries, but I still haven't visited mainland Africa. I've heard it's not safe there, and I don't know much about it yet, so I'm not sure when I'll go. But I have many more countries to visit, and out of the 216 countries in the world, I've only visited 59—it's just the beginning. :)

Is your electric wheelchair specially equipped with things like a battery, extra hooks for luggage, etc?

Yes, my wheelchair is fully automatic, and it weighs only 23 kg. It's a gift from my brother-in-law, and it changed my life forever. It's an amazing chair to travel with because of its weight, which is the main issue most of the time. I've added some extra accessories for convenience, like a hook for luggage.

2021

SAM SCHMIDT

I feel normal

Sam Schmidt graduated from high school and, at the age of 25, bought out his father's business. He aspired to be a race driver and entered the racing world at the relatively late age of 31. Despite this, he found success in his first season and quickly secured his first win. He competed in the famous Indy 500 race three times, but in 1999, he suffered a serious crash that left him badly injured. In early 2000, while testing at the Walt Disney Circuit, he had another accident that resulted in paralysis from the neck down.

Remarkably, within 14 months, Sam established his own racing team. His Schmidt-Peterson Motorsports (SPM) team went on to become the most successful team in the Indy Light Series. When we learned that Sam had obtained a driver's license to operate an Arrow Electronics-built car using only head movements and breathing into a tube, we were intrigued and reached out to him. Within hours, we received responses

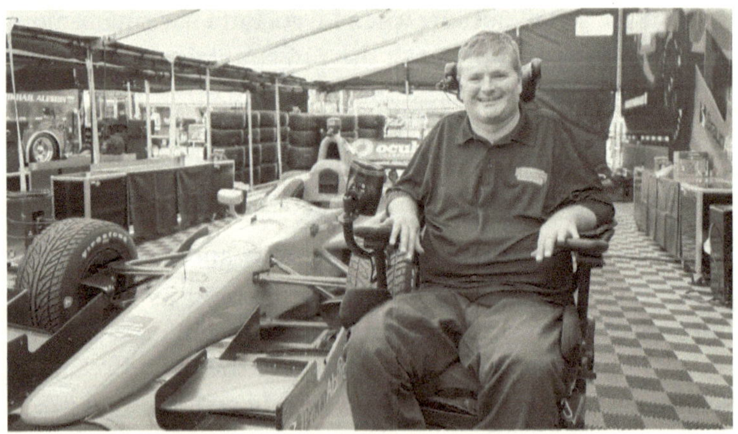

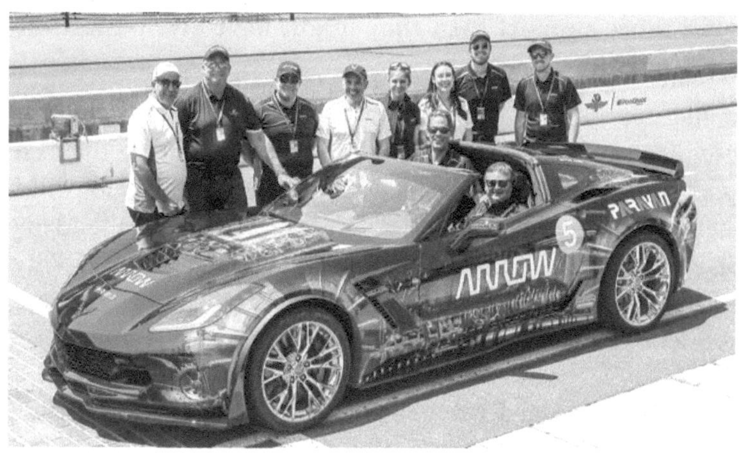

not only from the team's PR officer, Veronica Knowlton, and Arrow Electronics executive Joe Verrengia, but also from Sam Schmidt himself. We extend our thanks to all of them for their cooperation.

When Sam had his near-fatal crash in 2000 and became paralyzed, what motivated him to establish his own team?

Sam: I wanted to continue living fully and supporting my family. At the time, my kids were just six months and two-and-a-half years old. I had been competing in motorsports since I was five years old, and while I had other ways to make a living, I felt a deep need to compete in the IndyCar Series. Additionally, my father had faced paralysis when I was 10 years old. Doctors said he would never walk or talk again, yet he battled back to become a successful businessman. His determination, combined with our faith and a strong support system, gave us the strength to succeed.

How did sponsors and drivers react to Sam? Did they see him as a reminder of the dangers of racing and consider it bad publicity, or did they admire his perseverance and

offer more support than they might have given a healthy team owner?

Joe: Arrow got to know Sam personally and observed his race team, Schmidt-Peterson Motorsports, during the first year of the SAM car project. Our decision to sponsor SPM stemmed from this positive experience. We saw firsthand his strategic intelligence, commitment to excellence, and ability to leverage technology for competitive advantages. From there, the sponsorship decision became a natural development.

How did the SAM car project come about? Was Arrow already developing the technology and looking for a qualified quadriplegic driver like Sam, or did Sam approach Arrow seeking such a solution?

Joe: Arrow wanted to create a high-profile humanitarian technology project. We chose to focus on developing technology for the disabled community because it could be done

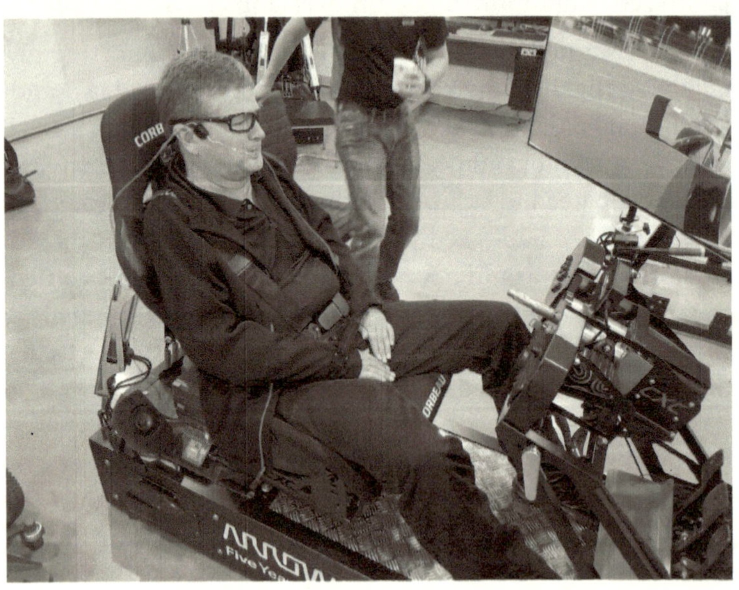

quickly and didn't require extensive regulatory approval, unlike medical care innovations. We also decided to use a fast sports car to make a bold public statement and draw attention to mobility and automated vehicle technology.

Once we set this goal, we realized we needed a highly skilled driver willing to accept the risks of experimental high-speed driving. A mutual friend introduced us to Sam via text, and we quickly began specific discussions. Sam had one condition: the car had to reach at least 100 mph. When we agreed, we knew we had our driver! Recently, Sam drove the SAM car at 190 mph.

How long did it take to develop the project from your first meeting with Sam to him receiving his license? What were the costs?

Joe: The project began conceptually in the summer of 2013. Within 10 months, Sam was driving demonstration laps at the 2014 Indy 500, reaching 107 mph. Every year, we set new driving goals in January, test improved systems within a few months, and demonstrate them publicly by April or May.

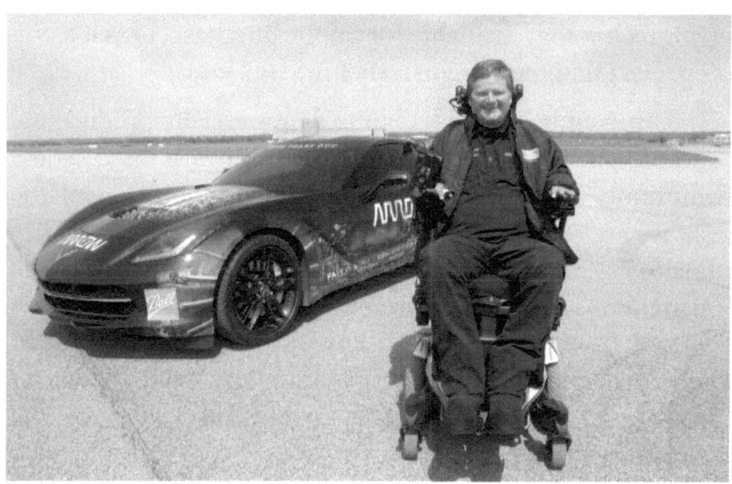

Sam received his driver's license in September 2016, making the SAM system legal for public roads. The car costs about $500,000, which includes the purchase of the Corvette, co-driver controls, and all the electronic modifications for steering, acceleration, braking, and voice commands. This does not account for ongoing engineering staff costs or expenses for driving events.

Did Sam contribute to the development process, for instance, by using simulators to suggest improvements, or was the project presented to him as a finished product?

Joe: Simulator sessions with Sam have been invaluable. They allow him to practice courses virtually and provide feedback. For example, when preparing for the Pikes Peak International Hill Climb—a demanding 12-mile course with 156 turns—the simulator helped us fine-tune steering calibration and gauge Sam's stamina. While the simulator wasn't an exact replica of the actual drive, it gave us confidence in both the system's capabilities and Sam's readiness. He completed the Pikes Peak course in an impressive 15 minutes.

Is this technology available for public purchase, or is it a one-off project designed exclusively for Sam?

Joe: Currently, we don't plan to commercially produce the SAM system for cars. Its purpose is to inspire the disabled community and encourage technological innovations. However, we are exploring applications for slower, repetitive-use vehicles like farm tractors and warehouse equipment to create broader opportunities for disabled individuals.

Does Sam intend to use the car for daily driving, or was obtaining the license mainly a demonstration of the technology's potential?

Joe: At this point, Sam's driver's license requires a trained co-driver. For now, the SAM car is reserved for Arrow demonstrations. We plan additional demonstrations next year with a variety of disabled participants, including military veterans.

I've read that Sam requires a co-driver and a safety car in front of him when driving. Doesn't this make the process both expensive and logistically challenging?

Joe: Yes, the SAM car always includes a trained co-driver. On the track, Robby Unser—an experienced retired racecar driver who competed against Sam—fulfills this role. Robby's knowledge of the car and the risks of high-speed driving have been instrumental in pushing performance limits. He has also contributed valuable insights for improving the car's equipment, including Sam's helmet.

On public roads, a lead safety car is required to reduce risks, such as other vehicles unexpectedly turning in front of Sam. This precaution stems from the fact that other drivers wouldn't know Sam is operating the car through head movements and breath control. While this adds expense and complexity, it's an essential part of the program. In the future, we aim to reduce these requirements to enhance Sam's driving freedom and normalcy.

Is the SAM technology specific to this car, or could it be adapted to other vehicles?

Joe: The SAM system combines existing electronic components in a unique way, driven by custom software. Leveraging existing technology allows us to innovate quickly without the need to develop new hardware from scratch. For example, the steering system in Year 1 was adapted from a video game system. While this particular configuration was designed for the Corvette, similar systems could be adapted for other vehicles.

Is Sam involved in other projects for quadriplegic individuals where his status as a public figure helps raise awareness?

Sam: Yes, I am a shareholder in BraunAbility (known as AutoAdapt in Europe) and sit on its Board of Directors to influence future mobility solutions for disabled individuals. The SAM Project has garnered global attention over the past three years, positively impacting the industry. Additionally, I am the founder and chairman of Conquer Paralysis Now, an organization dedicated to researching cures for paralysis.

In simple terms, how does the Arrow system work?

Joe: In essence, Sam steers by moving his head left and right. Infrared cameras track these movements and send the data to the car's wheels via a computer. To accelerate, he blows air into a tube, and to brake, he sucks on the tube. Voice commands allow him to control additional features such as lights, windows, and wipers.

What happens if Sam sneezes or hiccups? Would it disrupt the car's operation?

Sam: (Laughing) Fortunately, that hasn't happened during tests, but I'm confident Arrow's engineers accounted for such scenarios in the software. **Joe:** Exactly. The steering system is designed to respond only to smooth, deliberate head movements within a specific range. Vertical motions, such as nodding, are ignored. Similarly, the car will maintain its speed if Sam isn't actively blowing or sucking on the tube, so brief reactions like sneezes or hiccups wouldn't interfere. And if they did, his co-driver would step in—probably with a tissue for Sam!

Can you share Sam's thoughts after his first drive? Did it trigger memories of his crash, or did he simply feel exhilarated?

Sam: I expected to feel the thrill of driving again, but what truly surprised me was the profound sense of normalcy I experienced. For the first time in 15 years, I was in complete control of something, and it was incredibly emotional. **Joe:** His first words after that drive were, "I feel normal." That statement has become the motto of the SAM car project. Everything we do now is aimed at extending that sense of normalcy, with a little help from technology.

2017

SHEELA SHARMA

I lost my mother, brother and hands at the same time

Sheela Sharma is a foot-painting artist from India. We chose to feature her because she lost her arms and nearly a foot in a train accident when she was only four years old. As if that wasn't enough, she also lost her mother and brother in the same tragic accident. Despite these immense challenges, Sheela never gave up. While studying at a boarding school in New Delhi, she encountered an artist who inspired her. Though her father never understood art, Sheela pursued her dream and began drawing with her foot. We would like to thank IMFPA (Indian Mouth and Foot Painters Association) coordinator Ayswaya Pillai for assisting us with this interview.

India is a country of stark contrasts, with very poor people and very rich people. What is your background, and how big is your family?

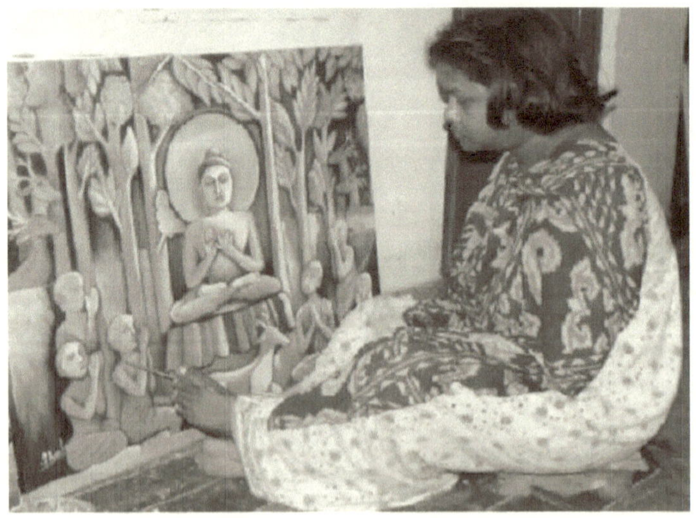

There are five members in my family: my husband, two children, my mother-in-law, and me. We come from a middle-class background.

What was your childhood like? Were you accepted by neighbors and classmates, or were you treated as a rarity and often bullied because of your disability?

I lost my hands in a train accident when I was just four years old. Growing up, I had two types of friends: those who always supported me and those who teased and made fun of me.

When did you realize you were different from others and that part of your body was missing? Can you live independently, or do you need assistance for basic needs?

The accident that took my hands also took my mother and brother. It was a very difficult time. Initially, I struggled with daily activities, but slowly and gradually, I adapted. Now, I manage most of my activities on my own and rarely need help. However, I do require someone to accompany me when I travel.

Did you always love painting and pursue it at any cost, or did someone suggest it to you as a way to express yourself, and you discovered your passion for it?

I have loved painting since I was a child. I started drawing at a very young age, and one of my teachers noticed my talent and encouraged me. I eventually completed a five-year degree from an arts college. However, not everyone appreciated my work. Some thought my painting style was strange and told me I shouldn't continue because it wouldn't lead anywhere. Their discouragement only strengthened my determination to succeed. I believe that instead of holding people back, especially those with disabilities, others should offer support and encouragement to help them achieve their goals.

Using your foot as a tool for painting is unconventional. How difficult was it to learn to hold a brush with your toes, dip it in paint, and create what you envisioned? Are you self-taught, or did you have a teacher or join a group of painters?

I didn't find it particularly difficult to hold a brush or dip it into paint with my foot because I've been using my feet for all kinds of activities since childhood. I started by making greeting cards with my foot in 8th grade, and people really appreciated them—some even kept them as keepsakes. When I joined art college, my teacher, Arya Sir, who was a wash painter, guided me and became my mentor.

Do you paint what you feel or see around you, imitate others, or express your inner emotions? How long does it take you to complete a painting?

Most of my paintings are inspired by nature and women. I've done a lot of work on the theme of mothers and children, showcasing the unconditional love between them. It usually takes me about a week to complete one painting.

When you started painting, how long could you work before getting cramps in your toes or legs? Has this improved over time?

When I was younger, I could paint continuously for four to five hours without any issues. Nowadays, at the age of 53, I take breaks every hour, as I can no longer paint for such long stretches without resting.

When did you realize that you had found your own painting style and stopped experimenting with other techniques?

I found my style over time and now focus solely on perfecting it. I paint whenever I feel inspired.

Did you approach the Indian Mouth and Foot Painters Association (MFPA) for help, or did they contact you after discovering your work?

After completing my education, I worked at Lalit Kala Kendra. An article about me was published in *India Today*, and through a friend who is also a foot artist, I learned about MFPA and connected with them.

How does your relationship with MFPA work? Do you need to apply for membership and submit a certain number of paintings each year to receive support?

Yes, we apply for membership and regularly submit our paintings to the head office each year. In return, we receive a monthly stipend and bonuses for artwork selected for sale.

Do you think your disability has allowed you to see more of the world, meet more people, and grow into a more enriched person than you might have as an able-bodied individual?

I've always been passionate about the arts and would have pursued them regardless. If not for painting, I might have become a singer. I love everything related to art.

Have you ever exhibited your work outside of India?

No, I haven't held exhibitions outside India, but I did have the opportunity to visit Singapore in 2012 for a workshop in collaboration with MFPA. I would love to hold exhibitions abroad if given the opportunity.

2021

SIMON FITZMAURICE

A triumph of human will

Film fans marvel at new tricks, animations, 3D technology, and other miracles of the big screen. As technology advances, we may soon see feature films created entirely without live actors.

The Irish film *My Name is Emily*, directed by filmmaker Simon Fitzmaurice, had its premiere at the Zlín Film Festival in the Czech Republic. At first glance, this might seem unremarkable amid the flood of films released every year, but Simon is a man living with Motor Neuron Disease (MND), which means he can communicate only with his eyes. The fact that he directed an entire film this way is astounding, and we were eager to learn more. We reached out via email to producer Jerry Li, who kindly connected us with producer Kathryn Kennedy. Kathryn answered some of our questions on Simon's behalf, while others were answered by Simon himself.

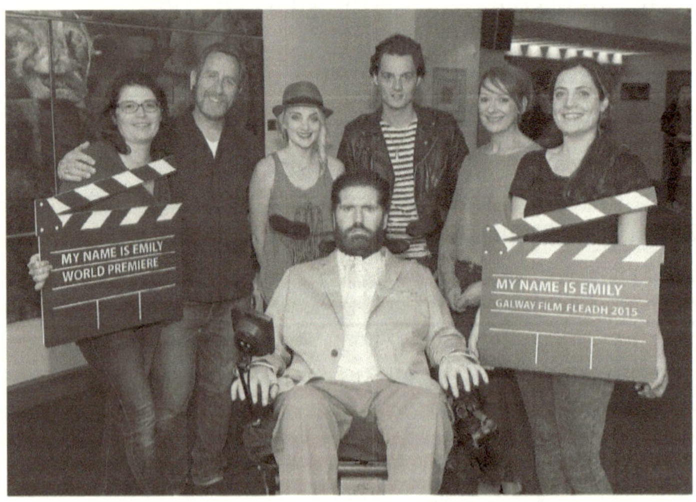

From the age of 14, Simon loved writing stories and going to movie theaters. His idols were directors Peter Weir and Wim Wenders. Simon directed two acclaimed films, *The Sound of People* and *Full Circle*. In 2007, he attended the Sundance Film Festival with his debut film and achieved great success. At that time, his wife was expecting their third child. Upon returning from the United States, Simon began to notice something wrong with his body. He was diagnosed with MND, and his condition deteriorated rapidly.

Three years later, Simon was unable to move or talk, could only breathe with a ventilator, and was fed directly through a tube as he could no longer swallow. Doctors gave him little hope and advised his family to disconnect life support, but Simon refused. He returned home and received round-the-clock care from a nurse. Despite his condition, Simon conceived another child, and to everyone's surprise, his wife gave birth to twins. While his wife cared for him and their children, Simon began writing the script for *My Name is Emily*, a project he had started as a healthy man.

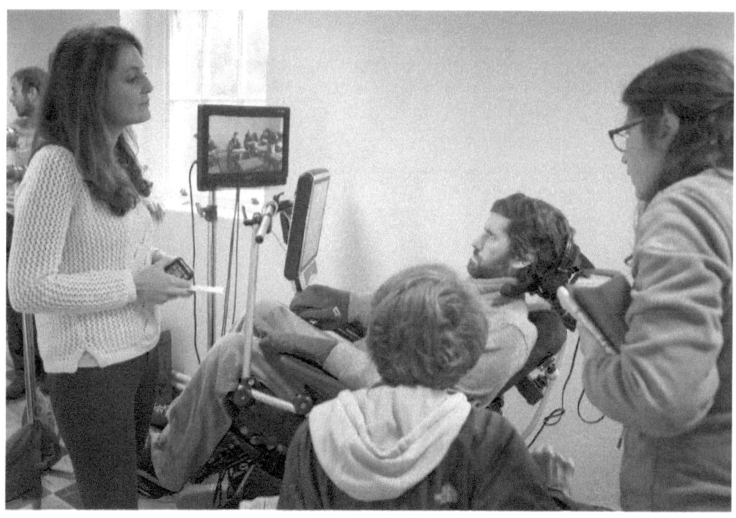

With support from the Irish Film Fund, Simon got to work. When he needed additional funding for equipment and tools for his assistant director, Alan Rickman launched a campaign that raised over £120,000, with contributions from stars like Colin Farrell and Sam Neill. Simon communicated with his crew through a specialized device that tracked the movement of his eyes. He directed a film that won accolades at festivals and earned widespread respect for his extraordinary perseverance. Simon not only pushed human boundaries but also became the first person to direct a film entirely in this way.

Doctors gave Simon four years to live, but he is still working. Is it difficult for him to live with the idea of 'borrowed time'?

As far as we know, Simon doesn't dwell on this too much. He focuses on living for today and avoids making long-term plans. His disease has progressed to its final stage, affecting his entire body except for his eyes. While infections remain a

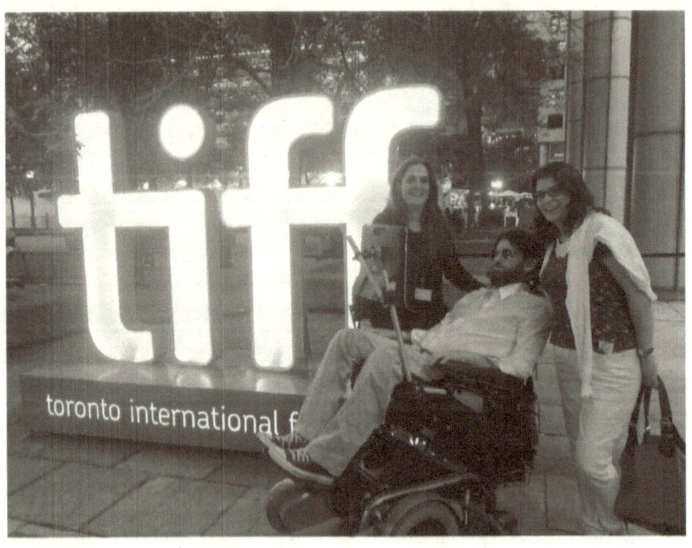

constant threat, Simon lives for his family, which is his greatest motivation.

How does Simon communicate with his children? It must be challenging for both sides.

Simon's relationship with his children has evolved as his condition has progressed. His eldest son remembers him as a healthy man, but the twins have only ever known him as severely disabled.

Directing a film is a massive responsibility, even for an able-bodied person. What was the hardest part for Simon?

(*From Simon*) The biggest challenge was meeting new people who didn't know anything about me. They often felt awkward or embarrassed, and it took time for them to adjust. During the shoot, I had to interact with many people to move the project forward, which was exhausting but also energizing. Filming recharged me with energy I didn't know I still had. Since communication took longer for me, I had to prepare thoroughly to minimize time lost. My crew made the process much easier, but it was still a significant challenge.

Technically, how does Simon communicate when he can only move his eyes? Was his device developed especially for him?

Simon uses an "Eye Gaze" computer manufactured by Tobii Dynavox, supplied through the Irish Motor Neuron Disease Association. This technology is widely used by others with similar conditions. A sensor beneath the screen tracks the movement of Simon's eyes, which acts as a computer "mouse." Wherever Simon focuses his gaze, the system "clicks." Though the device can be configured to respond to winks, Simon prefers to click by staring.

Transitioning from writing by hand to writing with one's eyes is a huge shift. How long did it take Simon to learn the technology, and can he convey exactly what he envisions?

(*From Simon*) It took time to adjust to using a computer with just my eyes, but after six years, it's second nature. There's nothing I can't do when it comes to writing on a computer.

Simon was determined to make the film. Did he expect the crew to treat him as a healthy director, or did everyone have to adapt to his condition?

Simon was treated like any other director. He handled emails, creative briefs, and on-set responsibilities just like anyone else, though responses took longer due to the nature of his communication. Crew members adapted by framing questions to elicit "yes" or "no" answers, which Simon could blink or stare to indicate. Simon also had a Support Director, Liz Gill, who relayed his instructions. Despite the unique setup, Simon worked as hard—if not harder—than any other director.

What impact did directing have on Simon? Did it distract him from his illness, inspire others, or push the boundaries of filmmaking?

(*From Simon*) Directing the film kept my mind focused on what I could achieve rather than what I couldn't. Yes, it was a remarkable achievement, and we hope Simon's work inspires others in all walks of life. As far as we know, no other film has been directed entirely through Eye Gaze technology, so Simon has certainly pushed the boundaries of filmmaking.

We don't know how *My Name is Emily* was received by the public and critics, but do you think the way it was made may be even more extraordinary than the film itself?

When promoting the film, it's tricky to discuss both *My Name is Emily* and Simon's condition simultaneously, as audiences might assume the film is a documentary. Many critics and viewers were unaware of Simon's condition before watching the film. From our experience, critics judged the film on its own merits, praising the script, acting, cinematography, and artistry, rather than focusing on Simon's condition.

Simon also wrote a book, which is an incredible achievement. Was the process of writing it similar to that of filmmaking? Is there any risk that excessive use of his eyes might weaken them over time? Is he the first author to write a book this way?

Yes, Simon's book was written using Eye Gaze technology, just like his script. While it's hard to predict the long-term effects, there's no evidence suggesting that his eyes will weaken from use. Simon isn't the first author to write a book this way; *The Diving Bell and the Butterfly* was also written through similar technology.

A person with Simon's condition could inspire deep sympathy. How did the actors respond to working with him? Was it emotionally challenging for them, or did they work extra hard to make him happy?

Everyone on the cast and crew was aware of Simon's condition before meeting him, so they were prepared for the unique challenges. Communication took some getting used to, but everyone worked incredibly hard. There was a strong sense of dedication on set, as people saw how much effort Simon put into his work and wanted to ensure the project succeeded.

What about post-production tasks like editing, production, and promotion? Was Simon involved in these processes?

Simon was involved every step of the way. He showed incredible energy and commitment, surprising everyone with how much he could do. Initially, the team planned for Simon to be on set for only four hours a day, but he arrived on day one at 8 a.m. and stayed with the crew until wrap each night. This dedication carried through to editing and promoting the film. Simon gave his all throughout the entire process.

How long did it take to complete the film? Was the crowdfunding campaign necessary to cover unexpected costs, or was it planned from the start?

The filming process lasted five weeks, with Simon present every day. The total budget was €2 million, which couldn't be financed entirely from a single source. The Irish Film Board was a key supporter, providing both financial support and guidance. Additional funding came from BAI, TV3, Ireland's S481 tax incentive, and co-production partners in Sweden and Norway. The crowdfunding campaign was specifically launched to cover Simon's unique requirements, such as a Support Director, a customized van, a new Eye Gaze computer, and other essential tools.

Was Simon able to attend the film's premieres at festivals? Does he have plans for another project, or was *My Name is Emily* a one-time breakthrough?

Simon attended three festival screenings. His first was the domestic premiere at Galway Film Fleadh in Ireland, which was special as it allowed his family and friends to attend. He also made it to the North American premiere at the Toronto International Film Festival, marking his first trip abroad in five years. The third festival was the Edinburgh Film Festival, where Simon traveled by boat from Ireland to Scotland. He hopes to attend the London Screenwriters

Festival soon. Simon is currently writing and hopes to make another film.

P.S. Simon Fitzmaurice sadly passed away on October 26, 2017.

2016

SWAPNA AUGUSTINE

I can't imagine how my life would have been if I had both hands

We wanted to interview a disabled Indian artist, and our search led us to Swapna Augustine, a remarkable woman born without arms. Swapna, now 43, hails from Paingottoor in Kerala's Ernakulam district. Her mother was shocked when her first child was born without hands; in the late 1970s, medical technology was not advanced enough to detect such conditions during pregnancy. Swapna's siblings—a daughter and two sons—were born later and were perfectly healthy. Despite her challenges, Swapna has lived life to the fullest and become a respected foot-painter. Her stunning artwork caught our attention, and, thanks to Ayswaya Pillai, coordinator for the Indian Mouth and Foot Painters Association (IMFPA), we had the opportunity to interview her.

India is a country of vast contrasts, with both extreme poverty and great wealth. What is your background, and how large is your family?

I come from a middle-class background and belong to a joint family with many members.

What kind of childhood did you have? Were you accepted by your neighbors and classmates, or were you treated differently because of your disability?

I was born in a typical village in Kerala where my neighbors and schoolmates were kind and supportive. I was never treated as a rarity. My parents, however, faced difficulties, especially my mother, who assisted me with all activities until I was four years old. Then, we met a local tutor who taught me how to hold a pencil between my toes. Though it was initially painful and my legs didn't bend properly, we persisted. Within two years, my legs effectively became my hands.

When did you realize you were different from others? Was your condition due to a genetic disorder? Are you able to live independently, or do you need assistance with daily tasks?

I attended a normal school in Changanassery, Kerala, before transferring to a boarding school for disabled children at age six. There, we learned to perform daily activities independently and support one another. My parents were initially concerned about my future, but they ensured I received a good education and training for a normal life. At first, I wasn't eager to interact with able-bodied people, but attending regular schools enhanced my social skills. I believe it's essential for disabled people to mingle with others to foster mutual understanding.

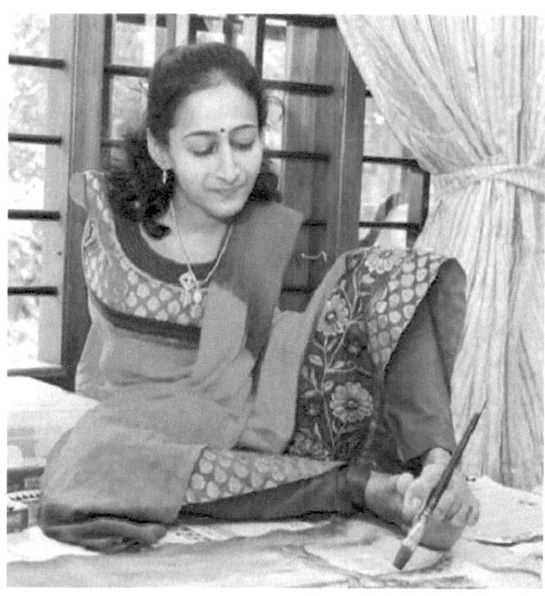

Today, I don't need a caregiver because I can handle 80–90% of my daily activities independently. I didn't truly notice the absence of my hands until I reached eighth grade.

Have you always loved painting, or did someone encourage you to try it?

I've loved painting since childhood. It feels like a gift from God. I started drawing at age seven, initially sketching flowers and other simple designs. My early drawings weren't perfect, but I kept practicing. After attending a workshop on acrylic painting, I transitioned to proper canvas work.

Painting with your feet is unique. How challenging was it to learn this technique? Did you teach yourself or have formal training?

I first learned to write and eat using my feet at around three years old. Later, I began drawing with pencils, which gradually led to painting. Since I rely on my feet for most activities, it felt natural to adapt. However, I only received formal training after joining MFPA-India in 1999.

What inspires your artwork? How long does it take you to complete a painting?

Most of my paintings reflect nature and my imagination. It usually takes me five to six days to complete a piece.

When you started painting, could you work for extended periods without discomfort? How long can you paint now?

I've never experienced cramps while painting. Even in the beginning, I could paint for four to five hours continuously.

How long have you been painting, and when did you find your artistic style?

I've been painting for 20 years. Joining MFPA-India was a turning point that deepened my passion and refined my technique.

How did you connect with the Indian Mouth and Foot Painters Association?

I initially applied to a Canadian organization, unaware of MFPA-India. They helped me join MFPA-India in 1999.

What is your relationship with MFPA-India? Do you need to submit paintings regularly?

Yes, we must apply for membership and submit paintings to the head office annually. In return, we receive a monthly scholarship and bonuses for artworks selected for sale.

Do you think your disability has given you a unique perspective and enriched your life?

I can't imagine how my life would have been with both hands. I believe we should embrace and utilize the talents we're given. God created me this way, and I'm content with who I am.

Have you showcased your work internationally?

I haven't participated in any exhibitions outside India, except for one in Qatar organized by MFPA.

2021

TOMÁŠ JANOUŠEK

I Dream About Painting a Winter Landscape at Night

Life can change in a split second. Czech youngster Tomáš Janoušek knows this all too well. In 1998, just three days before the end of the school year, he went to his art school to pick up a report. On his way, he was hit by a car, fracturing his spine between C1 and C-2. Tomáš became paralyzed from the neck down and is connected to a ventilator to breathe. Despite these challenges, he managed to finish school with great effort. Now 26, Tomáš devotes much of his time to mouth painting. He began with watercolors and now uses acrylics and oil paints. We admired his work and asked his mother, Iva Janoušek, to assist us with this interview.

After the accident, you spent three full years in the hospital. When you returned home, did your parents have to adapt your house for wheelchair access? Was the return home a culture shock for you, and how did you cope with the life change?

We live in a family house, so the first floor didn't need major changes. My parents only had to add more sockets in my room, remove the carpet, and lay down linoleum. Since I shared the room with my sister and brother, they moved into my parents' bedroom, and my mom shared the room with me. Coping with the situation? I was eight years old when it happened, so honestly, I don't know. For me, it just became normal somehow.

What or who introduced you to mouth painting? Did you try other forms of self-expression before settling on painting?

I've been painting since I was very young and started attending art school at age five. While I was in the hospital, my mom saw a documentary on TV about artists who paint with their feet and mouths, so we decided to try it. At first, it was hard—I couldn't figure out how to hold the brush or control it since it kept rolling in my mouth. A doctor in the Children's Department told us about another boy with a similar injury who was working on a computer. We got in touch with his family, and they showed us how to make a special mouthpiece to hold the brush. That's when things really started.

I didn't enjoy drawing with crayons, so I began with watercolors. Then I moved on to aquarelle, acrylics, and now I prefer oil painting. I tried working with a computer and playing games, but they didn't interest me as much. I love painting, watching TV, and sports. While in the Prague hospital, my mom and I started painting together, but then we were introduced to ergotherapy. After returning home, my mom arranged for an ex-art school teacher to coach me. Later, I started attending the UMÚN (Czech Association of Mouth and Foot Painters) studio in Prague, where I was guided by wonderful teachers.

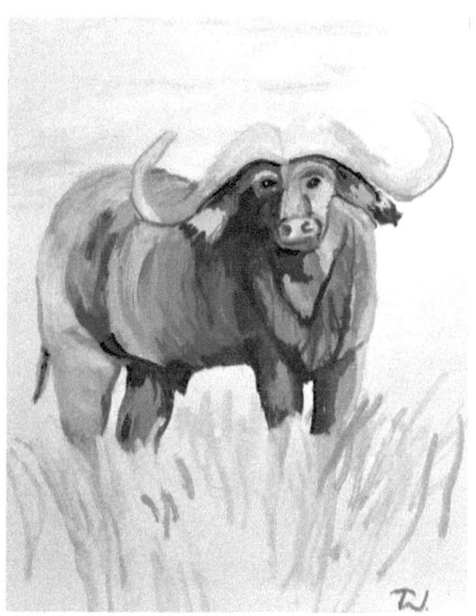

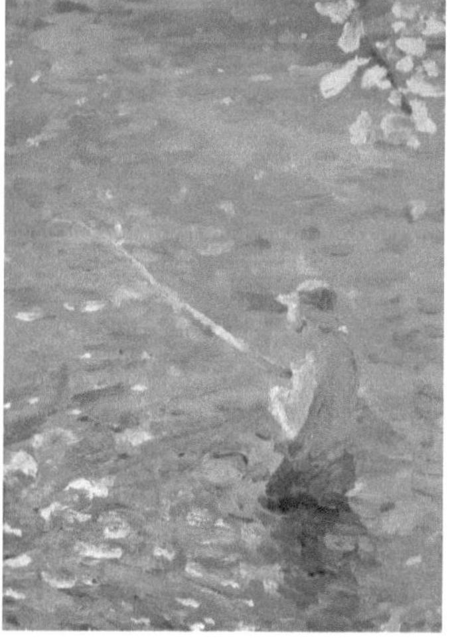

Your paintings often feature trees from Tuscany or rocks from a Czech national park. Have you traveled to these places? Which trips have left the deepest impression on you, and is there a dream destination you'd like to visit?

The furthest I've been is the Swiss Alps, which was an incredible experience. I also travel around the Czech Republic, and twice a year, we have exhibitions in various locations. Besides that, I visit our family cottage, but honestly, I love going anywhere—it's beautiful everywhere.

How long did it take for you to develop your artistic style? Have you ever considered giving up?

It took a long time. My progress was very slow, and there were times when I didn't enjoy painting. There was even a three-month period when I didn't paint anything at all. But I always realized in the end that painting is the best thing I can do.

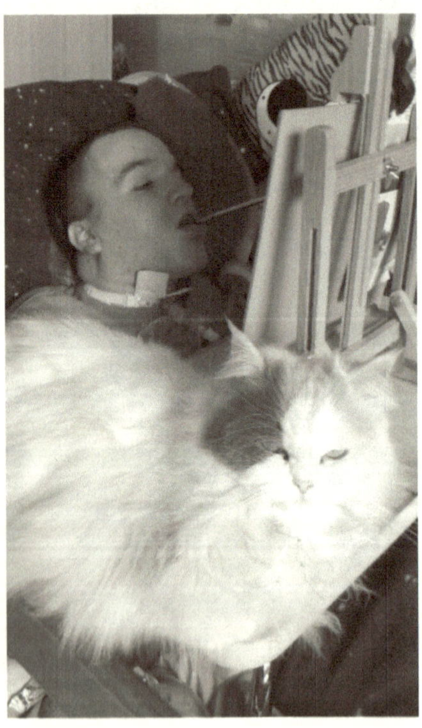

Do you paint every day, or only when inspired? How long does it take to finish a painting?

Painting with my mom and dad doesn't really work—we don't understand each other when it comes to this. Once a week, I go to the UMÚN studio, and once a week, my ex-teacher visits me at home. A single painting takes me about 15 hours to complete, but I can't do it in one go. I get tired after about three hours and need to rest.

Do you have a dream picture in your mind that you'd like to paint but can't manage technically?

Usually, I paint based on a pattern, which is easier with oil paints. I often dream about painting a beautiful winter landscape at night.

You also paint live animals. Is it difficult to capture their expressions? Do you feel anything when a kitten sits on your lap?

I love animals and enjoy painting them, but landscapes are my priority. I try to capture animals' facial expressions—sometimes I succeed, and sometimes I don't. At home, we have many pets, including three cats. I remember when they were kittens—they were scared of the ventilator and wouldn't come near me. Now they're much more comfortable, sleeping with me in my bed and being incredibly cute.

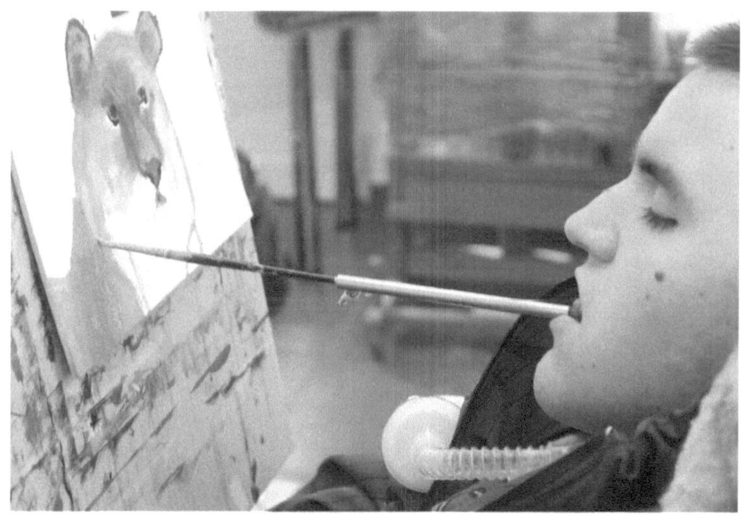

Have your paintings been featured in exhibitions or publications?

I've had two solo exhibitions, one even before I joined UMÚN. In 2002, I exhibited in Budapest with an international group of disabled painters, and the same happened in Prague the following year.

Do you connect with other painters? Have you received any accolades for your work?

Yes, I meet other disabled painters regularly, even outside of UMÚN activities. We often meet on vacations as well. I've received many diplomas and trophies at various exhibitions.

Do you think your disability has given you something you wouldn't have experienced otherwise?

I was paralyzed at the age of eight, so I didn't understand much about life or what I could or couldn't do. While my life is different—I'm in a wheelchair, paralyzed from the neck down, and use a lung ventilator—I have my family who cares for me, and life goes on.

Is there a difference between painting with watercolors, oil, or acrylic paints?

Yes, there's a significant difference, especially in the final result. Painting with oils is much more complicated.

2015

TOMÁŠ KVOCH

Adventurer

Life changed dramatically for Tomáš one summer afternoon when he planned to attend a music festival with friends, traveling by train from Pardubice to Brno in the Czech Republic. A stubborn female conductor insisted their tickets were invalid and said they'd need to buy new ones at the next stop. She gave them incorrect information about the waiting time for the next train. Tomáš, who went to buy the tickets, had to run to catch the moving train. The same conductor told him not to jump onto it and pushed him roughly off the wagon's footboard. He fell under the wheels, which severed both his legs above the knees. At the time, Tomáš was 21 years old and an active hockey, table tennis, and tennis player.

After the injury, Tomáš turned to sports for purpose and direction. He became the most famous Czech sled hockey player, with remarkable achievements. In 1999, he summited the highest Czech mountain, Sněžka (Snowhill, 1,603 m), in his wheelchair. The following year, he climbed it again—this time using only his hands—and was included in the Guinness Book of Records. With the Czech national sled hockey team, Tomáš finished second in the European Championships in 2007 and repeated this feat at the Boston World Championships the following year. He also competed in the Paralympic Games in Vancouver. Living life to the fullest, he became a father to his son Jakub in 2004.

When you woke up and realized you had lost both your legs, you initially wanted to give up. What changed your mind and helped you take the next step in life?

You're right—when I woke up, I really wanted to end it all. But after the initial panic, I started thinking calmly about what would happen and who I would hurt if I gave up. That's when I decided to keep going and give life a try.

What inspires someone to pick themselves up and move forward after such a traumatic experience? Was there a particular moment, book, or film that gave you the push?

For me, it was sport. I was an athlete before the accident, so I started wondering how it would work without legs. That became my first challenge. In my case, it wasn't about a book or a film—it came from within me. I've played basketball, tennis, table tennis, sled hockey, and done athletics, but recently, I've focused on sled hockey and tennis.

When someone loses their legs and begins the process of recovery, how does it work? Do you start from scratch and learn your new limits, or is it better not to set boundaries and just take it step by step?

When something like this happens, you have to start from scratch. You learn what you're capable of doing without help and gradually overcome what seems impossible. It's a slow process.

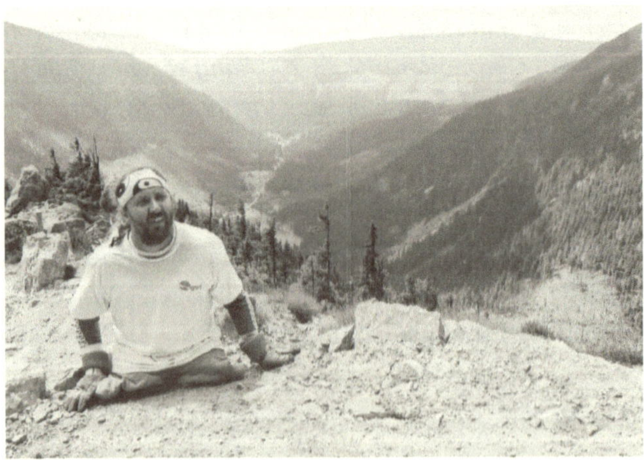

Before the accident, you had many friends. How did your relationships change afterward? Did you discover who you could count on, or did anyone surprise you? Was it hard to distinguish honest help from pity?

I can tell you this: I don't like pity. I prefer people to be direct. It's true that I had many friends before the accident, and many of them stayed with me afterward. Some didn't know how to talk to me and were afraid to say anything that might upset me. But once they realized I was open to talking about anything, everything worked out fine.

Your accident occurred during the communist regime. Aside from the mental and physical challenges, did you face bureaucratic hurdles or a lack of support? Do you think conditions for disabled people are better today?

Yes, the accident happened during the old regime, and it was very difficult back then. Today, things are much better. You can easily find information about available resources, the best wheelchairs, accessible apartments, and more. Everything is different now.

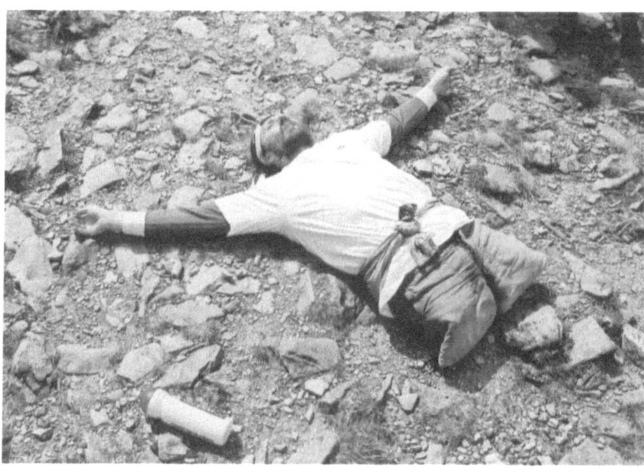

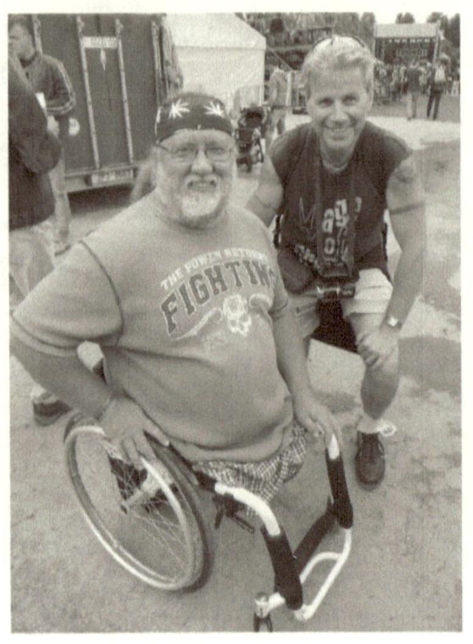

Did you take up a job through a protected workshop program, or did you focus on sports because it offered better opportunities?

Finding a job isn't easy for anyone, and it's even harder for someone with a disability. I was lucky to be hired by Ivana Špeldová, the co-owner of Missiva. Through this job, I met many inspiring people who showed me the way forward. I repaid them by sharing my own experiences and helping others overcome their challenges.

You've accomplished extraordinary feats, such as climbing Sněžka using your hands. What motivated you to take on such challenges? Was it for attention, to prove something, or just a natural part of who you are?

Climbing Sněžka wasn't easy. The idea came from my TAI-CHI teacher, Jan Pletánek. We talked about it during a trip to the mountains, and we decided I would push myself to the summit in my wheelchair. We succeeded and descended by cable car. Later, he suggested we try the more difficult route, and I agreed. It was a real challenge, and I didn't succeed the first time, so I trained hard and made it on the second attempt.

People often say it's not the length of life that matters, but its quality. Do you think your accident, paradoxically, gave you a fuller life?

Absolutely. The quality of life and values are different now. I can't compare what my life would have been like if I were able-bodied to what it is now. I just focus on living fully and appreciating what I have.

We see many disabled athletes but few disabled politicians, sculptors, or actors. Is sport particularly accommodating to disabled individuals because it offers a way to demonstrate willpower and effort?

Sport helps disabled people in many ways. Whether it's an individual or team activity, sport builds resilience and fosters growth. At the top level, it can be very physically demanding, and that's where athletes truly shine.

You've traveled extensively for sports. Have you encountered ignorance or a lack of support, or have you generally received the help you needed?

I've visited many countries, and Vancouver stands out as exceptional. The people there were incredibly kind and supportive. They would help if we were lost or needed something. In the Czech Republic, we still have a lot to learn from that kind of openness and support.

It's said that you plan to climb an 8,000-meter mountain to celebrate your 50th birthday. Is this a realistic goal, or more of a daring statement?

Yes, I've said I want to do that when I'm 50. I don't want to prove anything to anyone—just to myself. I'm a born adventurer, so I definitely want to try. I'll need to talk to a mountain climber to figure out what's possible and what's not. I'm not saying I'll succeed, but I will try.

2014

TORSTEIN LERHOL

Happy life weighing just 37.5 lb

Thirty-year-old Norwegian Torstein Lerhol is an extraordinary man. Born with Spinal Muscular Atrophy, like his sister, his body weighs only 17 kilos (37.5 pounds). Despite this, he leads a happy and full life, working as a teacher, giving lectures and talks, actively engaging in politics, and pursuing his passions. Photographer Henrik Fjortoft, who captured his images, even photographed Torstein naked in nature. Initially unsure how to approach the interview, we were surprised when Torstein responded within days, making it easier than expected.

What sort of childhood did you have? How did your neighbors and other children treat you—with disdain and sarcasm, or with understanding, care, and love?

My childhood was quite normal. I was raised in a family with four siblings, and my parents are farmers (they still

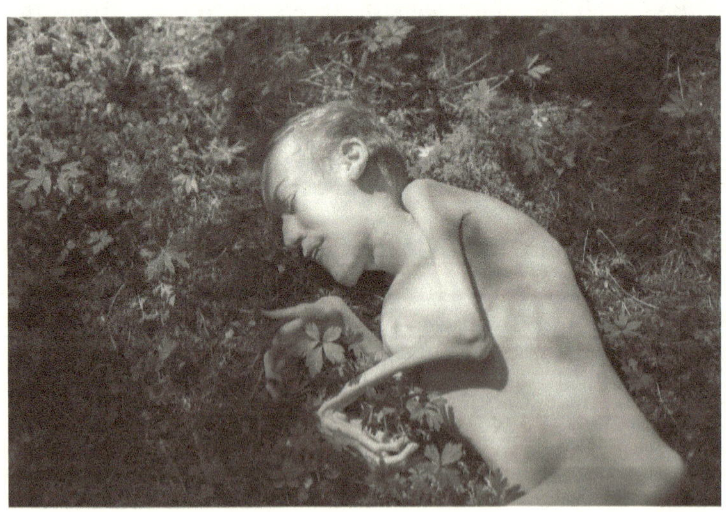

are). We lived in a small mountain village in central Norway. My sister and I were the only two children in wheelchairs, but I only had normal, healthy friends who treated me with understanding, love, and tolerance. I was never bullied and always felt part of the 'gang.' The main activities in our community involved being outdoors, so my friends included me in everything—sleeping in snow caves, climbing mountains, snowkiting, fishing, and more. My parents treated me like any other child, with the same expectations and boundaries as my siblings. This upbringing, surrounded by supportive family and friends, is a major reason for my success in life. My parents and the whole village believed in me and encouraged me to follow my dreams.

Did you attend an ordinary school, or did you receive special treatment? Did you have a specific dream for your future?

Yes, I attended regular schools—elementary, junior high, high school, and university—on a normal timeline. As a child, I dreamed of becoming a soldier in the special forces, but I realized that wouldn't be possible. So, I changed my dream

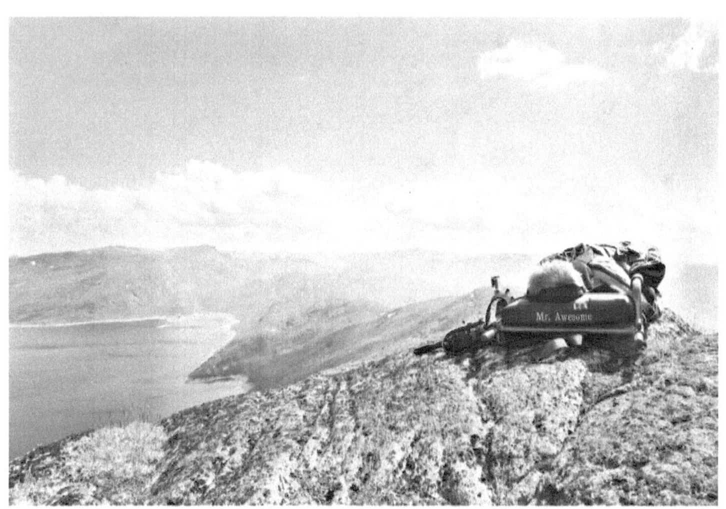

to becoming a teacher—and I achieved that. I'm a qualified history teacher with a master's degree.

When deciding on a career, do you have the same opportunities as others, or are there special exceptions?

In general, everyone in Norway has the same opportunities. People with disabilities receive additional support when needed, such as specially adapted apartments, which I also benefited from.

Politics can be brutal. Why did you choose that path? Have you faced unfair treatment from rivals?

Politics in Norway isn't as brutal as in some places. I chose politics for two reasons: I wanted to join a party that could influence national policies and keep Norway out of the European Union. I'm a member of the Senterpartiet, a centrist party. Secondly, political experience is great for building a resume, which is important for job opportunities in Norway. I've never experienced unfair treatment from political opponents.

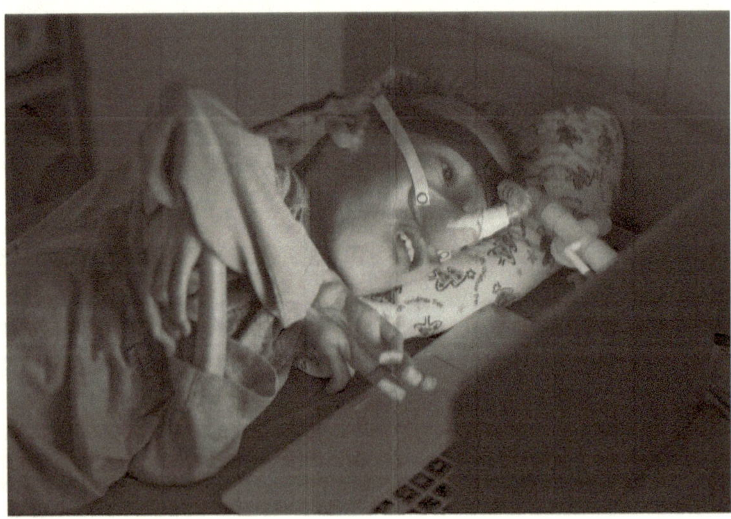

What do you hope to achieve in politics? Does being in the public eye help or hinder you?

I aim to create a better society where everyone, no matter where they live, has equal opportunities. I advocate for farmers to earn fair incomes while producing clean, natural food. I also fight for the right to work for everyone, including people with disabilities. Being in the public eye doesn't bother me; in fact, it helps advance some of my initiatives.

How do you manage life at just 17 kilos? Do your internal organs work normally? Is your condition purely muscular?

I live perfectly fine at 20 kilos now, and as far as I know, all my internal organs function normally. My condition is purely muscular.

Do you think your condition has led you to meet more interesting people or visit unique places?

Not necessarily. I'm a people person and naturally drawn to meeting interesting individuals and exploring exciting places.

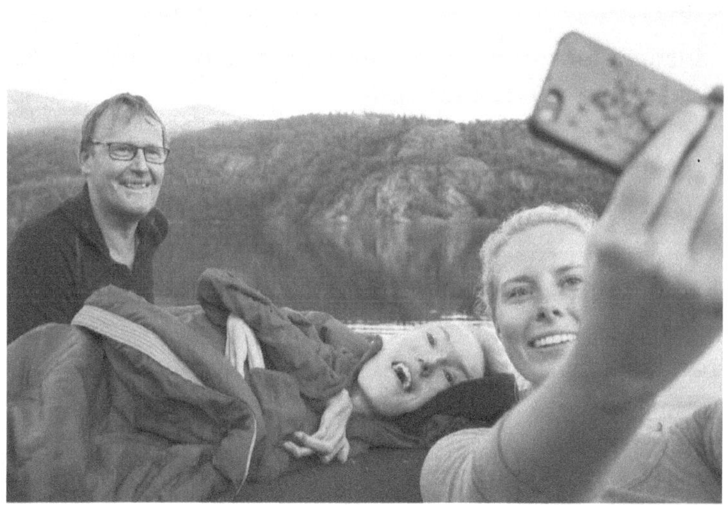

My situation has certainly provided some unique experiences, but I believe I'd still be the same adventurous person without my disability.

Do you believe in destiny or God? Do you feel you've been gifted in areas where others might be average?

I believe in destiny to some extent, but I don't think I'm more gifted than anyone else.

If you could turn back time, would you change your life?

No, I wouldn't change a thing. I'm incredibly happy with my life as it is.

Do you give motivational speeches to inspire others to follow their dreams without boundaries?

Yes, motivational speaking is my side job, and I love it. I travel across Norway and Scandinavia, meeting interesting people and sharing my message, which I believe resonates with many.

You were also a history teacher. How was that experience? Did students respect you, or were there challenges?

I taught for two years and always received respect. I never felt like I wasn't taken seriously.

What does a typical day look like? What does it mean to be CEO of a building company?

I've since changed jobs and am now a department manager for Scandinavia's largest private health company, Aleris. I live in a company apartment in Oslo during the week and spend evenings with friends. On weekends, I usually visit my parents' farm to spend time with my family, especially my young nephew.

2016

VIKTOR KEMETY

How to swim across Lake Balaton without arms

A couple of years ago, we stayed at a hostel in Prague and met a man with no arms in the corridor. We didn't think much of it at the time, but the following week we realized he was a Slovak swimmer. Intrigued, we tracked down the contact details of his coach, Ladislav Struhár, who shared the remarkable story of his prodigy and helped us get our questions answered by Viktor.

Viktor Kemety was born on November 12, 1995, in the Slovakian town of Nove Zámky, the second child of a deeply religious family. Born healthy but without arms, Viktor's right arm was completely missing, while his left side had a 15-cm (6-inch) limb with two fused fingers. Before Viktor, his sister was born with Cerebral Palsy but tragically passed away when Viktor was five. At age eight, Viktor's healthy brother Adam was born, and he tried swimming and tennis. The youngest sibling, Nicola, was also born with Cerebral Palsy and is entirely dependent on their mother for care.

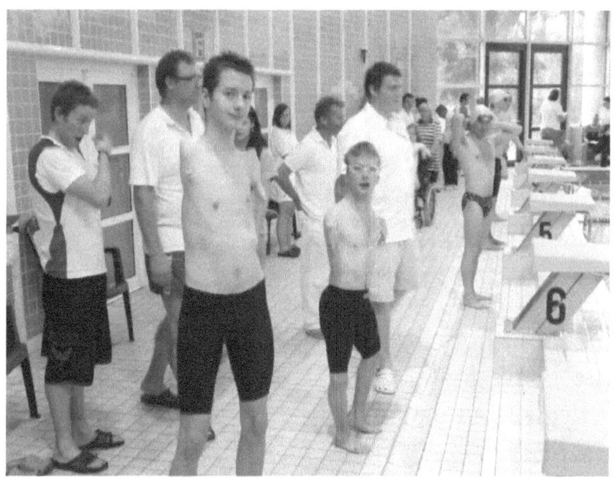

Do you remember the moment you realized you have no hands, that something was missing, and that you'd have to live with it?

As far as I can remember, no one treated me as disabled. I was raised by my grandparents. My grandmother often took me to the garden, where my grandfather would inflate a pool for me to play in. I enjoyed the water, grabbing toys and other items with my feet. Over time, I developed techniques to adapt.

How was life with a disability in your childhood? How did other kids, teachers, and classmates treat you—respectfully or otherwise?

I'd say it was 50:50. Some kids were amazed by what I could do with my feet, while others stared as if I were an alien. Some laughed at me, while others didn't. I attended elementary school like any other able-bodied child but had an assistant to help with certain tasks. I learned to manage on my own. Now, I'm in my third year of secondary school and still have an assistant, but I continue to learn independently. I've earned a certificate in German and have loved English since childhood. Watching movies in German and English helped me a lot.

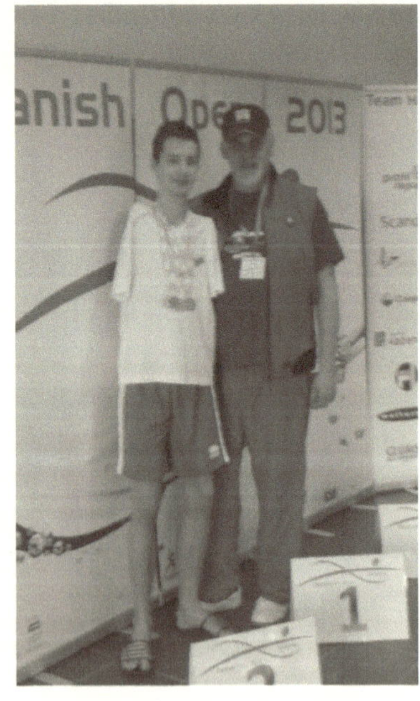

Sorry for the personal questions, but how do you manage basic tasks like eating, hygiene, or using an artificial arm?

These days, you can have anything if you have money. But there's no point in getting an artificial arm that can't connect to nerves or function properly. For example, I know a respected professor missing both wrists who tried artificial ones but had problems like accidentally pinching someone or getting stuck on tram handrails. She eventually stopped using them. As for me, I manage quite well. If food is in front of me, I use my feet to handle utensils and eat faster than most people. I blow my nose by holding a handkerchief with my feet, although I can't always put the tissue back in my pocket. Clothing can be a challenge—putting on jeans or handling buttons and zippers is difficult. I don't tie my shoelaces, and I rely on help for using the bathroom, whether from my mom at home or my coach when traveling.

Do you feel like something is missing, or has your brain adapted to accept your body as it is?

I think others might be better at answering that! I can open doors, scratch my back, wash myself, and even shake hands—

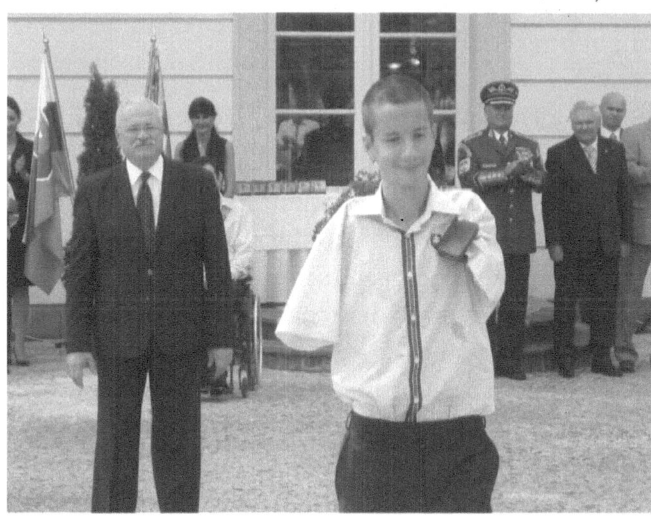

well, shake feet—with people like the prime minister and the British ambassador. My brain has fully adapted to my body, and I function as if it's normal.

Did you have dreams for your life, or was sport always your passion?

My coach makes sure I focus on my education. If I didn't, he'd drop me immediately—I couldn't even work as a garbage collector, as he jokes. I like languages and technology. Last year, I considered teaming up with our blind swimmer, Karina Petrikovičová, in Bratislava, but she had some personal setbacks. She later returned and even won a bronze medal at the World Championships in Canada.

Why swimming? Why not soccer or athletics? Was it because swimming seemed the hardest and you wanted the challenge?

I couldn't run properly for years—my legs tangled, and I kept falling. Now I can run on a treadmill at the gym. Swimming started because a neighbor of my grandfather, a swimming coach, introduced me to it. I had so much fun that I got hooked.

What does an ordinary day look like? Do you swim like other athletes or use a different technique?

You should come and see, haha. I get to the pool, my coach helps me undress, pats my shoulder, and I jump in. I swim using standard techniques like any other swimmer. My routine is quite demanding, especially during the season. I wake up at 5:15 a.m., eat at 5:45, and then train. By 7:30, my coach helps me dress and takes me home. At 8:00, I'm at school studying with an assistant. After lunch at 2:00 p.m., I go home, do homework, and then return to the pool for a second training session. Three times a week, we include dry exercises, followed by two hours of swimming. On weekends, I swim from 8:00 to 10:00 a.m., then relax at home or on my PC.

You swam across Hungary's Lake Balaton. Can you tell us about that?

Yes, I've done it several times. My father encouraged me, and my coach motivated me further, having done it himself. It's a great experience to swim for hours when you have the time.

You've competed in India, Denmark, Germany, Hungary, and Canada. Do you set goals with your coach or simply attend as a Slovak representative?

You forgot the 2012 Paralympic Games in London! I'm also a champion and vice-champion of the Czech Republic. My coach always says, "Work hard, get results, and I'll take you around the world. If not, get lost so I can relax at my cottage." So far, we've worked hard and succeeded, traveling often.

How did you feel about finishing seventh at the London 2012 Paralympic Games?

It began with tough training and qualification. Our initial goal was 11th or 12th place, but after the first round, my coach said, "You're in good form; you can do better." With no pressure, I swam relaxed in the finals and finished seventh. We flew home the next morning due to accommodation shortages and watched the rest of the games on TV.

How are limits set for disabled swimmers to ensure fairness? How does your coach balance pushing you while avoiding unrealistic demands?

The IPC Swimming Rankings categorize swimmers into groups (S1-S10 for various physical disabilities, S11-S13 for visual impairments, and S14 for intellectual disabilities). Officials determine which group a swimmer fits into. Success requires hard work, regardless of ability. My coach knows what's achievable and what's excessive, ensuring I stay within realistic limits.

2013

MARISA HAMAMOTO

We use the wheelchair as a tool to express emotion, not to highlight physical disabilities

Marisa Hamamoto, an American of Japanese descent, loved ballet and dancing. Then, out of the blue, she became paralyzed, and it seemed like her life had come to a standstill. But she didn't give up. Instead, she established *Infinite Flow - An Inclusive Dance Company*, which connects disabled and able-bodied dancers—people of all kinds who love to dance as a form of self-expression. By breaking barriers, Marisa sparked a wave of interest in inclusive dance. Since neither of us are dancers, we were curious about how it all worked and asked Marisa for an interview.

How did you get hooked on dancing, and what drew you to it?

I started dancing when I was six years old, and it quickly turned into an obsession. As one of the few Asian kids at

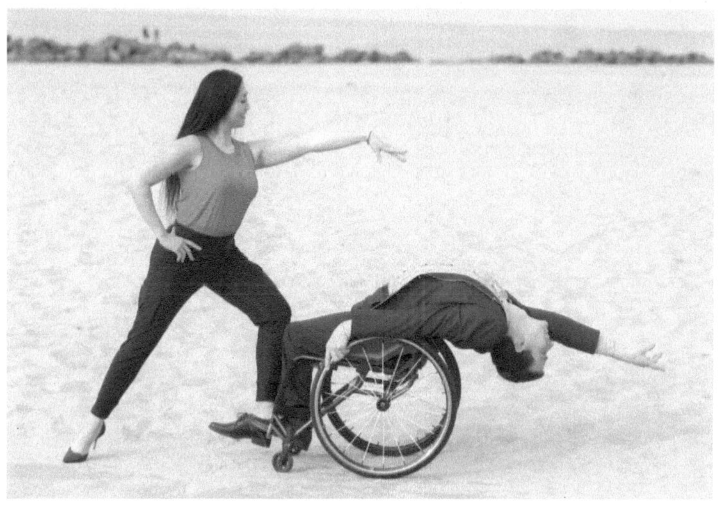

school, I often felt out of place. But in dance lessons, I felt equal to everyone else—accepted and free from judgment. It was my sanctuary. Outside of dance, it was a different story. I looked different, spoke without an accent, and was bullied by classmates who called me a "f***ing immigrant." I had few friends, and my peers often excluded me, which was incredibly painful.

Did dancing become a way for you to gain respect and prove you were just as capable as others?

Yes, it was my only outlet. I dreamed of becoming a ballet dancer, but despite studying at the prestigious Kirov Academy, I wasn't progressing. I kept facing rejection, which was devastating because dance was my only source of happiness. The worst blow came from someone I trusted—a mentor who tried to rape me before I was even 20. It shattered my world. I felt betrayed and utterly alone, with no one to confide in about my pain.

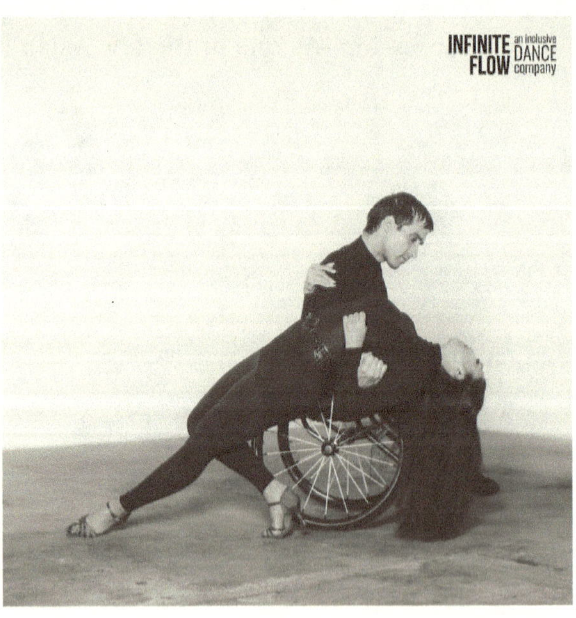

What happened next?

I moved back to Tokyo and enrolled at Keio University, a prestigious school. I continued dancing, holding on to my dream of becoming a ballet dancer. But in 2006, during a training session, I felt my elbows shake, and I collapsed. I was paralyzed from the neck down. The doctors diagnosed a spinal stroke and told me I'd never walk again, let alone dance.

That must have been a devastating diagnosis.

It was, but strangely, it motivated me to fight. Less than eight weeks later, I walked out of the hospital on my own. Yet, inside, I felt empty. The constant rejection, the mocking laughter of my mentor, and his curse for not giving up my dream haunted me for years. It wasn't until four years later that I found hope again.

What gave you hope?

Social dancing. I discovered the joy of moving with a partner. Unlike ballet, which can feel isolating, social dancing is about connection, touch, and shared motion. It brought me back to life. Two years later, I moved to Los Angeles to pursue social dancing in the entertainment industry. But once again, rejection followed me. At auditions, I was told flatly that no one on TV wanted to see an Asian dancer. That's when I decided to create something for people like me—those who are different

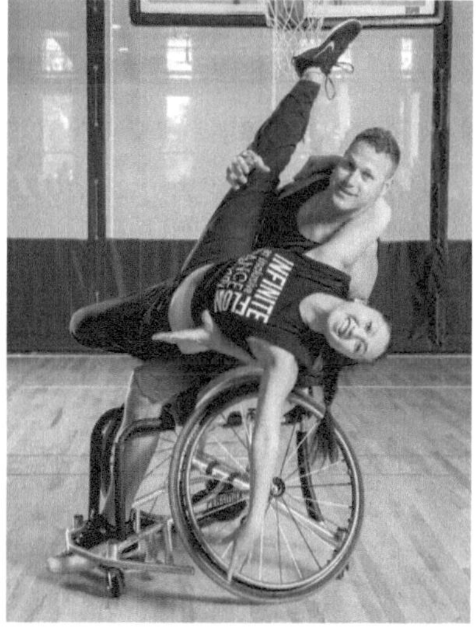

and often underestimated. By chance, I came across the world of dance for disabled people and realized how little attention it received. Millions of disabled individuals in the U.S. would love to dance but lacked opportunities. I decided to change that.

How did you begin working with disabled dancers?

I started searching for a disabled partner but couldn't find one with dance experience. Eventually, I found a disabled athlete who agreed to give it a try. After countless hours of rehearsing, something magical happened—the wheelchair disappeared, and I was simply dancing with a partner. It was a profound moment of mutual joy and connection. I realized dance could be a universal language for people of all backgrounds, abilities, and experiences. This led me to establish *Infinite Flow* to provide a space for those who are often rejected because of their differences but still want to enjoy the beauty of dance and movement. Soon, our company began receiving invitations to perform at corporate events. Suddenly, no one cared that I was a Japanese immigrant. I became a certified social dance instructor, traveling to share my story and inspire others to never give up.

Could you explain the choreography for wheelchair dancing?

I work as the creative director, production manager, and choreographer. But when someone else can do a task better, I happily step aside. Social dances have specific steps, and my job is to adapt them into a language wheelchair users can understand. Each person's body is unique, whether they have all their limbs or none, so I encourage dancers to interpret my instructions in a way that works for their own body.

How do you ensure your choreography is accessible to people with varying levels of disability?

It's inspiring to see how people help each other find solutions. One dancer might excel at something another struggles with, and vice versa, but they inspire each other in the process. We treat all dancers equally, regardless of the severity of their disability. We teach the same techniques to everyone. For instance, if I demonstrate an arm movement, I might ask dancers to replicate it with their legs or another part of their body. This allows them to discover what works best for them and how to complement their partner.

Is it important for choreographers to physically experience what it's like to dance in a wheelchair?

Absolutely. Empathy and understanding are crucial. Many of our choreographers try movements in wheelchairs themselves to understand the experience and translate it effectively for wheelchair users. Dance is about expressing emotions through the body, and everyone feels it differently. Skill levels also vary—some dancers master complex moves with ease, while others struggle. Interestingly, wheelchair dancers often achieve things that able-bodied dancers cannot. For example, a wheelchair dancer can glide across the room with a single push, while an able-bodied dancer might struggle to slide as far on their knees. In our work, the wheelchair becomes a tool for motion and expression, not a symbol of disability.

2019

These are the stories of disabled individuals who achieved extraordinary things and refused to give up on their lives and dreams. But dreams aren't limited to those who face physical challenges—everyone has aspirations, both waking and sleeping, that they strive to fulfill. Here are some inspiring stories of people who turned their dreams into reality. May they serve as motivation for anyone who feels like giving up before even starting.

DREAMS THAT BECAME REALITY

HAL NEEDHAM

One fulfilled American dream

America is often called the land of unlimited possibilities. While we won't delve into that claim, it's worth noting that another great nation once declared, "Tomorrow means yesterday." Every American has their own version of the "American Dream," which often centers around financial success and the idea that even the poorest person can become a millionaire. We won't argue the merits of this idea, as many people in our own country have also risen from poverty to wealth—though we might question how fair their path to success always was.

The story of Hal Needham, however, is a classic example of someone achieving the American Dream through sheer dedication, hard work, and determination. Born in 1931, Hal rose from humble beginnings to become one of the most renowned figures in Hollywood, transitioning from stuntman to actor to director. Along the way, he achieved several notable firsts: he was the first to test an airbag, the first director to include unused scenes in the credits, and the owner of the first car to reach supersonic speed. Conducting this interview took seven months, but the resulting story is worth the effort.

What sort of childhood did you have? The 1930s weren't exactly the happiest time in America, were they?

I grew up during the Great Depression in a poor part of Arkansas. There were seven of us, and my father left my mom when I was born. My stepfather, though a crook, never hit me and made me tough. He earned just $400 a year, so I hunted rabbits and squirrels to put meat on the table. I didn't go to school much—just eight grades—and my clothes came from the Salvation Army. When I was ten, we moved to St. Louis during WWII because my father got a factory job making weapons. That was the first time I saw a city, a car, or a cinema. Since I'd been working from a young age, I got a job in a shop. Later, when I left school, I worked cutting branches on high streets for $1 an hour. I never feared heights.

Did you have any idea what you wanted to do with your life?

Not really. I spent three years chopping branches, wondering what was next. Then I visited an Army recruitment center and was impressed by what they offered. The Korean War was underway, and I saw it as a challenge. I trained with the Rangers, learned to operate light and heavy weapons, and trained in desert and arctic conditions. After being discharged in 1954, I returned to tree work, where I met a paratrooper working in TV. He invited me to join a dangerous stunt: jumping from a plane onto a galloping horse. I loved it and asked him to call me for future stunts. That's how I became a stuntman.

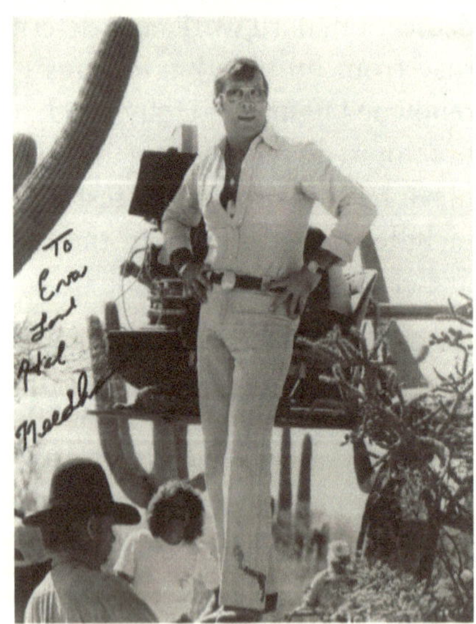

Do you remember your first real movie?

Yes, it was *The Spirit of St. Louis*, starring James Stewart as Charles Lindbergh and directed by Billy Wilder. I had to stand on the lower wing of a biplane and transfer to the undercarriage of another plane mid-flight. I earned $1,000 per take, so I didn't mind the repeats. I made more money during that shoot than I ever had before. After six weeks, I knew my future—I was going to be a Hollywood stuntman.

Starting from scratch must have been tough, wasn't it?

It wasn't easy, but I wasn't afraid of hard work. Luck helped, too. I lived near the studios in California, and most stuntmen around me went to work on John Wayne's movie *The Alamo.* Since I wasn't chosen, I ended up being one of the few stuntmen left in town. While they were away for four months, I was so busy that I sometimes worked on five films in one day. It boosted both my income and my reputation. I doubled for many actors, including Burt Reynolds, who became a close friend. Directors noticed my willingness to do anything, and I became a key stuntman for Andrew McLaglen.

How did you land film jobs?

There were several ways. You could work for a stunt coordinator who would call when needed. You could also check industry papers like *The Hollywood Reporter* for information about ongoing productions. I took a different approach—I never refused a job. Soon, productions began calling me directly. Once I made some money, I bought 250 horses, built barns, and trained them for rental to studios. This meant I worked on movies, got paid, and earned extra income from my horses. James Stewart, for example, rode a horse named Pie in all his films.

Were there any tragic or fatal accidents during filming?

Safety is always a priority, with strong trade unions overseeing procedures. That said, there are risks. I've broken 56 bones and fractured my back twice. For *Kings of the Sun,* we wore metal boards under our costumes while real arrows with metal tips were shot at us—still, it wasn't pleasant. In *Little Big Man*, we used arrows with rubber tips, but one stuntman lost an eye. We do everything possible to minimize risks, but danger is part of the job.

How did you transition into directing?

It was a gradual process. As I gained experience, directors asked me to coordinate stunts or serve as a second-unit assistant director. I prepared scenes, positioned actors, set up cameras, and shot sequences without main stars. These opportunities taught me everything I needed to know about directing.

What kind of director were you?

I valued camaraderie. Unlike some directors, I let the crew watch the daily footage so they knew where we stood. A happy crew works harder. I ate the same food as everyone else and often paid the bar tab after we wrapped. For my first film, I invited my devout mother to pray for the crew and the movie's success. The whole crew joined in, and it became a tradition for all my films.

How many projects did you complete as a stuntman, actor, and director?

I worked as a stuntman in 4,100 TV shows and 310 movies, acted in 50 films, and directed 10 features. My first movie as a director, *Smokey and the Bandit*, had a $4.3 million budget, with $1 million going to Burt Reynolds. It grossed $300 million, so a sequel was inevitable. Altogether, my films cost $110 million to make and earned $1.4 billion.

You were among the first directors to show unused sequences during credits and use product placement. How did that start?

Unused scenes debuted in *Hooper*. We had so much leftover footage, and I thought it would be a shame not to use it. As for product placement, it tied into my NASCAR team sponsorships. For *Smokey and the Bandit*, I pitched Pontiac on a car-themed film. They gave me six cars. After the movie's success, demand for that model skyrocketed. For the sequel, Pontiac asked how many cars I needed—I got 70 and wrecked them all.

You were the world's highest-paid stuntman. Why?

I focused on getting stunts right on the first take. I charged $5,000 per stunt, which was cheaper than hiring someone less experienced who might need multiple takes. For particularly dangerous stunts, like testing airbags at high speeds, I asked for $25,000—and got it.

What do you think of modern films with CGI?

It's a shame that the old ways of filmmaking are disappearing. In my day, I managed 1,200 real horses for a scene. Now, CGI generates herds of 5,000. While technology has its place, people will always be essential to filmmaking.

2013 P.S. Hal Needham sadly passed away from cancer on October 25, 2013.

2013

HOMER HICKAM

I wanted to be part of a big adventure

When we watched the movie *October Sky* a few years ago, we were captivated by the story of a boy who followed his dreams and reached for the stars. We discovered that the author of the book behind the film, Homer Hickam, was still alive, so we wrote to him for an autograph. His reply came quickly, with the note: "Aim High." About a decade later, we revisited the life of Homer Hickam, taking a deeper interest in the man whose bestseller has inspired countless people worldwide to pursue their dreams.

Hickam, born in 1943, has a remarkable range of experiences: he served in Vietnam, became an expert diving instructor, and worked at NASA training space crews for their missions. Despite his accomplishments, he shows no sign of slowing down. Encouraged by his advice to "Aim High," we reached out for an interview. To our surprise, his response came within two weeks, and it was as fascinating as we'd hoped.

You fought in Vietnam. Did you volunteer, or were you drafted? Can boot camp really prepare a young man for war?

To Eva –
Aim high!
Homer Hickam

I served in Vietnam for a year, from 1967 to 1968, which included the Tet Offensive—a challenging year for American forces. I volunteered and trained at Fort Leonard Wood in Missouri. I was commissioned as a First Lieutenant in the 4th Infantry Division. While training helps, combat is entirely different. Still, I did the best I could.

Were you turned into a "killing machine" as some claimed, or were you an ordinary soldier with a heart and conscience?

I was never a killing machine, nor were most of the soldiers I knew. Many were draftees doing their best. I was in an armored unit, tasked mainly with protecting truck convoys. I also participated in medical missions to help local communities. We respected the Vietnamese people and even our enemy, though we had to fight them—and fight we did.

Did your experiences in Vietnam inspire you to write a book?

I haven't written about Vietnam, and I'm not sure I ever will. It just doesn't call to me as a subject, at least not yet.

Where did you serve in Vietnam? Were you wounded, and did you lose anyone close to you?

I served near Pleiku in the Central Highlands. I was wounded, possibly by friendly fire—there's no way to know for sure. Sadly, I did lose friends who didn't make it. Those memories stay with you. I occasionally encountered North Vietnamese soldiers, though face-to-face combat was rare.

In the 1950s, you had your finger on the button to launch rockets into space. In Vietnam, it was on the trigger to kill. Did you reflect on the contrast?

All I can say is that I did my duty. I preferred my work in peacetime.

Your first book, *Torpedo Junction*, took 15 years to complete and focused on submarine warfare during WWII. Why choose that topic instead of your experiences as a diver?

Writing *Torpedo Junction* became an obsession. Once I start something, I have to see it through, no matter how long it takes. I'm glad I did. The book was recently optioned for a movie, which is exciting. I did write a scuba diving novel years ago, but it needs significant revision before it can be published. Maybe someday!

You dreamed of rockets and space as a student and later worked for NASA, training astronauts. Did you consider becoming an astronaut yourself?

By the time I joined NASA at 38, I was already focused on other things, including my writing career and scuba instruction. I didn't seriously consider becoming an astronaut—I was just happy to train them.

In the 1950s and 1960s, astronauts were seen as heroes, almost like characters from Jules Verne novels. Do you think that's changed today?

It still takes tremendous courage to ride a rocket, so astronauts should always be considered heroic. Public interest, however, fluctuates. My main hope is for humanity to expand into space, particularly to the moon, where there's much work to be done, including mining.

The movie *October Sky* portrays your father as hard and unfriendly and your teacher as a major motivator. How accurate is that depiction?

The movie isn't entirely accurate—most films "based on a true story" take liberties. I wrote a book, *From Rocket Boys to October Sky*, to explain the differences. My parents weren't as they were depicted, I never met Wernher von Braun, and I didn't quit school to work in the mine. The real story is in *Rocket Boys*.

Do you remember how you felt when you first saw Sputnik in the sky?

When I saw Sputnik, it was as if God himself were flying across the sky in a golden chariot. It was awe-inspiring and set me on the path to becoming part of the space adventure.

Are you still in touch with the other Rocket Boys?

Yes, I'm in touch with the four living Rocket Boys. We gather annually at the Rocket Boys Festival in West Virginia.

When you speak to audiences, do you encourage them to follow their dreams?

I don't always talk about *Rocket Boys* since I've written many other books, but I often encourage young people—especially in poor communities—to find a passion, make a plan, and persevere. I call it the three P's of success. Dreaming is essential, but so is balancing responsibility to one's family. Fortunately, my family ultimately supported me in everything I did.

Is it true that your wife is your first reader and critic?

Yes, she's an excellent editor, and I value her feedback. Still, there are times when I have to trust my instincts and go in a different direction.

You write across genres. Is that to avoid being typecast?

Exactly. Moving between genres helps me stay creative and avoid being pigeonholed. Some writers get caught up in publisher deadlines, rushing out books that may not be their best work. That can tarnish their reputation. I try to stay outside that system and focus on quality.

Did you always want to write, or did it come later?

As a student, I enjoyed literature and disliked technical subjects. If Sputnik hadn't launched, I might have become a university professor. But Sputnik opened the door to an entirely new adventure for me.

Do you think people read less today, preferring the internet or e-books?

Yes, people probably read less now, which motivates me to write books they'll truly enjoy. My latest book, *Carrying Albert Home*, has already been well-received by readers, and that brings me joy.

2016

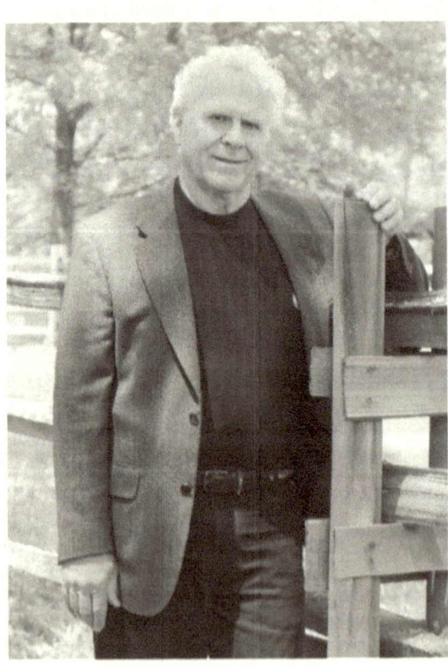

IVAN RINGEL

With animals you know the score with, it doesn´t work with people that way

Ivan Ringel (1947) always loved animals and dreamed of working with them. For eleven years, he worked as an animal orderly at the renowned Czech zoo in Dvůr Králové nad Labem, where he first stepped into a tiger's cage. In 1972, he left the zoo and, with his wife Olga, joined the Czech Circus, becoming one of the world's top lion tamers. His first show was a groundbreaking act featuring eleven different big cats, and he later staged another world-first: performing with a hippopotamus named David alongside tigers. Ivan became a star in the Moscow circus scene, with his pinnacle act being the daring moment he put his head inside a tiger's jaws.

In 2008, Ivan and Olga established a small home zoo, *Ringeland*, in Habrkovice near Kutná Hora, housing tigers and David the hippopotamus. He also owns Europe's largest collection of circus posters. Since Olga's death, his animals have been his sole companions. Sitting in his office—next to the tiger cages, surrounded by photographs of his glory days—it felt like stepping into a magical world reminiscent of Charlie Chaplin's *Limelight* and *The Circus*. Ivan shared his remarkable story with us, rewinding the reel 50 years to a life filled with passion and danger.

You worked with Josef Vágner at Dvůr Králové Zoo, who overcame great odds to establish the Czech Safari. What was it like working with him?

It's a tragic flaw in Czech society: envy and resentment of success. We struggle to celebrate others' achievements. Josef Vágner was a once-in-a-century figure, and my best years were spent working alongside him. Building the Safari Zoo with limited support and funding took an extraordinary vision and determination, and he had both. He would finish his official work at 4 p.m., change into overalls, and shovel alongside us.

We younger workers were inspired by his dedication and gladly helped him without expecting pay. I loved it so much that when I returned from two years of national service, I slept in the barn on hay for two years. Vágner's dream of creating the Safari Zoo allowed me to fulfill my own dream of working with animals. It was a tragedy when, during his time in India, 44 giraffes in his zoo were shot. To this day, I believe it was orchestrated by the Czech secret police.

Why do you think someone becomes an animal trainer? Is it about asserting dominance over creatures?

No, not at all. We are not "lords" over animals—we're more like the cancer of this planet, its greatest threat. Animals possess superior senses. For example, an elephant can sense a storm 500 kilometers away, while humans remain clueless.

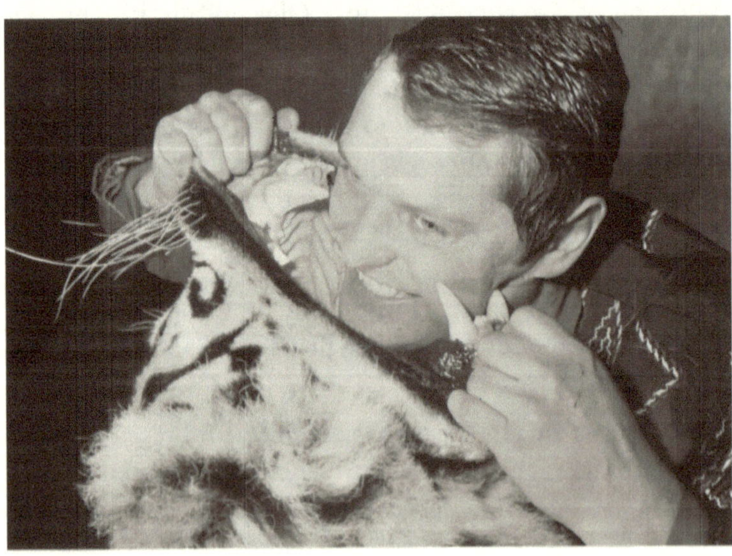

In the ring, you become part of their world. I've had up to 15 animals around me during a show—it's a magical experience. Before the war, German circuses could hold 10,000 people and featured 100 lions and 90 polar bears. It was a different time, with no TV or radio to compete with.

When training lions and tigers, do you need to establish trust while also showing courage? How long before you start actual training?

You must always enter and leave the ring as the winner. Animals can sense fear or anger. Each animal has its own "running distance"—the space it allows you to approach. For some, it's two meters; for others, just a few feet. Out of 100 animals, only a rare few will allow close contact, like letting you embrace them or put your head in their jaws. Crossing that distance prematurely triggers a warning, like roaring. It's a way of saying, "Don't come closer, or you're in trouble."

Tamers often speak to animals during performances. Is this to maintain control or reassure them?

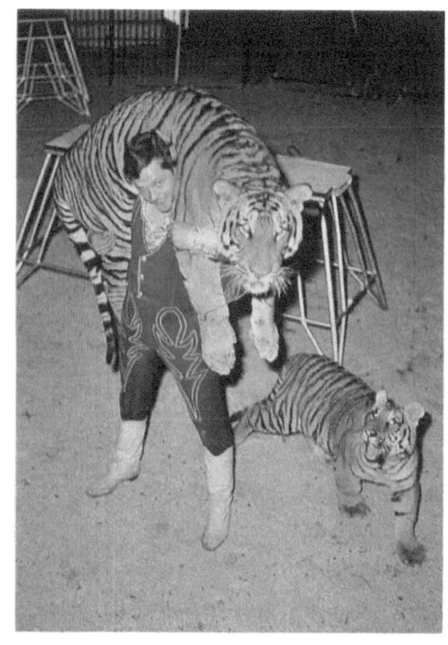

It's both. Speaking softly reassures the animal, while raising your voice signals something is wrong. Rewards play a key role—I prefer treats over whips. If you strike a tiger, it will remember and eventually retaliate. Tigers are incredibly powerful, with razor-sharp claws up to 12 cm long. A year in the ring teaches you more than a university degree. You learn about animals, life, and yourself. I've often lain beneath a tiger, anticipating an attack, yet I've survived every encounter. There must be something extra—a spark—that's kept me alive.

How did you gain the confidence to perform the head-in-the-jaws trick? How long did it take to train for it?

This trick is rare today, but my sons and I performed it as a "family jewel." In my lifetime, I trained over 90 tigers but only performed the trick with two of them. It's the ultimate test of trust between trainer and animal. I practiced every day. At the Moscow circus, I trained tigers from 8 a.m. and performed five shows daily.

At the climax of the act, the band would stop playing, and I'd cross the tiger's "running distance." The tiger would roar as I approached, open its jaws, and let me place my head inside. The audience would go wild.

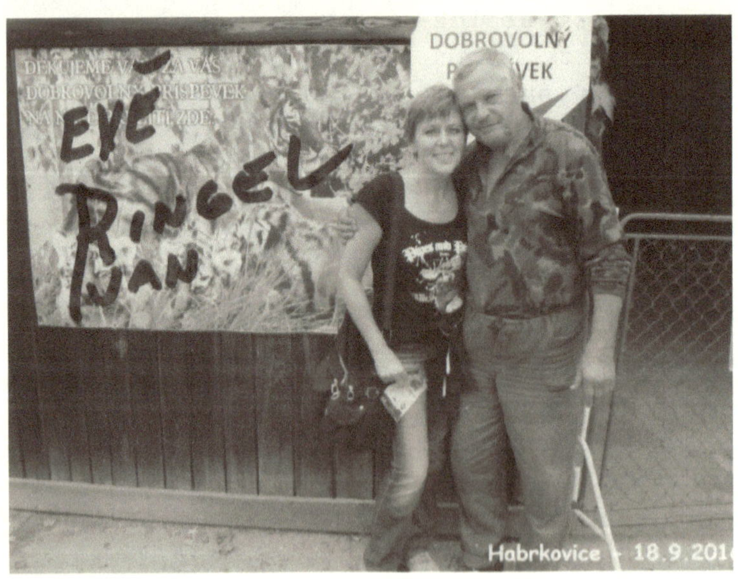

Do you think the tiger enjoys the act?

I don't know. But to perform it, you must fully trust the tiger. You place your head deep inside, grit your teeth, and hope your instincts are right.

The circus life is grueling. Why do people endure such hard work for applause?

If I could have worked with animals at the zoo, I never would have left. But I had to sign a paper agreeing not to enter cages, so I joined the circus. The work is relentless, and death is a daily risk, but those ten minutes in front of an audience are worth it. The adrenaline, the connection—it's addictive. My wife Olga stood by me through it all, and for that, I am deeply grateful.

The Soviet Union was a circus superpower. What was it like working there?

The Soviet circus was prestigious, like performing at Prague National Theatre. The venues were luxurious, and shows sold out months in advance. Each performer had assistants, but I worked alone, which made me stand out. I spent every moment with my animals, feeding and cleaning them. This constant contact built trust and allowed me to understand their moods, health, and capabilities.

Can you describe a moment when things went wrong during a performance?

In Astrachan, I opened a tiger's jaw and found it full of blood from boils—it lashed out, biting me. I fell under another tiger and thought I was done for. My brain went into overdrive, and I managed to stand despite bleeding heavily. The tiger began licking the blood, which only heightened the tension. But the act finished, and the audience erupted in applause. Moments like that are victories earned through sweat, blood, and trust.

In 2008, you founded *Ringeland*. Was it to settle down while staying close to animals?

Yes. I'll care for these animals until my last breath. Our hippopotamus, David, was devoted to Olga, and after her passing, he listens only to me. If I die before him, it's agreed he will be euthanized, as no one else could manage him safely. Animals are my family. Unlike people, animals are honest—what you see is what you get.

Looking back, are you satisfied with your life and achievements?

I've lived a rich life and achieved much, including unique shows with tigers and a hippo. However, circus management often treated me poorly, and I regret not being able to save the elephants after the Velvet Revolution. That failure will haunt me forever.

2017

MARGARET KEANE

"All Our Abilities and Talents Are Gifts"

In the 1950s and 60s, paintings of children with big, sad eyes signed "Keane" became a global sensation. These images adorned the walls of Hollywood stars like Kim Novak and Joan Crawford, as well as anyone who wanted to be "in" and could afford them. They even earned a mention in Woody Allen's brilliant film *Sleeper*. The market was flooded with prints, postcards, and even a dedicated gallery showcasing the works.

The paintings were promoted by Walter Keane, a mediocre artist but a masterful businessman with charisma to spare. He lived lavishly, graced the cover of *Life* magazine, and compared himself to Michelangelo on talk shows. But in 1970, the façade crumbled. The true artist behind the paintings was Walter's wife, Margaret, whom he had locked in a room, forcing her to paint for up to 16 hours a day. The truth led to a court case, and Margaret was awarded $4 million in damages, though she never saw a dime, as Walter squandered the money.

Interest in Margaret's work waned until Tim Burton reignited it with his 2014 biopic *Big Eyes*, starring Amy Adams and Christoph Waltz. Inspired by her story, we wrote to Margaret, then 90 years old and still painting daily. To our delight, she responded within a month.

What was it like to see yourself portrayed on screen?

I was in shock for two days after watching the film. Seeing everything I went through from an outside perspective was overwhelming. Amy Adams was incredibly precise in her performance. Before filming, she spent time with me to learn how I hold a brush and apply paint to a canvas, so the movie was very accurate.

How did the movie come about? Did Tim Burton approach you directly?

Tim had been a fan of my paintings for years and had bought some before the film was even conceived. Later, when interest in my story grew and a book about me was published, it caught his attention. That's when the idea for the movie took shape.

Did you have input into the script or casting?

Yes, I contributed to the script, and they often discussed it with me to ensure accuracy. I didn't have any say in the casting, though. They paid me for my input and invited me to the premiere, where I met Amy Adams again and congratulated her on her performance. Watching her portray my experiences was traumatic but also rewarding, as it reminded me how beautifully the film was made.

Did the film renew interest in your work after years of anonymity?

Oh, absolutely. Suddenly, everyone wanted to write about me and hear my story, and a new wave of interest in my paintings began. However, I no longer paint sad eyes—I focus on happy faces now.

Walter claimed his inspiration came from children he saw in post-war Germany. Why were their eyes so sad?

Those eyes reflected my inner feelings—emotions I couldn't express and wasn't allowed to share. I was like a prisoner, and those sad eyes became my only outlet for my emotions.

Didn't you feel like a robot, painting to order? Did it make you hate those paintings?

No, I never stopped loving my paintings. Pouring my emotions into them helped me survive the hardship.

Why didn't you ever say "no" to your husband?

I was scared. I feared that if I left him, I wouldn't be able to support myself or my daughter. Walter constantly reminded me that no one would buy my paintings without him, claiming he had the magic to sell them. He mentally tortured me, breaking my confidence. He even threatened me, saying he had Mafia connections and would harm me if I ever spoke out. When he was away, he called me hourly to ensure I was painting and hadn't left the house. He lived lavishly while I worked endlessly.

Did you receive any money for the paintings?

No, Walter handled all the deals and took the money. He became a celebrity while I worked in silence. Even after winning the court case, I never saw the $4 million in compensation because he had spent it all and died in poverty, forgotten.

Is it true that meeting Jehovah's Witnesses gave you the strength to tell the truth?

Yes. They helped me realize I could no longer lie to anyone. I found the strength to speak the truth I had suppressed for years, and in doing so, I destroyed Walter's facade. I regret letting it go on for so long, but at that moment, I reclaimed my voice.

Do you feel your life was wasted working for your husband? Would you live differently if given another chance?

I don't feel my entire life was wasted. I did the best I could under the circumstances. If I had a second chance, I wouldn't lie or let things go so far—that was my mistake.

Do you know how many paintings you created? Do you see people's souls through their eyes?

I have no idea how many paintings I've made—countless, for sure. The eyes are part of the brain, and they reveal so much about a person.

Do you believe painting is a gift, or can it be learned through hard work?

It's definitely a gift. All our talents and abilities are gifts from our Creator. When we use them with goodwill and acknowledge His name, we are blessed beyond imagination. I owe my ability to paint to Jehovah, the source of all creativity. The world around us is filled with His artistic acts, created for our inspiration and well-being. The fact that a movie was made about my life is one of the greatest blessings I've ever received.

P.S. Margaret Keane sadly passed away on June 26, 2022.
2017

MICHAEL COATS

Per Ardua ad Astra

Michael Lloyd Coats was born on January 16, 1946. After attending Ramona High School in California, he entered the United States Naval Academy, where he earned his first degree. In September 1969, he joined the Navy Air Force, and after completing training, he served aboard the USS *Kitty Hawk* from August 1970 to September 1972, flying 315 combat missions during the Vietnam War.

After the war, he pursued advanced pilot training and became a test pilot for the A-7 and A-4 aircraft. Between 1976 and 1977, he worked as a test pilot in the Navy, which led to his selection as an astronaut for NASA in August 1979.

Coats' first space mission was in 1984 with the STS-41-D crew, marking the maiden flight of the Space Shuttle *Discovery*. The launch faced significant challenges, including three aborted attempts in two months and even a fire. In February 1985, he was slated to command STS-61-H, but the mission was canceled following the *Challenger* tragedy. His next mission came five years later with STS-29, and he returned to space a third time in 1991 as commander of STS-39. In total, Coats spent 463 hours in space before transitioning to the civilian sector.

After 14 years in private industry, he returned to NASA in 2005 as the Director of the Johnson Space Center, a role he held until his retirement in 2012. Intrigued by his experiences as an astronaut and leader, we reached out to Mr. Coats, who graciously answered our questions within a few months.

Did you dream of becoming an astronaut as a child, and were the first space explorers your heroes?

The Gemini and Apollo astronauts were certainly my heroes, but as a child, my dream was to become a Navy pilot and land planes on aircraft carriers. Fortunately, my eyesight was good enough to fulfill that dream. Becoming an astronaut was beyond my wildest imagination.

In 1968, you became a pilot and soon after served in Vietnam. Were you young and hungry for adventure?

Earning my Naval Aviator wings and landing on aircraft carriers was a significant achievement, but I wasn't "hungry" for war. The Vietnam War was a reality, and I was fortunate to survive all my missions—many of my friends did not.

You studied at three technical universities. Was this to gain as much experience as possible, or did it naturally lead to NASA?

I earned two Master's degrees because I was interested in the subjects and believed they would benefit my Navy career. At the time, I hadn't considered applying to the astronaut program. In hindsight, the degrees likely weren't a major factor in my selection as an astronaut.

What drives people to become astronauts today? It seems the public isn't as engaged as in the days of Gagarin, or Glenn.

I was an instructor at the Naval Test Pilot School in 1977 when Apollo astronauts John Young and Vance Brand encouraged test pilots to apply for the first Space Shuttle astronaut class. My wife wasn't keen on the idea, and I was content with my Navy career, but I decided to apply "just to see how far I'd get." When I visited Johnson Space Center for interviews and physical exams,

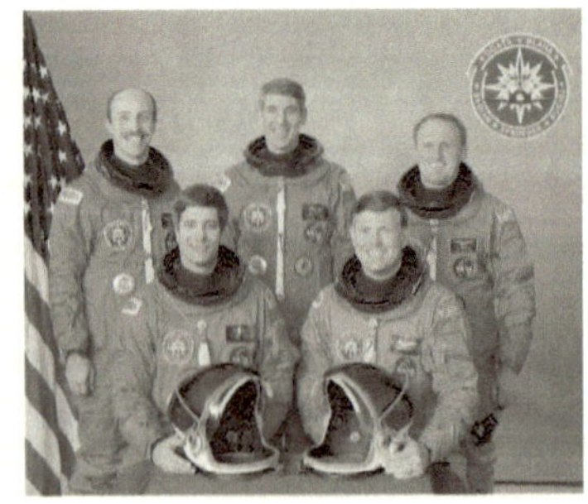

I was inspired by the dedicated people at NASA and hoped to join them. Fortunately, I was selected.

During your service on the USS *Kitty Hawk*, you flew 315 combat missions. What did that entail?

The Navy didn't allow napalm to be flown from aircraft carriers. My missions involved bombing bridges and trucks to disrupt supply routes and dropping mines in Haiphong Harbor to block shipments to North Vietnam. We avoided strafing civilians, and many American pilots lost their lives trying to minimize civilian casualties.

You joined NASA in 1979 but didn't fly until 1984. What did you do during those years?

After selection, astronaut training lasted three years. Once we were assigned to a mission, we trained specifically for that flight.

Your first mission on *Discovery* faced three aborted launches and a fire. How did you stay calm during such challenges?

Crews train extensively and are eager to fly, but no one

Michael L. Coats

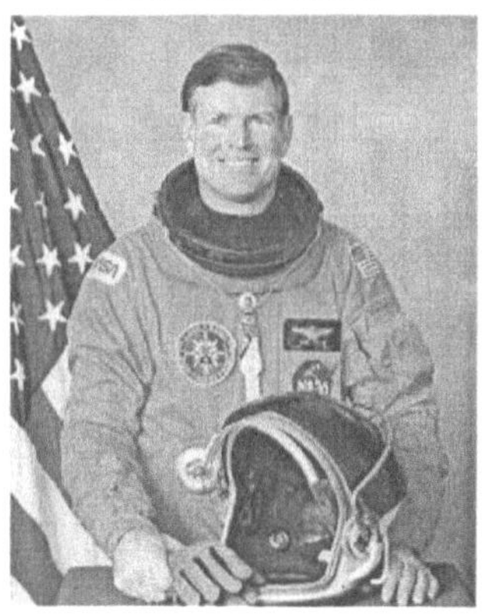

To EVA ~
Dare to Dream!
Mike Coats

wants to launch unless the spacecraft is 100% ready. The fire got our attention, but we trusted the ground crews at Kennedy Space Center, and they resolved the issue effectively.

Your second mission was canceled after the *Challenger* disaster. What was it like at NASA during that time?

After *Challenger*, we were committed to finding the cause of the accident and ensuring it wouldn't happen again. Following a period of mourning, we worked hard to make the Shuttle safer while supporting the families of our lost friends.

Before your second mission, post-*Challenger*, were you apprehensive? Did you pray during the launch?

NASA trains crews to handle every manageable emergency. Spaceflight is inherently risky, but we focus on what we can control. As the first explorers likely said, "The only way to be perfectly safe is to stay home." A few prayers don't hurt, though.

Why did you leave NASA after three missions?

After my third mission, my wife said, "That's enough." She en-

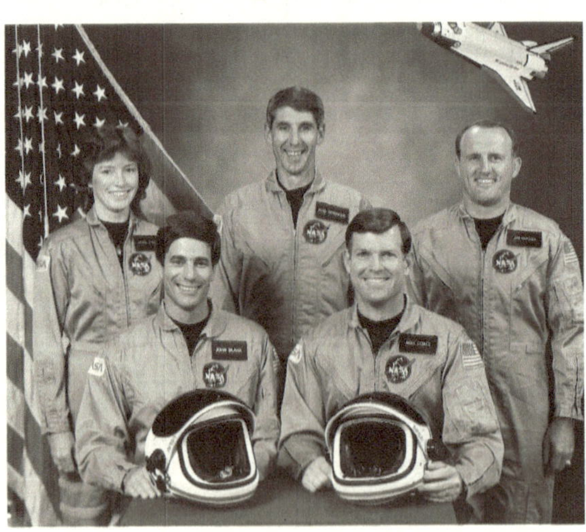

dured the pad abort and lost friends in *Challenger*, so asking for more missions would have been selfish. Fortunately, I received several private-sector offers and was curious to explore that world.

With no Space Shuttles and reliance on Russian rockets, do you think NASA plays second fiddle to Russia?

It's frustrating to pay Russia over $80 million per seat for ISS transportation—about half a billion dollars annually that supports Russian engineers and scientists. Hopefully, Boeing's Starliner and SpaceX's Dragon will soon carry our astronauts, allowing us to invest in our own people.

Was there a moment in space when you felt it was all worth it? Were there any close calls that made you reconsider flying?

The breathtaking view of Earth from orbit made every challenge worthwhile. Seeing the vibrant greens, whites, blues, and browns of our planet alongside the blackness of space is unforgettable. It reinforced my gratitude for the opportunity to be there.

Did spaceflight change your perspective on life?

Yes. Observing the beauty of Earth and the starkness of space made me appreciate our planet deeply. It strengthened my belief that we must protect "Spaceship Earth" for future generations.

As Director of the Johnson Space Center, what were your responsibilities?

I led the JSC, home to the astronaut training facilities and Mission Control. With 3,000 civil servants and 10,000 contractors, my role was to support them in any way possible, ensuring human spaceflight missions were successful. 2017

PATCH ADAMS

How to Change the World for the Better

Patch Adams was born on May 28, 1945. He became a doctor in 1971 and spent many years in pediatric practice before founding the Gesundheit Institute. His guiding principle has always been: *"Medical treatment should be a human-loving process, not a business transaction."* He believes the health of an individual is intrinsically linked to the health of their family, community, and the world.

Between 1971 and 1983, Patch treated 15,000 patients for free. In 1983, he stopped house visits to focus on raising funds for his dream hospital—a 40-bed facility with its own theater, garden, gym, and workshops. He also became a professional clown, traveling the globe to promote peace and joy. His work inspired the practice of "clown doctors" in hospitals worldwide, bringing smiles to young patients.

The movie *Patch Adams*, starring Robin Williams, moved audiences with the story of a doctor navigating a tough, profit-driven medical system with kindness, humor, and humanity.

We wrote to Patch Adams, and he responded with a handwritten letter. Over five years, we exchanged dozens of letters and became friends. He even shared his love of stamp collecting with us. Patch Adams is a remarkable person, and if there were more like him, the world would undoubtedly be a better place.

How did you find a different path in life than most people?

When I was 16, I faced a life crisis. My uncle shot himself, I was hospitalized with ulcers, and I attempted suicide, ending up in a mental hospital. I shared a room with someone worse off than me, which shifted my focus. I started making jokes to cheer him up, and I forgot my own problems. That's when I realized humor could heal.

Friends visiting me would lift my spirits, and I noticed that laughter and connection improved my condition. I concluded that *friendship* is the ultimate healing force. By 18, I was asking myself how to tackle the world's problems. I realized everyone suffers in some way—issues with life, parents, jobs—and most people are locked in their suffering. We rarely celebrate the miracle of being alive.

When I sat with patients, they could talk endlessly about their suffering but struggled to describe their joys. I realized society programs people to dwell on pain and negativity. I've spent my life trying to teach others that it's better to focus on joy, happiness, and love. Even when patients were near death, I reminded them, "*You're still alive—enjoy the time you have left.*"

A wise person once said the most important thing is to serve others and be kind-hearted. Do you agree?

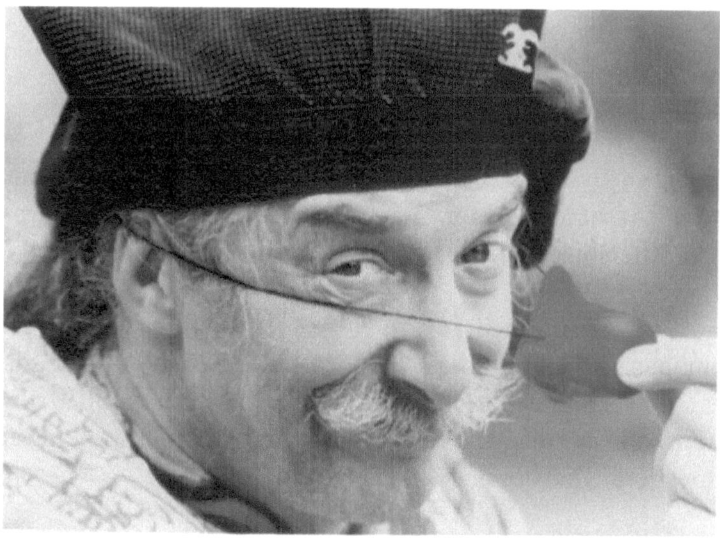

Absolutely. The greatest gift is giving to others. Look at Mother Teresa or Gandhi—they cared deeply for others and inspired nearly religious devotion. Joy is so rare that when we find a truly joyous person, we regard them with suspicion or awe. Perhaps figures like Buddha or Jesus were revered because they loved life more deeply than anyone else.

What advice would you give to the younger generation?

If you want to change the world, start by being happy. Celebrate your life and let it flow freely. Most importantly, follow your dreams. Be grateful you're alive, and ask yourself, "*Who can I help today?*" When people complain endlessly, I tell them, "*Stop moaning and live your life with purpose.*"

What are your core life principles?

Friendship, friendship, and more friendship. We need each other far more than we realize. Use your imagination, live in the moment, and devote your life to making the world better. Don't waste a single day.

Healthcare today is big business. Can anything be done about that?

Money and power dominate modern values. People are lonely and bored, so they seek meaning in material possessions. To me, it's unethical for medicine to be treated as a business. A sick person can never feel they belong somewhere if they're viewed as a client.

At the Gesundheit Institute, we treat people for free and emphasize the bond between doctor and patient. Friendship is a powerful healing force. When patients trust that I truly want to help them, they let me into their lives in ways I never imagined. That connection is magical.

You built your dream hospital. How does it differ from others?

Hospitals are often sad places. Staff rarely exude joy, and patients are left feeling isolated and fearful. At our institute, we aim to create a happy, supportive environment.

We start with a four-hour intake interview to understand the patient's story. Families are included in the process, and they participate in activities like gardening, cooking, or workshops while their loved one undergoes therapy. Volunteers play a big role, helping with anything from growing vegetables to playing music.

Patients feel a sense of responsibility and independence, which is part of the healing process. Our goal is for patients to leave not just healthier but also happier. Many stay in touch and return for yearly visits, remaining our friends.

Your hospital treats patients for free. How do you sustain it financially?

We keep costs low by living as a community and relying on part-time jobs, donations, and practical gifts. Over 20 years, I worked multiple jobs to save $900,000 for the hospital. People donate everything from money to hospital equipment, food, furniture, and even their time.

It takes sacrifice and hard work to realize a dream, but it's worth it.

Why did you name your institute Gesundheit?

Gesundheit means "good health." It's meant to make people laugh, which is central to our therapy. While work is important, we approach it with joy and humor—not the grim seriousness of *Arbeit macht frei.*

How do you approach death and terminal patients?

When I was a child, my father died alone in a hospital, and we weren't allowed to visit him. That still haunts me. I believe death should be a celebration of life.

Many terminally ill patients tell me they want to die surrounded by loved ones, laughing and sharing happy moments—not alone in a sterile hospital room. Death is inevitable, but we can choose to face it with love and connection.

You travel the world with clowns, spreading joy. Do you have a story of directly helping a patient?

In Ecuador, I visited a five-year-old girl, Valencia, who had been raped and hadn't spoken, eaten, or cried for two months. She was wasting away, and doctors planned a stomach operation to keep her alive.

I spent an hour with her. She showed no signs of life—her face was the saddest I've ever seen. I held her hand, cradled her, and lay on the floor with her. By the second day, the doctors canceled the surgery, and within two days, she woke up, hugged people, and began eating again. She returned to school a week later.

Three months later, I received her photo, and I barely recognized her.

How did your story become a film?

My first book gained attention, and Hollywood producers quickly showed interest. I didn't like their initial ideas, so I asked my friend Mike Farrell from *MASH** to take the project to Universal Studios.

Were you happy with the movie?

Robin Williams did an excellent job given the simplistic script. I wasn't thrilled with how they left out my radical work for peace and justice, but the film still inspired people. Over 3,000 projects worldwide were started because of it.

Where do you find the energy to keep going?

At 18, I decided to find joy in simple things—rain, snow, birds, trees, silence in the woods. People recharge me with their love and belief in what I do. Letters from around the world inspire me to keep going.

I wish you love and peace.

2014

PHILIPPE PETIT

I Am an Artist, Not a Stuntman Risking His Life

Frenchman Philippe Petit, born in 1949, is a man of many talents. He excels at juggling, rock climbing, equestrianism, fencing, and even built his wooden house using 18th-century tools. But his greatest passion is high-wire walking.

Petit discovered climbing, magic, and juggling at an early age. By 14, he began walking on high wires, teaching himself tricks, and performing as a street juggler in Paris. In 1971, he secretly set up a wire between the two towers of Notre Dame in Paris and performed a daring walk. More public performances followed, but the newly constructed World Trade Center in New York soon captured his imagination.

The Twin Towers became an obsession, and over six years, Petit meticulously prepared for what would become his most famous performance. He secretly visited the site numerous times, studying the structure to determine the best way to anchor his cable. On August 7, 1974, just after 7 a.m., Petit stepped onto the wire, 410 meters above the ground. Over 45 minutes, he made eight passes across the wire, performing stunts before rain ended the act.

The feat garnered widespread media attention, and the charges against him were dropped in exchange for a free aerial show for children in Central Park. Petit was later granted a lifetime pass to the Twin Towers' Observation Deck.

In 1989, as part of France's bicentennial celebrations, President Jacques Chirac invited Petit to perform a high-wire walk from the Trocadero to the Eiffel Tower's second floor. An audience of 250,000 people watched. His extraordinary life inspired the 2008 documentary *Man on Wire* by James Marsh and the 2015 film *The Walk* by Robert Zemeckis.

To mark Petit's 70th birthday, we sent him a card along with a letter of questions. He graciously responded within a few months.

We read that you weren't a great student and were expelled from school. Were you a 'rebel without a cause'?

I wasn't expelled just once—I was expelled five times! I discovered magic and spent my time practicing card tricks under the desk. Eventually, I had to choose between school and magic, and for me, magic was far more important.

Was high-wire walking your dream, or did you want to break records and be the first in something?

I simply loved art, magic, and performing my own program in the streets of Paris. I was never interested in breaking records. I'm self-taught—I learned everything on my own, including high-wire walking. I started with three wires, then two, and within ten days I was walking on a single wire.

Within a year, I could do backflips, front flips, and even ride a unicycle on the wire. But I always wanted to go higher. After my first public walk between the towers of Notre Dame, the Twin Towers became my obsession for six years. I don't see myself as a stuntman risking his life; for me, it's an art—a theater performance for a large audience.

Have you ever abandoned a walk because something felt wrong—a bad omen or a sixth sense?

Never. I would never take the first step if I weren't sure I could take the last one victoriously.

When you stood atop the Twin Towers with a 410-meter drop below, were you nervous? Did you doubt your abilities?

I wasn't nervous—I didn't have time for that. I was behind schedule, and workers were about to start their shifts, so I had to hurry. I had worked too hard and prepared too thoroughly to give up just before realizing my dream.

How did you feel when the Twin Towers were destroyed in 2001?

I had an intimate connection with the towers—I loved them. Watching them collapse and take thousands of lives was devastating. To honor the victims, I offered to walk between the new towers as a symbol of respect and resilience. Unfortunately, the design made it technically impossible.

Is tightrope walking a natural gift, or is it something anyone can master through training and effort?

It's not a gift—it's the result of hard work, effort, and determination. Even now, I train six days a week for three hours a day. Confidence is essential, and you can't achieve it without putting in the work.

Can you walk a tightrope without a balance pole, or is it essential?

The balance pole is essential. It wouldn't be possible without it.

After a successful walk, do you feel elated or exhausted?

I'm completely exhausted—physically and mentally. The satisfaction and joy come later.

When you're on the wire, do you create a mental bubble where you feel in control of everything?

No, I don't create a bubble. I enjoy the void around me. When walking between trees in a park, I've played with leaves and talked to birds. At greater heights, clouds can pose a danger, but otherwise, I feel at home up there.

Were you satisfied with Robert Zemeckis's film about your life, *The Walk*?

Yes, I was. I actively participated in the project and even taught the lead actor how to walk on a wire. I had received many offers in the past, but they were only interested in buying the rights to my story. This time, I worked with the right people, and it was worth the wait.

2019

MARK BOYLE

In the Past, Systems Were Changed by Revolutions. My System Is a Long-Term Evolution

I discovered the name Mark Boyle by pure chance when Eva pointed out his book *The Moneyless Man: A Year of Freeconomic Living*. Intrigued, I bought the book and found it both fascinating and thought-provoking. It raised many questions, so I set out to find his address. After learning that he had moved from England to Ireland, I sent him a letter in November 2016, along with the book cover for a signature. To my surprise, he replied within two weeks.

I admire his commitment to rejecting a consumerist lifestyle and embracing a return to nature, living in harmony with it and with gratitude. I also respect how he practices what he preaches: when he gives speeches, he's content to sleep on the floor of a host's home, considers a sofa a luxury, and prefers to travel by bike, train, or even hitchhike. Unlike some ecologists who preach one thing and do another, Mark leads by example.

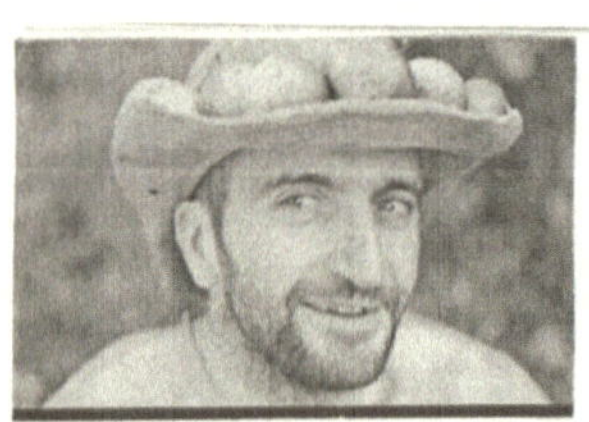

To Eva.
Thank you for all you do.
Much love,

Where do you come from? Were you used to living without money, or did you grow up wealthy and become disillusioned?

We were very poor. You could say we lived hand to mouth, week by week. Despite that, we always had food on the table and a loving family, so I'd call my childhood happy. In the neighborhood where I grew up, no one had a car or phone. The only phone belonged to one family, and they left their door open so anyone could use it, leaving a few pennies on the table for the call.

We all knew one another, played together in the streets, and parents swapped clothes for their kids. If someone faced financial difficulties, everyone chipped in to help. When I visit now, people are better off financially, but that sense of community is gone. Everyone lives behind closed doors, focusing on themselves. Happiness has shifted from friendships to money, and that's deeply sad.

What inspired you to start living without money?

I was studying economics and aiming for a well-paid job, but I began questioning the system. Something felt inherently wrong. My professor encouraged me to ask questions, and the more I learned about how the system worked, the less sense it made.

In 2007, a friend challenged me: "If you're so against money, why don't you give it up?" That pushed me to try. I sold my houseboat and started the *Freeconomics* website. I'll admit, I was scared for the first three months. I'd given up the financial security I was used to, but I found a new kind of security in friendships and relationships.

What began as a year-long experiment to prove it was possible turned into a way of life. I've now lived without money for eight years, and I love it.

Weren't you worried about becoming an outcast or alienating people by living on the margins of consumer society?

Initially, yes. But I felt more like an active participant in my own life rather than a passive consumer. I thought I might alienate people, but I discovered many who also dream of leaving cities to live in peace with nature.

At first, my parents weren't thrilled, but once they understood my reasons and motivation, they supported me. The first three months were the hardest, but I soon began enjoying the freedom and new perspective.

Life without money taught me so much. It freed me from the daily worries that plague most people—fears of losing a job or not having enough for the mortgage. Each day brought something new, and I thrived on finding creative solutions.

I also became healthier and happier. I ate fresh, healthy food, spent my days outdoors, and felt physically and mentally free. This way of life enriched me in ways money never could.

You've talked about creating a new system. What does it look like?

I'm exploring a long-term evolution, not a revolution. Past systems—like capitalism and communism—were driven by money as the safety net. I envision a system where people have stronger relationships with their environment and treat it, and each other, with dignity and respect.

Our addiction to money is dangerous. The more we have, the more we want. That cycle leads to stress and overwork. My approach is to move away from this addiction gradually, by fostering community and generosity.

What are your goals for The Free House project?

Using royalties from my book, I bought land in Ireland—my only financial transaction in recent years. We're constructing a building made entirely from natural materials, which will serve as a free community center.

About 14 people are helping me with this project. Once completed, we'll host seminars and educational courses. The surrounding nature offers a tranquil setting where visitors can stay for free, experience this way of life, and decide if it's for them.

2017

BENJAMIN MEE

Hard Work and Determination Help Fulfill a Dream

We first became familiar with Benjamin Mee's story through the film *We Bought a Zoo*, which was based on his book. However, his real-life story is even more colorful—full of action, drama, and heartbreak. Moved by his journey, we decided to reach out to him and wrote him a letter.

Benjamin's passion extends beyond his zoo; after the passing of his beloved wife, he has dedicated himself to raising his two children, writing, and traveling the world. In his talks, he shares not only his deep connection with animals but also his insights on how people can turn their dreams into reality.

Is it true that you were born in Australia and raised in Surrey? If so, when exactly were you born? I couldn't find that information. What prompted the move to England? Do you think experiencing bushfires and wildlife in Australia subconsciously shaped your determination, stamina, and love for animals?

In 1965, there were serious bushfires around Melbourne, Australia. I recently met some visitors at the zoo who still remember them. My parents were in Australia on a three-year contract—my dad, a mathematician, was working for the Australian census. I returned to the UK at six months old but still have an Australian passport as well as a UK one. I don't remember Australia, but knowing that my parents, both from working-class backgrounds, had moved there for a time made me feel that anything was possible in life.

We heard you were expelled from school. Was that because you disliked the system, refused to learn, or were you simply

a rebel who didn't fit in?

I hated school from the moment I was first dropped off as a small child to the last time I was expelled as a teenager. The pressure to conform to unexplained rules bothered me the most. Plus, I had an exciting family life with much older brothers who knew lots of interesting things, and school just didn't feel like the right place for me to learn. Later, I studied at the Open University, then UCL and Imperial College in London, where I realized that the subjects they had tried to teach me in school were actually very interesting—just not taught in a way that resonated with me. My son, Milo, is now homeschooled and started with the OU at 15. Ella, on the other hand, prefers school and fits in very well.

When working as a decorator and bricklayer, what was your idea of a good life? Did you have dreams, or was it simply a struggle to make ends meet? Was that where you learned the DIY skills that you later turned into a book and found so useful while building the zoo?

I liked living hand to mouth by bricklaying, laboring, and decorating. As a young adult, I was carefree but somewhat bemused that I hadn't found anything I was truly interested in. That all changed when I read about dolphin intelligence (see my TEDx talk). The DIY skills I learned gave me a niche that other journalists didn't have, allowing me to write as if I were speaking to friends who couldn't hold a power drill properly.

It's written that an encounter with a dolphin sparked your fascination with animal intelligence. Could you share more about that experience? What was it about that moment that made you decide to study psychology?

The first time I saw a dolphin, I was about 16 or 17 and unimpressed by most things. But the way the dolphin looked back at me—sadly and knowingly—through the glass at the UK's last dolphinarium stopped me in my tracks. I had always wondered about animal minds, but that look was so profound it left a huge impression. A few years later, when I read about dolphins assisting at human births, something clicked. A light went on inside me, and I knew I had to go to university to study them.

You were a journalist for 15 years. What kind of articles did you write? Were you a freelance writer, or did you work for an editor? Did you have your own column and build a regular audience, or did you write about anything and everything just to earn a living?

I wrote about art, restaurant reviews, and anything I could, but my background in psychology gave me an edge as a science writer over most journalists at the time. I especially loved writing about health and later adventure travel. Freefall parachuting, dog sledding in Canada and Finland, learning to dive off a 7-meter board, riding the halfpipe on a snowboard—it was incredible to get paid to do these things. I knew I was lucky to be there, especially considering that just a few years earlier, I had been a laborer with no qualifications. It made me appreciate that with hard work and a clear goal, people can achieve a great deal.

Your sister sent you a brochure for Dartmoor Zoo with a note saying, "A dream scenario." Had you ever actually dreamed of owning a zoo before? What was the experience like?

I never wanted to buy or own a zoo, but I've always wanted to work closely with animals. As I suspected, the daily reality of running a zoo isn't exactly fun. Everyone else enjoys themselves, but when you're the one paying the bills in a rain-soaked recession, it's a different story. Yesterday, some guys were filming a 3D tour of the zoo, and I heard they were throwing grapes for the monkeys. Meanwhile, I was inside, sweating over a spreadsheet. But the zoo allows so many people to develop a better understanding of animals, and in the end, that makes it worthwhile. And my kids absolutely love it.

Was that dilapidated zoo actually a proper zoo that had been badly run down by its owners, or was it just a large property with too many animals that had gotten out of control? Could you share what the asking price was?

It was a zoo that had operated for nearly forty years, almost without rules, and by the time we bought it, it was closed. It was on the market for £1.2 million—the same price as a five-bedroom house in Surrey, near London. But a zoo comes with big bills from day one.

When you became an impromptu director, did you have to learn the rules and regulations first, or did you start by studying animal care to ensure their well-being and avoid any legal issues, with the director's role coming second?

The rules came quickly from the outside. Government regulators were tough on us in the first few months, making sure we understood the seriousness of the position—which we did. We hired skilled keepers to take care of the animals' basic needs, and I focused on encouraging enrichment and diet programs to ensure the animals were as stimulated as possible.

When did you realize your book, *We Bought A Zoo*, would be turned into a film? Did you have any input in shaping the story, or did the studio simply buy the rights for a set amount, leaving you out of the process? Was the film fairly accurate, or was it a typical Hollywood adaptation?

I got a call from Hollywood around 2010 with an offer to buy the rights. In the end, the money from the film covered one winter's wages. They were generous in asking for my input on the script's direction and the casting (I chose Matt Damon). But once they had decided on the direction, there was nothing I could do to change it.

The story is about half of the book and set in perpetual sunshine. They wanted it to focus on recovery, so they moved Katherine's death to before the film starts, saying it was "too sad" otherwise. But they knew more people would see the film that way.

When did you realize *We Bought a Zoo* would be filmed? Did you have any input, or did the studio just buy the rights and take over? Did the film boost the zoo's popularity? Did Matt Damon or the crew donate to the zoo?

I got a call from Hollywood around 2010 with an offer to buy the rights. The money covered one winter's wages. They asked for my input on the script and casting (I chose Matt Damon), but once they had a direction, I had no say. The

Dartmoor Zoological Park,
Sparkwell,
Plymouth,
Devon,
PL7 5DG

2.12.13

Dear Vitek and Eva,

Thank you so much for your letter, I do apologise for how late my response is, I get a lot of letters and so along with the day to day running of the zoo it takes me a while to get through them. Please find enclosed the signatures you requested as well as a picture and flier.

It is a shame you missed coming to the Zoo when you were in the country, I hope you get to visit again. We do experience at the zoo so you could go in with the Meerkats. They are really wonderful animals and very very friendly. We don't have any chimpanzees as yet but we have Vervet monkeys, and are hoping to get some chimpanzees who need homes who are currently in America. We also plan on getting some Orang-utans in the near future.

We have Wallabies and many big cats. As well as many other animals. We have many exciting plans for the future. It has been a very big challenge as you have seen from the film, but it is all worth it for the magnificent animals. They are all so individual and amazing in their own ways.

I hope these things go well in your enclosure and we hope to see you at the zoo soon.

Best wishes,

Benjamin Mee

film covers about half the book and was set in sunshine. They moved Katherine's death before the story began, saying it was "too sad" otherwise.No one from Hollywood visited, but the film had a huge impact. Just yesterday, a family from Denmark came to shake my hand. Without it, the zoo might have closed. Donations? No, sadly not. Yet...

How do you balance running the zoo, writing, and giving talks? Do you see the public engagements as essential for funding the zoo?

Public talks help subsidize the zoo. Universities or organizations invite me to share my story, often offering generous fees. I enjoy motivating people to pursue realistic dreams and highlighting the importance of respecting and understanding animals.

2013

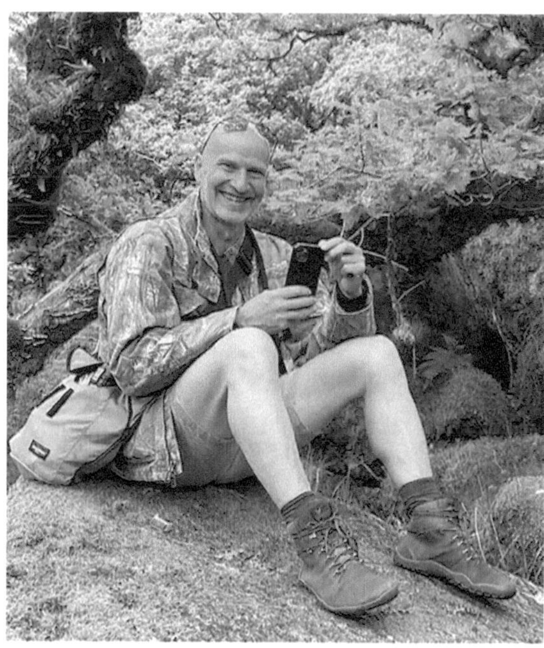

DAVID FRANKHAM

I Had Extraordinary Luck

British-born actor David Frankham graciously responded to our request for signatures, and we've stayed in touch ever since. This interview was compiled later as part of our conversations. David achieved something that would be nearly impossible in today's Hollywood—a story that sounds almost like science fiction. His experiences take us back to a time when the film business was far less ruthless.

What is your social background? What did your parents do, and what did they want for you?

My mother was the daughter of a Scottish shepherd. She met my father during World War I when she joined the British Navy's WRNS (Women's Royal Naval Service, popularly known as the Wrens). My father was an Able Seaman who worked his way up to Warrant Officer. When I was growing up, he was often away on two-year tours of duty, so I didn't really know him until I was 14, when he was finally based in England.

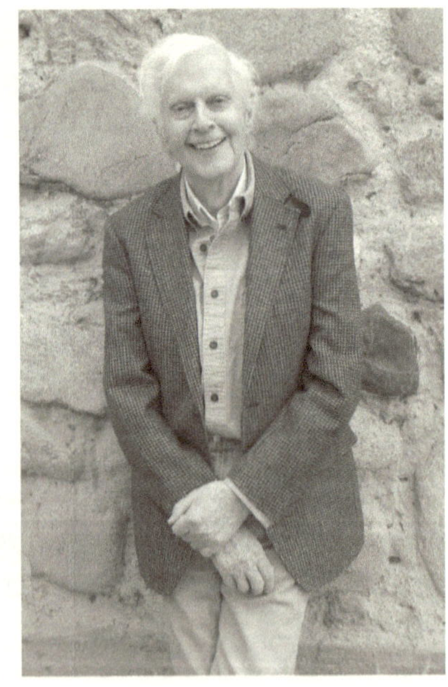

I was raised in Kent, thirty miles south of London, but during the bombings in 1940, my mother and I were evacuated to Scotland to live with her father and sister. I was an only child and always wished for siblings. My parents were neither artistic nor creative, and I often felt I didn't fit in with them. For example, I loved movies, but my father had to be dragged to the cinema. I was fascinated by actors, yet as soon as the credits rolled, my father would declare, "I'm not sitting through all that muck!"

When I was 16 and first expressed my desire to act, my parents were unsupportive. They insisted I study architecture, a subject I had no interest in whatsoever. I endured two miserable years of architectural school, but fortunately, the army intervened, putting an end to that chapter. Later, when I worked at the BBC, my parents were thrilled—it was a respectable career with the promise of a pension and retirement. However, when I gave it up to pursue acting in Hollywood, they were devastated. Even when I found success, their reaction was muted. My mother would sigh and say, "It's your life." It was a world they couldn't relate to, as if I had moved to Mars.

Still, I later discovered they were more supportive than they let on. My mother, diagnosed with cancer in 1955, delayed her

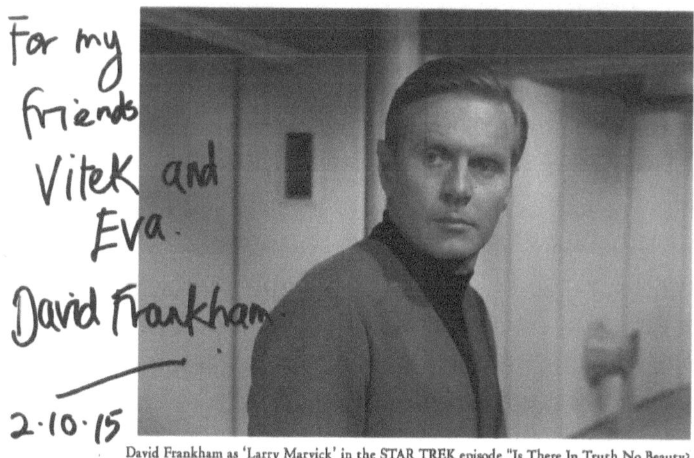

David Frankham as 'Larry Marvick' in the STAR TREK episode "Is There In Truth No Beauty?

surgery until after I had moved to the U.S., fearing it might hold me back. After my father's death, I found he had kept all the photos I sent from my films, with notes written on the back.

You served in WWII in Malaya and India. Did you see combat, and do you have any special recollections of wartime?

Fortunately, I was drafted after WWII ended, so I saw no combat. Initially, I thought those three years in the army were a waste of my youth, but that turned out not to be true. I was sent to pre-independence India, where anti-British sentiment was high, and our lives were often at risk. We had rocks thrown at us whenever we left the safety of the Red Fort in Old Delhi.

One pivotal event changed my life: on my 21st birthday in Kuala Lumpur, I collapsed from typhus and nearly died. The illness kept me from being sent away with my unit, and I remained in Kuala Lumpur, running a drawing office staffed by civilian Malayans. While there, I entered and won a contest to host a radio program featuring my favorite records. That experience led to an offer to work evenings at the radio station. When I returned to England, the station owner gave me a letter of recommendation for the BBC, launching a seven-year radio career I hadn't even dreamed of.

You worked for the BBC from 1948 to 1955. Was acting always your dream, or did it develop over time? What was post-war entertainment in England like?

I've wanted to act since I was 16, ever since seeing Gladys Cooper in *Now, Voyager* (1942). The defining moment came when I saw Laird Cregar's mesmerizing performance as Jack the Ripper in *The Lodger* (1944). I thought, "I have to do that someday." But with no parental support and my army draft, my dream was put on hold for years.

Working at the BBC as a radio interviewer allowed me to meet many Hollywood actors, keeping the dream alive.

Eventually, those connections enabled me to take the leap into acting. Nobody encouraged me—my parents and colleagues thought I was mad—but I never let go of the dream.

You made a bold decision to move to Hollywood in 1955 and got a job straight away—amazing. Was it really as easy as it looks, or did you have extraordinary luck? No waiter jobs in LA for aspiring actors like today?

I had extraordinary luck. After interviewing singer and actress Rosemary Clooney for the BBC, I asked her if she thought I could make a living in Hollywood radio. She said, "I think you'd do fine. Here's my secretary's number at the studio. Call me when you get there." It was as simple as that. Shortly after arriving in Hollywood, I began freelancing on Los Angeles radio. Rosemary Clooney changed my life.

I was too naïve to realize how difficult it was to break into acting. I just knew I had to try. My plan was to work in radio, build connections with film people, and work my way into acting, starting small. My extraordinary luck continued when, eight months after arriving in Hollywood, I got my first acting job—a lead role in a live TV play, stepping in for Roddy McDowall, who had to leave unexpectedly.

I knew many talented actors who weren't as lucky. They worked in shops between auditions and struggled to get roles. By contrast, after my initial TV appearance, I was offered five more leading roles on live television within five months. I worked hard, but I was undeniably fortunate. (I write about this in detail in my autobiography, *Which One Was David?*, published in 2012!)

What was Hollywood like when you arrived, and how has it changed since then? For example, when the creative moguls were replaced by the focus on the bottom line?

When I arrived in 1955, Hollywood was in the final days of the studio system, which was in decline due to the rise of television. Studio contracts offered actors security, but even major stars like my friend Angela Lansbury were being let go. Some actors appreciated the independence, but many struggled to promote themselves as freelancers.

For me, that time was thrilling. I had the chance to work with legends from the Golden Age of cinema: Stan Laurel, Boris Karloff, Claude Rains, Fred Astaire, Basil Rathbone, Peter Lorre, Vincent Price, and many others. To a movie fan like me, it was like being in heaven.

In the late 1950s, many legendary sci-fi thrillers were made. Was this trend influenced by the Cold War? Were the Martians just disguised Russians?

The Cold War certainly influenced the genre. The anxiety surrounding atomic bombs and monsters reflected the times. But I think it was also a passing trend—one studio had a hit, and others copied it. With the Baby Boom, there was a large youth audience, and sci-fi appealed to them.

Was there a Hollywood board supervising films for political content? Did you witness any of McCarthy's witch-hunting?

Yes, I saw the effects of the McCarthy era. My friends Betty Garrett and Larry Parks suffered greatly. Larry, star of *The Jolson Story*, was forced to testify before HUAC. Under immense pressure, he named names of people he had met, though neither he nor Betty had communist ties. His career ended the next day, and MGM pulled his current film. Betty's career slowed as well. By 1955, when I arrived in Hollywood, they welcomed me into their home despite their struggles. Larry was touring Canada to find work, as Hollywood had blacklisted him.

Your most successful film was *Tales of Terror*. Why do you think it became a classic, and why do modern remakes of 1950s films often flop?

Tales of Terror succeeded because it was well-crafted despite its low budget. It had a strong script by Richard Matheson, excellent acting from Vincent Price, Peter Lorre, and Basil Rathbone, and tight, focused storytelling. Modern remakes often fail because studios rely on title recognition alone, neglecting the original stories or characters. When filmmakers don't care, neither does the audience.

How did you land your role in *King Rat*? Was your WWII experience relevant? What was filming like?

My WWII experience had nothing to do with landing the part. The casting director had seen me play a similar role on television and recommended me. My scene in *King Rat* had no dialogue, just an emotional reaction. Director Brian Forbes trusted the recommendation and gave me the role.

The film was shot in California, where the Changi prison camp was meticulously recreated. Ironically, I had been stationed at the real Changi after the war, so I could vouch for its accuracy. Filming stretched over months due to delays, which worked in my favor as I remained on salary while waiting for my scene. When it came time to shoot, it took just one take. For my two days of work, I was paid far more than for many leading roles.

Acting is often seen as a thankless job—waiting for a phone call to get work. Did you ever feel truly independent?

The answer is both yes and no. It's frustrating to be dependent on others for opportunities, especially when many casting directors lack imagination. Sir Derek Jacobi once said that actors are essentially beggars, and I agree. Only the most successful stars can afford to create their own projects. I was a "jobbing actor," taking whatever came my way, much like a plumber or painter.

Do you think actors today are more independent, given that films are now made globally and not just by big studios?

Acting has never been easy, but I believe it's harder now. In the 1950s, the studio system provided a steady stream of work. Television series often ran for 39 episodes per season, creating stability. Studios were centralized in Hollywood, allowing personal relationships to develop between actors and casting directors. Today, everything is digital, making it harder for actors to make a personal impression. With far more actors competing now, the challenges are greater.

What's your view on current technology, animation, and 3D? Does it diminish the importance of real acting?

Actors will always be needed, no matter the technology. The real danger lies in studios prioritizing special effects over storytelling. Without strong scripts and compelling characters, even the most advanced visuals fail to engage audiences.

2015

EDDIE 'THE EAGLE' EDWARDS

It's Not Important to Win but to Take Part and Enjoy It

We're not sports fans, but the name Eddie Edwards stuck in our minds back in 1988 when Czechoslovakian TV aired highlights from the Winter Olympic Games in Calgary. I've always rooted for underdogs rather than the obvious favorites, so despite finishing last in the competition, Eddie won my heart. For more than two decades, we had no idea what Eddie was up to, but the recent film *Eddie the Eagle* brought him back into the spotlight. We loved the movie and set out to contact him. After trying his management and other channels without success (do management teams ever reply?), we reached out to his foundation, and—BINGO—Eddie responded.

In the movie, it seems that not only officials but even your friends looked down on you with disrespect. Was that true?

Within the team, many of the skiers were wealthy and could train whenever they liked because their families owned chalets in the Alps. I, on the other hand, could only practice on a training slope in Gloucester. The worst part, though, was the behavior of the sports officials. They acted as if they owned the entire federation and knew best how to promote skiing. They saw me as an embarrassment to British representation.

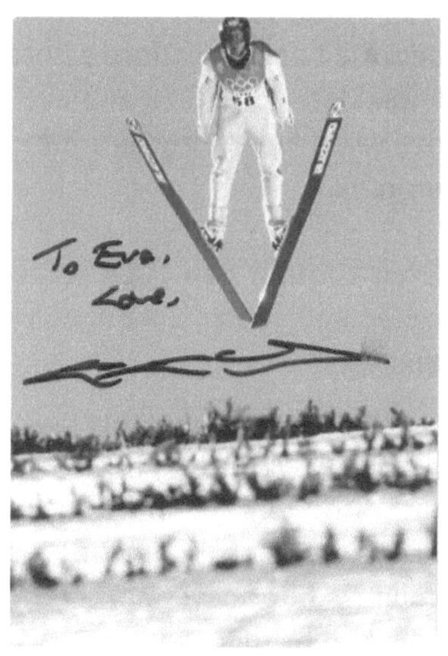

When I arrived in Calgary, people thought I couldn't even ski, which wasn't true—I was a good skier. The press, however, ran with that story because it made for good headlines. I spent a lot of time explaining myself. When I qualified for another Olympic Games and met all the required standards, the federation moved the goalposts, raising the target level to keep me out. They always seemed determined to throw a wrench into my plans.

It seems like you sacrificed everything for your dream of going to the Olympics. Did you really sleep in a cleaning closet and struggle to afford food?

We had plenty of skiers, but no jumpers, so I saw an opportunity to fill that gap and gave it a try. I was poor and quickly ran out of money. When I first went to Switzerland to train, I stayed in a chalet with Scouts who shared their Heinz beans with me. Otherwise, I ate whatever I could find, often scavenging from dustbins. Italian jumpers gave me goggles and a helmet because mine was old and didn't fit properly.

In Finland, I slept in barns and even in a lunatic asylum because I couldn't afford a hotel. I endured all of this because I was determined to achieve my dream. It typically takes five years to develop as a jumper—I qualified in just twenty months.

Even though you finished last at the Olympics, people celebrated you as a winner. Why do you think they reacted that way?

I think people liked me because I embodied the true Olympic spirit: it's not about winning, but about taking part. At that time, the Olympics were already highly professional, and I stood out as someone jumping on skis even though my country didn't have snow or proper ski jumps. I was genuinely happy to be there and enjoyed every moment.

I'm pleased that a film was made about my story and hope it inspires others to follow their dreams. We need more movies like that.

Ski jumping requires incredible courage. Is it true you psyched yourself up before each jump by swearing?

Yes, I was scared before every jump. Just before takeoff, I'd shout, "Shit!" It was enough fear to keep me focused, but not enough to stop me from jumping. I never got used to it. My goggles often fogged up, and I couldn't even see the landing spot.

You were a big celebrity, then faded into obscurity, and now you're back in the spotlight thanks to the movie. How did the film come about?

It's a long story. Back in 1999, I was approached with an offer to make a film, so I started working on the script with collaborators. But then problems arose—funding dried up, they couldn't find the right actor, and the project was shelved. I forgot about it. Then, in mid-2015, a producer called me out of the blue. He had bought the rights, and within six weeks, filming began. It all happened very quickly. Watching the movie was emotional for me—it reminded me of what I went through, what I sacrificed, and what I achieved.

Is the film 100% accurate, or were parts fictionalized?

It's very true to my story. The biggest change was combining several of my coaches into one character for simplicity. I hoped they wouldn't portray me as either a superhero or a fool, and I think they struck the right balance.

As a kid, I constantly heard, "You can't do this," or "You'll never manage that." Their doubt motivated me—I wanted to prove them wrong. I hope the film not only entertains but also inspires people to pursue their dreams despite obstacles. To me, the real loss isn't failing to reach the top, but not trying at all. If you try and fail, it's not the end of the world—you gave it your best shot.

Was it all worth it?

Absolutely. I'm the only athlete mentioned in the closing ceremony speech. When I returned home, the police were waiting for me, and I thought they were going to arrest me! Instead, they told me 10,000 people had gathered outside the airport to welcome me, and they were there to protect me. I had planned to take a bus or taxi home, but this reception was beyond anything I could have imagined. What more could I ask for?

2017

ACKNOWLEDGEMENTS

We extend our heartfelt gratitude to all the individuals whose stories are featured in this book. Your willingness, time, and effort are deeply appreciated.

We also thank you for granting us permission to use your images and photographs. Special thanks go to the Jamie Andrew Collection (Jamie Andrew), Alessandro Capoccetti (Alessandro Capoccetti and Andresa Ossola), Andrew Dow, Martin Maguire, Kathryn Kennedy (Simon Fitzmaurice), Mike Patrick, the John Somerville Collection (Erik Gundersen), Henrik Fjortoft (Torsten Lerhof), and Eva Csölleová (Evžen Erban, Tomáš Kvoch).

Finally, we extend our sincere thanks to Sastrugi Press for publishing this book.

ABOUT THE AUTHORS

Vítek Formánek (1963) lives in East Bohemia, Czech Republic. He has a deep interest in the Royal Air Force (RAF) since 1988. He befriended dozens and dozens of English ex-Guinea Pigs and POWs and has written 11 books about them. He also has written books about punk rock, speedway, film, autograph collecting, homelessness, and handicapped people, with 23 titles so far. He works as a social worker. Vítekhas had over 1500 articles published in the Czech and English media.

Eva Csölleová (1964) lives in Eastern Bohemia, Czech Republic. Along with Vítek, she has co-written 13 books about punk rock, film, the Royal Air Force (RAF), autograph collecting, handicapped people, and homelessness. She is a photographer and many of her photos have been used in her books and publications.

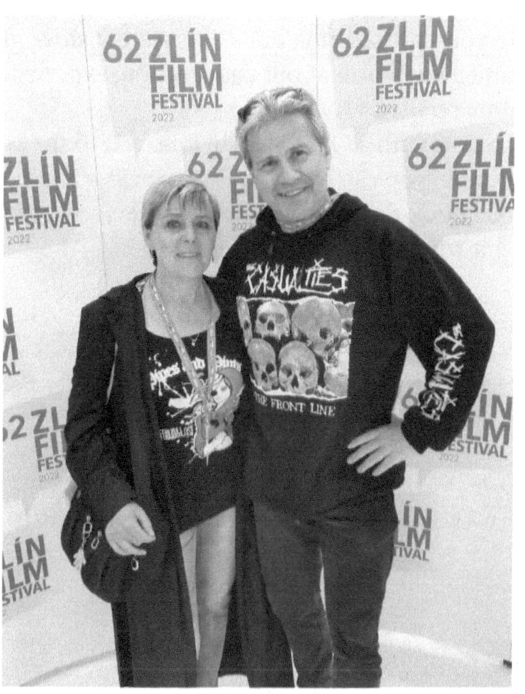

Vítek Formánek and Eva Csölleová at the 2022 Zlín Film Festival

AUTHOR'S NOTE

We hope you enjoyed this book. Please consider giving it a rating and add a few words about your reading experience at your favorite online retailer.

The link below with a QR code will take you to the book's web page. From there, you can follow links to various online retailers.

Giving our book rating and a short written review about why you enjoyed it will help us immensely.

Thank you!
Vítek Formánek and Eva Csölleová

www.sastrugipress.com/books/defying-limits/

Use your smart device to scan the QR code for the book's webpage.

ADDITIONAL BOOKS BY THE AUTHORS

Defying Limits

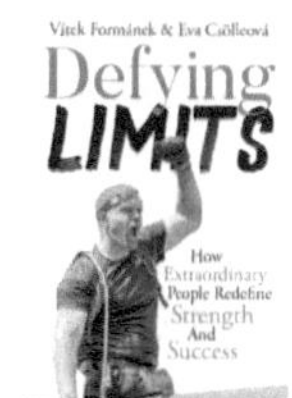

Discover the inspiring true stories of athletes, artists, and innovators who overcame every obstacle to achieve the extraordinary.

www.sastrugipress.com/books/defying-limits/

Wasted Lives of Unsung Heroes

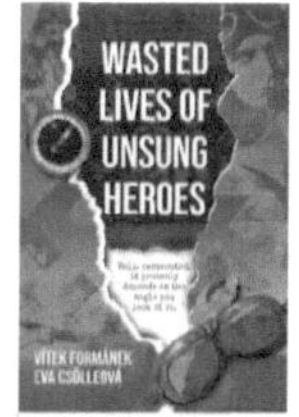

Experience the gripping stories of Czechoslovakian pilots who helped to defeat Nazi Germany in World War II only to be persecuted by Communist Czechoslovakia and Stalinist Russia.

www.sastrugipress.com/books/wasted-lives-of-unsung-heroes/

ENJOY ADDITIONAL SASTRUGI PRESS BOOKS

Black Ice

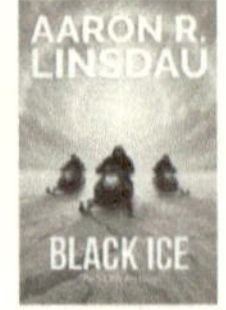

Some missions don't have a way back. When a hypersonic drone crashes in northern Finland, Grant Colson races against the elements and unseen dangers before the mission—and his team—are erased by the Arctic. *Free download.*

www.aaronrlinsdau.com/sera/black-ice/

50 Jackson Hole Photography Hotspots by Aaron Linsdau

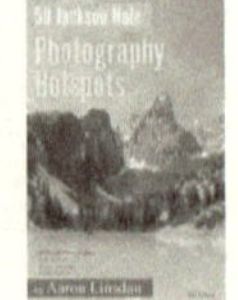

A guide to the best Jackson Hole photography spots. Learn what locals and insiders know to create the most impressive and iconic photography locations in the United States.

www.sastrugipress.com/books/50-jackson-hole-photography-hotspots/

50 Wildlife Hotspots by Moose Henderson Ph.D.

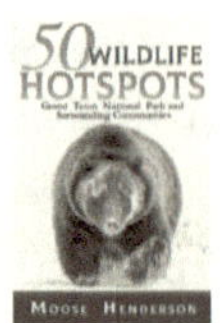

Find out where to find animals and photograph them in Grand Teton National Park from a professional wildlife photographer. This unique guide shares the secret locations with the best chance at spotting wildlife.

www.sastrugipress.com/books/50-wildlife-hotspots/

Adventure Expedition One
by Aaron Linsdau M.S.
& Terry Williams, M.D.

Create, finance, enjoy, and return safely from your first expedition. Learn the techniques explorers use to achieve their goals and have a good time doing it. Acquire the skills, find the equipment, and learn the planning necessary to pull off an expedition.

www.sastrugipress.com/books/adventure-expedition-one/

Antarctic Tears by Aaron Linsdau

Experience the honest story of solo polar exploration. This inspirational true book will make readers both cheer and cry. Coughing up blood and fighting skin-freezing temperatures were only a few of the perils Aaron Linsdau faced.

www.sastrugipress.com/books/antarctic-tears/

Blood Justice by Tim W. James

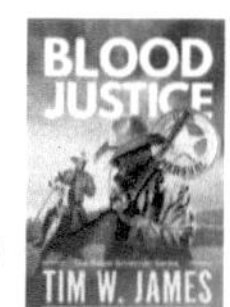

Two brothers, one a preacher's son, the other an adopted would-be slave, set out in opposite directions to avenge their family's murder only to cross paths in pursuit of the killer.

www.sastrugipress.com/iron-spike-press/blood-justice/

Counterfeit Justice by Tim W. James

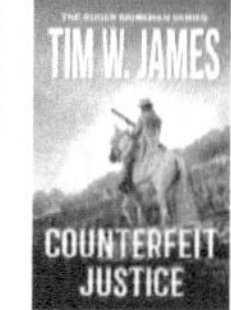

Preacher Roger Brinkman takes his crucifix and his Colt to fulfill a promise and help his lawman brother battle thieves, counterfeiters, and murderers in the Old West.

www.sastrugipress.com/iron-spike-press/counterfeit-justice/

How to Keep Your Feet Warm in the Cold by Aaron Linsdau

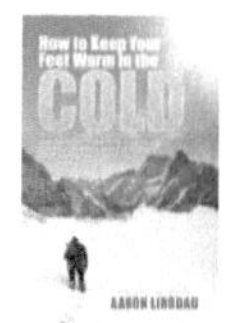

Keep your feet warm in cold conditions on chilly adventures with techniques described in this book. Packed with dozens and dozens of ideas, learn how to avoid having cold feet ever again in your outdoor pursuits.

www.sastrugipress.com/books/how-to-keep-your-feet-warm-in-the-cold/

Jackson Hole Hiking Guide by Aaron Linsdau

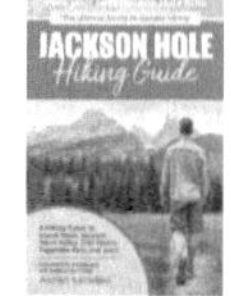

Find the best hiking trails in Jackson Hole. You'll get maps, GPS coordinates, accurate routes, elevation info, highlights, and dangers. The guide includes easy, challenging, family-friendly, and ADA-accessible trails and hikes.

www.sastrugipress.com/books/jackson-hole-hiking-guide/

Journeys to the Edge by Randall Peeters, Ph.D.

What is it like to climb Mount Everest? Is it possible for you to actually make the ascent? It requires dreaming big and creating a personal vision to climb the mountains in your life. Randall Peeters shares his successes and failures and gives you some directly applicable guidelines on how you can create a vision for your life.
www.sastrugipress.com/books/journeys-to-the-edge/

Lost at Windy Corner by Aaron Linsdau

Windy Corner on Denali has claimed fingers, toes, and even lives. What would make someone brave lethal weather, crevasses, and avalanches to attempt to summit North America's highest mountain? Aaron Linsdau shares the experience of climbing Denali alone and how you can apply the lessons to your life.

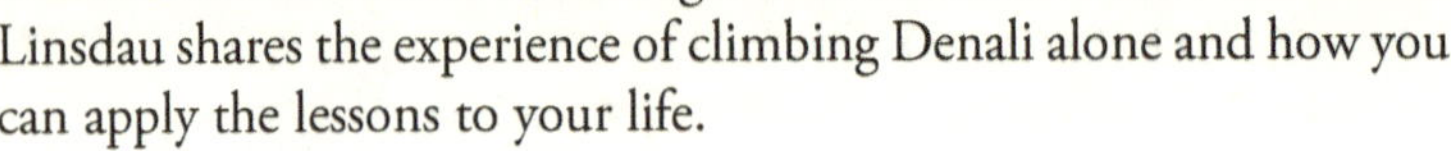

www.sastrugipress.com/books/lost-windy-corner/

So I Said by Gerry Spence

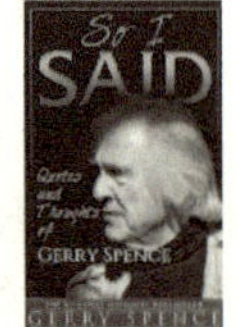

Venture into the mind of America's most famous lawyer. He shares his thoughts on hope, love, oppression, power, and life. Gain insight from a man who has fought overwhelming power and won from small-town Wyoming.
www.sastrugipress.com/books/so-i-said/

The Burqa Cave by Dean Petersen

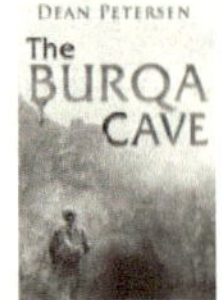

Still haunted by Iraq, Tim Ross finds solace teaching high school in Wyoming. That is, until freshman David Jenkins reveals the murder of a lost local girl. Will Tim be able to overcome his demons to stop the murderer?
www.sastrugipress.com/books/the-burqa-cave/

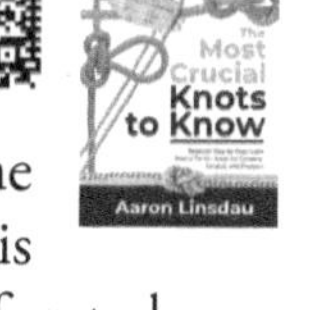

The Most Crucial Knots to Know by Aaron Linsdau

Knot tying is a skill everyone can use in daily life. This book shows how to tie over 40 of the most practical knots for virtually any situation. This guide will equip readers with skills that are useful, fun to learn, and will make you look like a confident pro.
www.sastrugipress.com/books/the-most-crucial-knots-to-know/

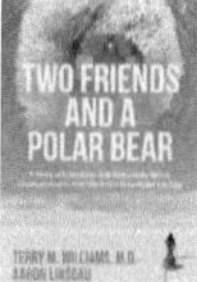

Two Friends and a Polar Bear by Terry Williams, M.D. & Aaron Linsdau

This story of friendship is about two old friends who plan to ski across the Greenland Icecap along the Arctic Circle in hopes of becoming one of the oldest teams to succeed.
www.sastrugipress.com/books/two-friends-and-a-polar-bear/

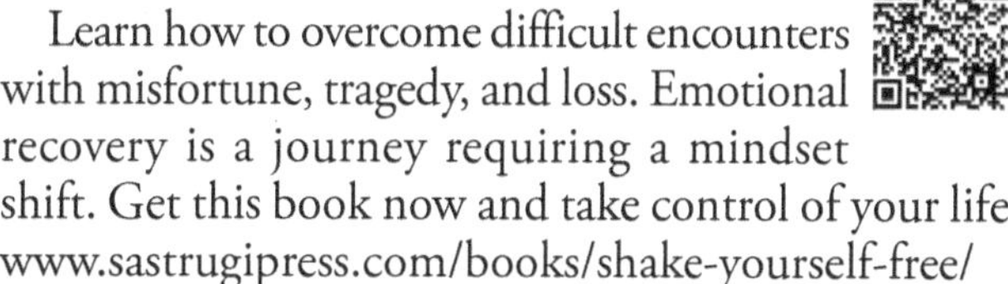

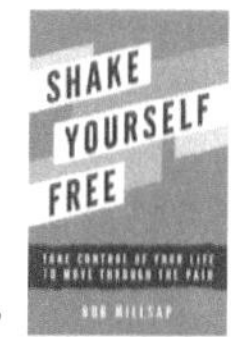

Shake Yourself Free by Bob Millsap

Learn how to overcome difficult encounters with misfortune, tragedy, and loss. Emotional recovery is a journey requiring a mindset shift. Get this book now and take control of your life.
www.sastrugipress.com/books/shake-yourself-free/

Use your smart device to scan the QR codes to visit website links.

Visit Sastrugi Press on the web at www.sastrugipress.com to purchase the above titles in bulk. They are also available from your local bookstore or online retailers in print, e-book, or audiobook form. Thank you for choosing Sastrugi Press.

www.sastrugipress.com
"Turn the Page Loose"

Pride and Prejudice by Jane Austen

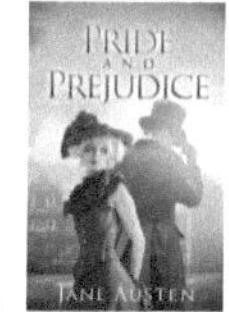

Follow the story of a family with daughters who struggle to find themselves as they grow up.
www.sastrugipress.com/classics/pride-and-prejudice/

Jane Eyre by Charlotte Brontë

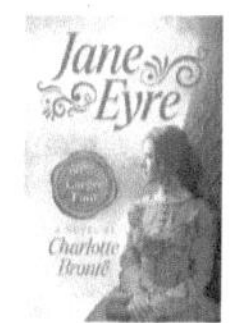

Follow the journey of a young orphan girl as she seeks to find her place in the world and discovers the transformative power of love and the importance of staying true to oneself.
www.sastrugipress.com/classics/jane-eyre/

Robinson Crusoe by Daniel Defoe

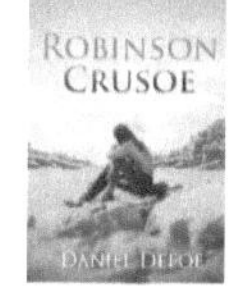

A man discovers he is the only survivor of a shipwreck on a deserted island and fights for survival against all odds.
www.sastrugipress.com/classics/robinson-crusoe/

Riders of the Purple Sage by Zane Grey

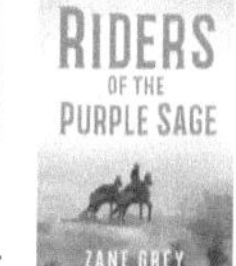

Zane Grey's classic cowboy story set the stage for an entire genre of books that continues today. Grey's story of fighting prejudice touches hearts and compels readers to examine how they deal with an internal struggle.
www.sastrugipress.com/classics/riders-of-the-purple-sage/

Treasure Island by Robert Louis Stevenson

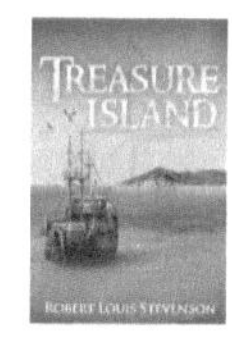

This seafaring tale follows the adventures of a young boy from an unassuming background who ends up intertwined with one of the most famous pirates in literature.
www.sastrugipress.com/classics/trcasurc-island/

Discover other Sastrugi Press large print books here:
www.sastrugipress.com/large-print-classics/

www.ingramcontent.com/pod-product-compliance
Lightning Source LLC
LaVergne TN
LVHW091022080826
845145LV00002B/330

* 9 7 8 1 6 4 9 2 2 2 4 3 5 *